This book addresses the central crisis in critical theory today: how to theorize the subject as both a construct of oppressive discourse and a dialogical agent. By engaging with a wide range of leading political, philosophical, and critical thinkers – Jameson, Habermas, Lyotard, MacIntyre, Rorty, Taylor, Benhabib, and West are all critiqued – Meili Steele proposes linking language with human agency in order to develop an alternative textual and ethical theory of the subject. Steele shows how constructivist theories fail to account for the ethical implications of the supposed contingency of all contexts, and how dialogical theorists fail to acknowledge the insight of postmodern critiques. Developing this theory through readings of texts that address issues of identity politics, race, and feminist theory, Steele illustrates that we do not have to choose between an idealized and a demonized modernity. This book maps new ways of confronting the problem of how politics and ethics are deployed in imaginative narratives.

Theorizing textual subjects

Literature, Culture, Theory 21

❖❖

General editors

RICHARD MACKSEY, *The Johns Hopkins University*

and MICHAEL SPRINKER, *State University of New York at Stony Brook*

The Cambridge *Literature, Culture, Theory* Series is dedicated to theoretical studies in the human sciences that have literature and culture as their object of enquiry. Acknowledging the contemporary expansion of cultural studies and the redefinitions of literature that this has entailed, the series includes not only original works of literary theory but also monographs and essay collections on topics and seminal figures from the long history of theoretical speculation on the arts and human communication generally. The concept of theory embraced in the series is broad, including not only the classical disciplines of poetics and rhetoric, but also those of aesthetics, linguistics, psychoanalysis, semiotics, and other cognate sciences that have inflected the systematic study of literature during the past half century.

Theorizing textual subjects

Agency and oppression

❖❖

MEILI STEELE

University of South Carolina

CAMBRIDGE
UNIVERSITY PRESS

Published by the Press Syndicate of the University of Cambridge
The Pitt Building, Trumpington Street, Cambridge CB2 1RP
40 West 20th Street, New York, NY 10011-4211, USA
10 Stamford Road, Oakleigh, Melbourne 3166, Australia

First published 1997

Printed in Great Britain at the University Press, Cambridge

A catalogue record for this book is available from the British Library

Library of Congress cataloguing in publication data

Steele, Meili, 1949–
Theorizing textual subjects: agency and oppression/Meili Steele.
p. cm. – (Literature, culture, theory: 21)
Includes bibliographical references and index.
ISBN 0 521 57185 5 (hardback). – ISBN 0 521 57679 2 (paperback)
1. Criticism.   2. Critical theory.   I. Title.   II. Series.
PN98.S6S75   1997
801'.95–dc20   96-26944   CIP

ISBN 0 521 57185 5 hardback
ISBN 0 521 57679 2 paperback

Contents

Acknowledgments

Earlier versions of parts of this book appeared in the following journals: *Boundary 2, Praxis International, Comparative Literature, New Literary History* and *Philosophy Today*.

In addition to my anonymous readers at Cambridge University Press, many people have read sections of the manuscript at different points during its composition and offered valuable suggestions. I want to name them: Amittai Avi-Ram, Carol Bernstein, Martin Donougho, Robert Dostal, Bill Edmiston, Robert Gooding-Williams, Michael Halberstam, Jane Hedley, Frank Kermode, Omar Lughod, John McGowan, Xavier Nicholas, Alfred Nordmann, Gerald Prince, Larry Rhu, Stephen Salkever, and Bill Thesing. Greg Jay read an early draft of the first three chapters and helped me clarify my ideas considerably. My daughter Laura Lane-Steele has contributed so much to this book, even though she hasn't read it. Lastly, I would like to thank my partner Cassie Premo who has given my work and my life extraordinary attention throughout the long development of the project.

❖❖❖

Introduction

❖❖❖

Most recent studies of the ethics and politics of literary theory focus on the polemical issues of literary value, multiculturalism, or canons.[1] The assumption of this book is that these questions cannot be fruitfully posed until we examine the theoretical commitments that drive discussions of textual politics. The commitments that I will address concern the relationships among language, subjectivity, and ethics. The influence of these commitments in contemporary debate can be seen in two assumptions made by most literary theory: (1) since any positive theory of the good life (good book) is necessarily ethnocentric, we should concern ourselves only with the political values of justice and negative freedom (freedom from social structures); (2) since the subject is a decentered site where social and linguistic forces converge, there can be no constructing ethical subject but only a constructed political subject. This is, of course, a simplification of the many positions I will examine in detail, but it captures enough of the problem for me to put the goals of this book on the table right away: to show how theory has boxed us into these unproductive positions and then to develop a way around the double impasse so that we can enrich the way we theorize textual value and read literary works. We do not need to decide what the canon is or what a good book is but rather to understand what is crippling our critical dialogue and how to find the resources to improve it.

The ethical/political dilemmas of literary theory can be seen in a conference on liberal education at the University of North Carolina. In one camp, there are conservatives, such as Allan Bloom, Lynne Cheney, and William Bennett, who attack the diversification of the curriculum because it ignores the need for "common ground,"

---

[1] The bibliography on canons and value is staggering. My concern is with the philosophical vocabulary in which value is theorized rather than with canon formation.

1

because it politicizes aesthetic issues, or because it leads to relativism. In the other camp, are those who form what Henry Louis Gates calls the "cultural Left" – that is, "that uneasy, shifting set of alliances formed by feminist critics, critics of so-called 'minority' discourse, and Marxist and poststructuralist critics generally, the Rainbow Coalition of contemporary critical theory" ("The Master's Pieces," p. 95).[2] The conservatives' attacks on the canon and the so-called "politicization" of the humanities make easy targets for the "cultural Left," which can point to examples of oppression and exclusion or to the inevitable political dimension in educational issues; however, the cultural Left's apparent unity masks its failure to address the question of what positive norms or guidelines should inform deliberation about education. This question brings out the emptiness of the word "Left" here, since it puts Stanley Fish with Michel Foucault. This vacuous alliance is made possible only by manifestly antidemocratic agendas, such as Bloom's and Bennett's. These agendas permit everyone to subscribe to different forms of a hermeneutics of suspicion that merely attack previous theories of cultural value with an unsituated appeal to justice and difference. A brief look at the remarks of three members of this Rainbow Coalition at the conference – Stanley Fish, Henry Louis Gates, and Gerald Graff – will highlight these problems.

In "The Common Touch, or, One Size Fits All," Fish shows how conservatives have made a fundamental epistemological error, not just a political one. Fish's essay aims to explode the myth of the common ground and shows how it is a "contested category": "Difference cannot be managed by measuring it against the common because the shape of the common is itself differential" (p. 247). Hence, he can point out that Lynne Cheney's writings result in "the marginalization and suppression of other traditions," that they "would arrest the play of democratic forces in order to reify as transcendent a particular and uncommon stage of cultural history" (p. 260). However, he never describes what political deliberation will look like once we have accepted this truth; instead, he leaves us with the dangerous platitude that everything is political: "Politics can neither be avoided nor embraced . . . [T]he political – the inescapability of partisan, angled seeing – is what

---

[2] There are other positions in this collection that do not fit this schema, such as Richard Rorty's "Two Cheers for the Cultural Left."

always already grasps us" (p. 249). He ends his essay not with democratic norms or guidelines but with a generalization about the production of values, a generalization that offers no ethical or political direction: "If values and standards are themselves historical products, fashioned and refashioned in the crucible of discussion and debate, there is no danger of their being subverted because they are always already being transformed" (p. 265). Fish describes the conditions that must inform any particular view of ethics, politics, and the self, but he never moves from this point to propose such a theory or to defend a positive agenda of his own.

In "The Master's Pieces," Gates revolts against a theory of difference that cuts through all identities. He does so not because he disagrees with the attack on conservatives but because he wants to talk about the constitution and achievements of individuals and communities and not just tell stories of oppression or mistaken epistemologies. It is not surprising that those who do not simply write about oppression but who are forced to live in communities whose ethical substance exiles them are not content only with an ethics/politics of negative liberty and difference. They know that only a rich axiology of existence, and not justice alone, can nourish them. As Cornel West says, "Those theories that try to take the place of wisdom disempower people on existential matters, just as those wisdoms that try to shun theory usually subordinate people to the political powers that be" (*The Ethical Dimensions of Marxist Thought*, pp. xxvii–xxviii). Hence, Gates does not flinch from offering an alternative position and rejecting strictures imposed by a deconstructive view of difference on identity for African Americans:

The classic critique of our attempts to reconstitute our own subjectivity, as women, as blacks, etc., is that of Jacques Derrida.

"This is the risk. The effect of Law is to build a structure of the subject, and as soon as you say, 'well, the woman is a subject and this subject deserves equal rights,' and so on – then you are caught in the logic of phallocentrism and you have rebuilt the empire of Law." To expressions such as this, made by a critic whose stand on sexism and racism has been exemplary, we must respond that the Western male subject has long been constituted historically for himself and in himself. And, while we readily accept, acknowledge, and partake of the critique of this subject as transcendent, to deny us the process of exploring and reclaiming our subjectivity before we critique it is the critical version of the grandfather clause, the double privileging of the categories that happen to be preconstituted. ("The Master's Pieces," p. 111)

Gates rightly claims that Derrida's theory of language cannot articulate satisfactorily the importance of agency and tradition in African American literature; however, instead of making a direct theoretical challenge to Derrida or making a meta-theoretical move that places Derrida's accounts of identity and history as one theoretical option within a broad hermeneutic space – which is the direction I will pursue in chapter 1 – he says Derrida's strictures do not apply to African American literature for political reasons. By simply walking away from the theoretical problem and pursuing a "vernacular criticism," in which the African American tradition is analyzed in isolation with its own critical language, Gates adopts an incoherent theoretical position and a flawed ethical/political one. First, his view remains vulnerable to a deconstructive critique, such as the one Barbara Johnson makes. She rightly claims that Gates "posit[s] the existence of pure, unified, and separate traditions, and spatializes the concept of identity" ("Response to Henry Louis Gates," p. 42).[3] This oscillation between deconstructing and essentializing is a familiar and vicious circle in contemporary theory that is produced precisely by the poststructuralist assumption that any account of the agent's self-constitutions is a humanist essentialism, an essentialism that ignores two of the presuppositions of contemporary cultural criticism, the decentered subject and the oppressiveness of ethical traditions.[4] Gates needs to take on both points: not all theories and practices of agency are essentialist; not all ethical traditions are so oppressive as to be incapable of recuperation. A satisfactory response to Johnson would provide a hermeneutics that could assess the different traditions that inform African American cultural identities and that could show how they enable and/or oppress. In characterizing the American/European traditions only in terms of domination, he does not account for the positive potential that African American writers have found in them or for the complex ways in which oppression

---

[3] Johnson's "Response" is to Gates's "Canon-Formation, Literary History, and the Afro-American Tradition," which is nearly identical to the Gates essay published in *The Politics of Liberal Education.*

[4] See Diana Fuss's *Essentially Speaking* for an account of these oscillations that unfortunately continues rather than ends them. I discuss her work in chapter 1.

works through internalization inside the texts themselves. Gates goes further than Fish, because he (Gates) does not simply unmask theories of tradition and affirm difference but actually goes on to characterize one kind of difference. Nonetheless, he still lets the tradition and the theories that sustain and critique it off too easily.

Gerald Graff's essay "Teach the Conflicts" pushes the arguments of Fish and Gates one step further since Graff does not just appeal to the truth and goodness of difference but proposes a way for thematizing alternative views of the true and the good. Graff shows how we need to get beyond poking holes in conservative proposals and "to concede that the curriculum is badly in need of coherence, but to reject its prescription for supplying that coherence. Instead of trying to superimpose coherence from above, we should try to locate a principle of coherence in the conversation itself in all its contentiousness" (pp. 50–60). Yet, Graff does not discuss the place from which we understand this conflict; his essay insists that we confront the familiar liberal dilemma of how a society should cope with the competing views of the good held by its members, but he does not offer new norms or other guidelines that would get us beyond liberalism's purported neutrality.[5] Instead of enriching the context of deliberation, he simply insists that conflicts be presented. However, Fish catches Graff's evasion in his critique of those on the Left who try to reconcile a theory of decentered difference with a positive agenda. "Each [those who, like Graff, propose teaching the conflicts and those who, like Betty Jean Craige, propose tolerance] fails to see that conflict and tolerance cannot be privileged – made into platforms from which one can confidently and unpolitically speak – without turning them into the kind of normative and transcendental standards to which they are constantly opposed" ("The Common Touch," p. 248). Fish tacks on "transcendental" to "normative," as if the two were necessarily linked. Norms do not need transcendental support. If

---

[5] Ronald Dworkin formulates liberalism's fundamental thesis with regard to the good life as follows: "Since the citizens of a society differ in their conceptions [of the good] the government does not treat them as equals if it prefers one conception of the good life or of what gives value to life" ("Liberalism," p. 64). When literary theorists employ the word "liberal," they usually refer to Matthew Arnold or Wayne Booth – if they drop a footnote at all – and not to contemporary political theorists. In political theory, the values of liberal democracy are not conservative museum pieces untouched by poststructuralist or Marxist theory. See William Connolly's Foucaultian liberalism in *The Politics and Ambiguity* and *Identity and Difference* or Habermas's recuperation of the Enlightenment.

the Enlightenment's democratic revolution linked the foundational-ist epistemological project with its political ideals, many philosophers now separate them.[6]

This separation means that strategies seeking merely to "de-stabilize," "undo," and "subvert" are inadequate, since this rhetoric of undirected change is justified only in the presence of something so awful that anything else is preferable; instead, these ideals can be criticized and renewed. Any theory of critique implies a theory of recuperation that makes that critique possible. What this means is that the Left will have to give up using only the vocabulary of power to characterize liberal democratic traditions, a vocabulary that justifies the quest for a revolution so radical that it is inconceivable. As Chantal Mouffe says, "The objective of the Left should be the extension and deepening of the democratic revolution initiated two hundred years ago" (*Radical Democracy*, p. 1).[7] Without a hermeneutics of recuperation that can reconstruct and valorize textual practices, a politics of difference threatens to become an indiscriminate appeal to diversity, a utopian projection that provides no language for discussing the identities and traditions of the oppressed or the dominant culture(s). It is precisely this need for positive norms that conservatives recognize, even if they come up with inadequate ways to fill it. Hence, both defenders and critics of the canon fall into what Amy Gutmann calls the false opposition of "give them liberty or give them virtue" ("Undemocratic Education," p. 75). As she says, "Cultivating character and intellect through education constrains children's future choices, but it does not uniquely determine . . . The question is not whether to maximize freedom or to inculcate virtue, but how to combine freedom and virtue" (p. 75).

What accompanies this particular ethical/political configuration in literary theory is the disappearance of agency, the absence of a theory of the constructing, as well as of the constructed, subject. In the poststructuralist paradigm, the "subject" becomes simply an

---

[6] See Hans Blumenberg's *The Legitimacy of the Modern Age* and Richard Rorty's *Contingency, Irony, and Solidarity*.

[7] Mouffe clarifies her proposal as follows: "For those who refuse to see 'really existing' liberal democratic capitalism as the 'end of history,' radical democracy is the only alternative . . . Such a perspective does not imply the rejection of liberal democracy and its replacement by a completely new political form of society, as the traditional idea of revolution entailed, but a radicalization of the modern democratic revolution" (*Radical Democracy*, p. 1.)

effect of forces working behind the back of the agent. We do not find theories of the subject's ethical constitution, commitments, or capacities but theories that display a self-consciousness for which they never account. In a world composed only of impersonal forces rather than agents and values, hermeneutics and ethics disappear in favor of political accounts of these forces and their effects. However, theorists who offer accounts of only a constructed subject avoid the hermeneutic circle by ignoring the agency of their own speech acts. This is not to say that poststructuralism's important critiques of humanistic views of subjectivity and value should be dismissed. Instead, they need to be accommodated as much as possible within a new space for hermeneutical and ethical reflection and serve as an ethical/political challenge to any closing of the hermeneutic circle. But where can we find theories that affirm agency and discuss the problem of articulating conflicting ethical goods?

When I began reading the works of ethical/political theorists such as Michael Sandel, Martha Nussbaum, Charles Taylor, Seyla Benhabib, Nancy Fraser, Iris Young, Cornel West, and Alasdair MacIntyre,[8] I noticed a concern for a host of issues about ethics/politics and identity that were important to literary theory but ignored within it, as Nussbaum and others note.[9] Since many of the theorists listed above have also addressed poststructuralist and Marxist critiques that inform literary theory, the question is why literary theory has ignored these debates. Among the many reasons, the most prominent is no doubt the one that Nussbaum offers when she says that literary critics are "constrained by the pressure of the current thought that to discuss a text's ethical and social content is somehow to neglect 'textuality,' the complex relationships of that text with other texts" (*Love's Knowledge*, p. 170). The Anglo-American philosophical tradition does not formulate its ethical/political concerns with linguistic terminology drawn from the structuralism and poststructuralism that currently dominate literary theory, and this abstention – combined with poststructuralist assumptions about the subject and ethical traditions

---

[8] See, for example, Sandel's *Liberalism and the Limits of Justice*, Taylor's "What's Wrong with Negative Freedom?," Benhabib's *Situating the Self*, MacIntyre's *After Virtue*, West's *Keeping Faith*, and Fraser's *Unruly Practices*.

[9] See "Perceptive Equilibrium: Literary Theory and Ethical Theory," *Love's Knowledge*. Unfortunately, Nussbaum speaks exclusively of Anglo-American ethical theory rather than Continental philosophy.

– has created the unfortunate assumption in literary theory that the only way to connect language to ethics is in the poststructuralist manner.[10]

Hence, the need for a new philosophy of language is directly related to the ontological problems of ethics and agency, since the ontologies offered by contemporary theory are linguistic. What Richard Rorty dubbed "the linguistic turn" many years ago is more accurately characterized as the "ontological turn,"[11] in which both the Continental heritage of Heidegger and the Anglo-American heritage of Wittgenstein offer competing views of the relationship of language and subjectivity. These debates point to the need for a meta-theoretical dimension, in which we can assess these alternative views in light of our theoretical needs. Moreover, they show the need to integrate ethics – or more broadly, axiology – into linguistic theory.

A good way to get hold of how language, ethics, and the self are connected is to think about the conflicts in daily life between understanding someone as an agent (what I will call a first-/second-person account) and understanding him or her as a constructed subject (what I will call a third-person account). In first-person accounts, we seek to articulate the subject's intentions, background assumptions, and the vocabularies used to constitute personal or community identities. In third-person accounts, we redescribe the subject's language or action in terms that do not respect the integrity of the subject's self-constitution. In first-/second-person accounts, we think of ourselves as agents; in third-person accounts, we redescribe ourselves as others with terms that cut across the

[10] Nussbaum makes no effort to join textual theories and ethical theory – which is at the heart of my book – and this explains why literary theorists do not have much dialogue with her or the ethical tradition she defends. Instead, she aims her work to Anglo-American ethical philosophers, urging them to consider her neo-Aristotelianism and her appropriation of literature. Anglo-American attempts to link language and ethics in the 1950s, such as the work of R.M. Hare and C.L. Stevenson, were narrow investigations of usage that have been largely abandoned and that perhaps have led philosophers to stay away from the linguistic dimension of ethics. See Bernard Williams, "The Linguistic Turn," chapter 7 in *Ethics and the Limits of Philosophy* for an account as well as Alasdair MacIntyre's critique in chapter 2 of *After Virtue*. I think such a dialogue is both possible and important. I discuss Nussbaum's work in chapter 4 after I have connected language and ethics in a way that is compatible with her work.

[11] *The Linguistic Turn.* I discuss the "ontological turn" in chapter 2 and in "The Ontological Turn and Its Ethical Consequences: Habermas and the Poststructuralists." For an excellent philosophical exposition of the character of agency from a Wittgensteinian perspective, see Charles Altieri's *Subjective Agency*.

action vocabulary of the agent so that the agent's vocabulary is determined by forces of which he/she is unaware. For example, we could redescribe a person's virtuous self-description in terms of a psychological mechanism – guilt, masochism – or in terms of an economic/social system – capitalism's ethic of consumption. We employ both of these modes in everyday conversation. With our friends, we are attentive to the language of self-constitution, but we also need to be aware of the patterns that operate "behind our friends' backs" and that help deepen our understanding – for example, the cyclical ways someone talks about her mother. Sometimes we will challenge our friends' language of constitution – for example, when we cannot endure the way they are hurting us or themselves. In this case, we will suggest a third-person description directly or indirectly: "I think you need to ask yourself why you keep falling in love with people who mistreat you?" Or, "In other words, what (third-person) forces are pushing you?" If we are in pain, we sometimes pay to have our language of constitution challenged by a therapist, whose job is to help us integrate the forces working behind our backs into our first-person accounts of ourselves. Third-person accounts often make unflattering redescriptions of our ethical self-understandings; however, these accounts are not views from nowhere; they ultimately appeal to a revised ethical self-understanding in which we can live.

If we often move back and forth between thinking of the subject as constructing and constructed in everyday life, we do not do so in critical theory. One reason is that the pains that interest critical theory are not usually accessible to dialogue with friends or therapists. These pains, such as the domination of women or the alienation of people from their work, require social change for them to be relieved. Moreover, the complex linguistic, social, and economic forces that produce pain cannot be grasped and laid out in front of us; rather, they are so pervasive that they do not just impinge on persons but constitute them. That is, the first-person accounts people give of their own actions employ ideas and languages that are complicitous with their own oppression and hence are epistemologically and ethically misguided. According to the assumptions of much critical theory, people do not have the autonomy they ascribe to themselves; moreover, the ethical ideas that inform their self-interpretations are better described as systems of power. Theorists, unlike therapists, do not have a dialogue with

9

these "persons"; theorists speak about not to these subjects. The dialogue is only with like-minded readers.

While there is little doubt about the importance of these third-person critiques, the theorists doing (and reading about) the unmasking account for neither their own agency nor the ethical resources that they use to make their critiques. If oppression is airtight, and if the ethical resources of the West are so bankrupt, how does the speaker get free, and where did he/she find an untainted language of justice and freedom in which to make an appeal? My point is not just to demonstrate a logical contradiction in these readings. Rather, I want to insist on the need to develop accounts of the constructing subject that can dialogue with accounts of the constructed subject. This project also requires a recuperation of our ethical resources that can respond to third-person stories that reduce ethics to power. I use the word "dialogue" because first-/second- and third-person accounts need to confront each other continually. We are both constructing and constructed subjects, and our deliberations need to be informed by both vocabularies. All unmaskings of our agency and our values are addressed by someone to someone (even if this is a future "someone") for some reason. That is, even the most anti-hermeneutical accounts, such as Foucault's or Derrida's, are appeals for a new kind of hermeneutics that avoids difficulties in the old ones.

Chapter 1 begins with the historical background to the contemporary arguments between third-person and first-/second-person perspectives, and I start with Kant's two realms and Hegel's critique of Kant before exploring latter reformulations from Marx to Heidegger and Gadamer. This exposition sets up my examination of the axiological and ontological assumptions that inform the work of Derrida, Foucault, Jean-Francois Lyotard, Jürgen Habermas, Edward Said, Judith Butler, and Fredric Jameson. My critical assessment of their work is done through the problematic of explanation and understanding, which is the philosophical background to the story of first/second-person (understanding) and third-person (explanation) I told above. I focus on two issues. The first is how a concern with domination eliminates ethics and agency. While Jameson and the poststructuralists think that our culture has become so deeply flawed that we cannot imagine an alternative, Habermas limits his conception of ethics and agency through a formalist universalism that abstracts ethics from cultural particulars. The second issue is the way claims of incommensurability among competing theories block discussion. The incommensurability issue can be dramatized through the following dialogue. Pragmatics says to Deconstruction, "You can't have signs without sentences." Deconstruction retorts, "You can't talk about the logocentric unit of the sentence until you've resolved the irresolvable aporias of the sign." "You can't talk about signs or sentences without background practices that underwrite your usage," says Habermas.[12] My goal is to create a space for ethics and agency and to reformulate this incommensurability in a positive way through meta-critical reflection. Hence, the dispute between Habermas and the poststructuralists can be reworked so that our theoretical choices are no longer framed as mutually exclusive alternatives. At the risk of leaping ahead of the argument, I will say that while poststructuralists do not theorize the shared presuppositions that underwrite their critiques, Habermas's holistic theory of background practices buries differences and obscures potential relations of power in the name of conditions necessary for intelligibility.

While chapter 1 reframes the debates so that agency and ethics are possible, it leaves open the question of which ethical resources are available and how to think about them. Chapter 2 looks at two philosophers who discuss the importance of language and ethics for a constructing subject, Richard Rorty and Alasdair MacIntyre. Rorty and MacIntyre are on opposite sides of the debate in ethical/political theory between liberals and communitarians. This debate is important to literary theorists for a number of reasons. First, it forces them to see that contemporary liberalism is not the caricatured strawperson that is so often evoked – that is, the autonomous liberal subject who takes *himself* as an epistemological and ethical ground. One of the curiosities of recent critical theory has been the outright dismissal of liberalism in the name of liberal values, such as freedom and justice, or liberal democratic institutions, as we saw in the papers from the conference on liberal education.[13] Second, the communitarian critique of

---

[12] Habermas goes beyond the holism of Searle, Rorty, or Wittgenstein to claim that communicative, not strategic, linguistic use is fundamental. This claim is the linchpin in his entire project, as we will see in chapter 1.

[13] I am indebted to John McGowan's *Postmodernism and Its Critics* for its excellent analysis of postmodern theory in terms of positive and negative liberty.

liberalism brings into focus the full range of ethical issues about the good life that literary theory's exclusive concern with domination and negative liberty leaves out. I selected these two philosophers as representatives in the debate because they both base much of their arguments in competing philosophies of language that will enrich the ways we think of texts. Rorty starts with a linguistic pragmatism from which he works out a postmodern liberal view of the self and community. MacIntyre's linguistic problematic is the "tradition," and he gives this troubled term an important philosophical bite by playing it off competing contemporary problematics for language and subjectivity and by using it to unfold the complexities and resources of cultural history. Both of these thinkers offer important alternatives to the theorists presented in chapter 1, though neither engages with the stories of oppression spun by these thinkers. Moreover, neither Rorty nor MacIntyre gives us a language for discussing the specifics of literary or social texts, preferring to keep their arguments aimed at competing meta-philosophical claims about language.

Chapter 3 develops a way of deliberating about the ethics/politics of language and subjectivity in literary contexts. For this, we need to bring narratives of agency, such as those in chapter 2, into dialogue with narratives of determination, such as those in chapter 1. To do this, I will use the model of a critical dialogue between friends as a point of departure for a theory of reading. This example shows how the work of critical dialogue, like the study of texts, asks us not simply to explain or unmask the past but to envision hopes for the future through renewal. By developing Charles Taylor's idea of "strong evaluations" and then connecting it to a concept of linguistic practice, I show how the ethical dimension of language shapes the constitution of the selves and communities. I argue that these shapes need to be articulated and not simply designated as "other" or "difference" if deliberation about ethics and politics in a multicultural society is to replace accusation. At the same time, we need critical language that cuts against the grain of these constructions, that redescribes them and listens for otherness. The democratic hermeneutics I develop here gives a place to the insights made available by liberal, communitarian, and poststructuralist problematics by revising the self-understanding of each theory. In the second half of the chapter, I develop my interpretive model through an analysis of the controversy surrounding Carol Gilligan's ethics of care and her reading of Susan Glaspell's "A Jury of Her Peers," a story that forces us to theorize how we interpret the distinctiveness and worth of women's practices generated under conditions of oppression. My reading of the story serves to break down the opposition in contemporary theory in which the oppressed are either idealized or reduced to discursive structures.

Chapter 4 turns from textual values of marginalized works to those of a canonized text, Henry James's *The Ambassadors*. I begin by enriching the theoretical connection between language and value sketched in chapter 3 and then trace the practices of truth, beauty, and goodness as they appear in the sentences that present Lambert Strether. My reading is principally recuperative – that is, I read the text for its positive potential for those interested in the postmodern dynamics of language and value. If the text is not to be only of historical interest, an example of rhetorical aporia, or an example of modernist reification, then it needs to be read from a position that allows it to speak to the present. This does not mean that we ignore gender, class, and race, which are crucial to the values in the text, or that we forget Walter Benjamin's famous remark that "there is no document of civilization which is not at the same time a document of barbarism" (*Illuminations*, p. 258). What it does mean is that the second movement in the dialectic of reading is a critique of James's text from the site of specific alternative textual spaces. In this way, "ideology" is not a vague and implicit claim but a specific site of interrogation.

Chapter 5 brings together all the theoretical and ethical/political threads of the book and shows how they can improve our dialogue about central questions facing critical theory – difference, democracy, and subjectivity. I do this in two steps. In the first, I look at the argument over race between identity politics and poststructuralism and show how neither side has the ethical/political vocabulary for addressing the major issues. (Gates's attempt to unify poststructuralism and identity politics in *The Signifying Monkey* is the focus for my discussion.) In the second part of the chapter, I read Ralph Ellison's literary and critical writings. Ellison draws on the ethical and political vocabularies of the three major groups we have examined thus far – liberals, communitarians, and radicals. He speaks the language of the liberal who affirms individualism, justice, and liberty; he also speaks the language of the communitarian who extols the virtues of different traditions and who is critical of liberal neutrality toward the good; lastly, he plays the role of the genealogist who unmasks the self-understandings of American culture across racial lines. For Ellison, the culture in which we are embedded is a deceptive, imprisoning one; however, unlike the poststructuralists, he does not set up the site of critique on an unspecifiable planet where cultural nourishment is problematic. He recuperates the very ethical/political traditions that he is attacking, sorting out the meta-philosophical and the first-order issues. Indeed, *Invisible Man* can be read as a meta-philosophical search for a site for telling the story. Ellison's writings show how he worked through the conflicts between the need for third-person accounts – in his time, these were Marx and Freud – the self-understandings of African American traditions, and the ideals of democracy.

1

❖❖

Stories of oppression and appeals to freedom

❖❖

Any attempt to characterize and critique in one chapter the diversity of contemporary theoretical practices will require a tight focus and purpose. What drives the exposition in this chapter is a cluster of pervasive and crippling philosophical assumptions about subjectivity and value. My goal is to ferret out these assumptions, show their possibilities and weaknesses and then propose a new way for these theories to speak to each other within a democratic hermeneutics. What I mean by "democratic hermeneutics" will emerge only through the argument of the entire book, but the first step toward such an understanding is through a meta-critique of the theories that claim our attention today. My way of focusing this meta-critique will be the hermeneutic issue of explanation and understanding, in which third-person accounts of the subject must negotiate with first-/second-person accounts of agents. The theorists whom I will discuss below – Jacques Derrida, Michel Foucault, Jean-François Lyotard, Diana Fuss, Judith Butler, Jürgen Habermas, Fredric Jameson, and Barbara Smith – were selected not only because they are influential but also because the problems in their work fit together nicely around this hermeneutic dilemma. This approach will clarify how we can think about the competing vocabularies of determination and constitution that now collide in discussions about race and gender, as we saw in the citation from Henry Louis Gates in the Introduction.[1]

But why should I begin with meta-critique? The answer lies in the nature of contemporary debate. These arguments are not between those who seek to ground a subject of epistemology and those who situate the subject in hermeneutic space. The epistemological strawperson – e.g., Cartesian subject – is no longer worth attacking. Instead, we have competing philosophical

---

[1] I have deferred examining gender and race until chapters 3, 4, and 5.

problematics that define the relationship of language and subjectivity in radically different ways, and these problematics underwrite political and ethical values. Debates on subjectivity do not thematize these differences but dramatize them, as we see in the recently published Derrida/Gadamer encounter and in Barbara Smith's sociological critique of axiology.[2] Thinkers in these debates are so committed to a theory that they either squeeze out meta-critical space altogether or they refuse to thematize the theoretical commitments in their meta-critiques. Habermas and Rorty are examples of the latter, while the poststructuralists and Smith exemplify the former.[3] Habermas's meta-critique never puts the theoretical underpinning of his philosophy of communicative action into question, while Richard Rorty rewrites his opponents in terms of pragmatism's linguistic instrumentalism. If poststructuralists follow the ontological turn initiated by Heidegger and Gadamer, they theorize the relationship of language and subjectivity so as to take apart the hermeneutics of the German philosophers. Unlike Habermas's critique of hermeneutics, which offers a double reading of the social text, one in terms of hermeneutics and another in terms of a critical sociology,[4] poststructuralists attempt to break with the hermeneutic circle entirely. They claim that Habermas's theory of language is narrow and oppressive. All parties run together their theoretical claims with normative claims so that the ethics/politics can be implied or even derived from a theoretical problematic. The two are connected but the connections are not inevitable and nonnegotiable. In order to make such negotiations, we need a meta-critical space that respects the powers of poststructuralists and Habermasians without succumbing to theoretical dogmatism or relativism. This chapter will create a meta-critical space for examining these competing problematics. I

[2] See Dianne Michelfelder and Richard Palmer, eds. *Dialogue and Deconstruction* and Smith's *Contingencies of Value*.
[3] Habermas wants to avoid the ontological turn initiated by Heidegger and Gadamer through his concept of the lifeworld (which I will discuss later), while Rorty ignores differences among contemporary theories through his assumption that the true relationship between language and subjectivity is an instrumental one. He is thus able to "split the difference" between Habermas and Lyotard ("Habermas and Lyotard on Postmodernity," *Essays on Heidegger and Others*) only by suppressing their different theories of language and making them pragmatists. In his response to Rorty, Habermas rightly refuses to let this difference be put out of play ("Questions and Counter-Questions," pp. 193–95).
[4] See Habermas, *The Theory of Communicative Action*.

use the argument between the poststructuralists and Habermas because their influential debate has framed the issues in a way that makes the recuperation of the Enlightenment's democratic political and ethical project difficult. This is why I bring Habermas into this chapter on third-person accounts and why I am more concerned with his limits than his strengths, which I will address later on.

This chapter falls into three parts. First, I give a brief exposition of the problem of explanation and understanding in political philosophy from Kant to Gadamer. This exposition will not simply serve as a background to contemporary discussions, it will also provide philosophical resources for the democratic hermeneutics I develop in chapters 2 and 3. After this introduction, I consider poststructuralists and Smith. The second half of the chapter looks at Habermas, Jameson, and Edward Said.

Explanation and understanding in political philosophy

The tension between these competing approaches to the subject gets its first important articulation in the work of Immanuel Kant, who wants to bring the first-order understandings of his culture to the bar of critique: "Our age is, in especial degree, the age of criticism, and to criticism everything must submit" (*Critique of Pure Reason*, p. 9). Kant seeks to correct "pre-modern" philosophers who conflated scientific questions about efficient causes with religious, ethical, and aesthetic questions. In pre-modern views of reason, such as Plato's or Aristotle's, ethics and epistemology come together; our knowledge of the world is inseparable from our attunement to the telos of the species and the universe. For Kant, it is necessary to distinguish between the subject as object in nature and the subject as moral agent. In the former case, the individual is an object that conforms to the mechanical laws of the universe. Kant's view of the subject as the product of natural laws does not account for the activity and continuity of the knowing subject. To solve this dilemma, Kant makes his well-known transcendental argument, in which the conditions for the possibility of knowledge are laid out. The result is the postulation of a transcendental "I think" that must be capable of accompanying the cognitions of the empirical self (*Groundwork of the Metaphysics of Morals*, p. 119; *Critique of Pure Reason*, p. 154). This "I think" is not available to introspection; it is a logical condition needed to make knowledge possible.

This account of science does not work for morality, however. For morality, Kant says, we need a completely separate point of view in which freedom and autonomy are possible, "for to be independent of determination by causes in the sensible world (and this is what reason must always attribute to itself) is to be free" (*Groundwork of the Metaphysics of Morals*, p. 120). Kant calls this point of view the "intelligible," which is opposed to the sensible world. In the intelligible world, the causality of natural law is replaced by the causality of the will. "The concept of the intelligible world is thus only a point of view in which reason finds itself constrained to adopt outside appearances and in order to conceive itself as practical. To conceive itself thus would not be possible if the influences of sensibility were able to determine man; but it is none the less necessary so far as we are not to deny him rational cause which is active by means of reason – that is, which is free in its operation" (p. 126). Autonomy is the self-legislating capacity of humanity to give itself laws. These laws are universalizing maxims separated from the ethical goods of the community and our personal desires, for consideration of such factors would undermine the universal validity of the moral "ought." Freedom and the will are beyond the reach of scientific explanation and empirical embodiment.

Hegel criticizes this Kantian project on several fronts. First, Hegel wants to reconcile the pre-modern ethical community of Aristotle with the modern freedom of Kant: "Individuals do not live as private persons for their own ends alone, but in the very act of willing these they will the universal in the light of the universal" (*Philosophy of Right*, p. 161). He also wants to heal the split inside the Kantian subject between desire and moral reason, so that desire is educated and reworked by reason. To do this, Hegel performs an immanent critique on Kantian notions, that is, he offers a critique aimed at the internal contradictions. For example, Hegel explodes Kant's methodological individualism by showing "I" presupposes a "we" and a struggle for recognition (*Phenomenology of the Spirit*, pp. 104–38).

What underwrites Hegel's immanent critique, however, is his historical narrative about how modern freedom emerges through an historical logic. In this view, historical periods shift when the internal contradictions among the dominant ideas become so great that they demand a new solution, a dialectical leap forward. This "solution," in turn, develops its own contradictions, and so forth. Hegel's historicizing story brings out a tension in his method. On the one hand, Hegel's phenomenological method brings out the points of view of the participants in history in an unprecedented way. On the other hand, Hegel's philosophical narrator stands above the intersubjective perspective of historical actors and posits a transsubjective agent, *Geist*, which is realized behind the backs of the historical agents. This is the famous "cunning of reason," by which history works through the particular actions of individuals: "It is not the general idea that is implicated in opposition and combat, and that is exposed to danger. It remains in the background, untouched and uninjured. This may be called the cunning of reason – that it sets the passions to work for itself while that which develops its existence through such impulsion pays the penalty, and suffers the loss" (*Philosophy of History*, p. 33). Thus, the failure of atomistic conceptions of society to see the social whole (*Philosophy of Right*, pp. 129–30) is not available to the agents (intersubjective perspective) of the time but only to an observer who can see the logic working behind their backs (third-person perspective). Seyla Benhabib articulates the tension between understanding and explanation in Hegel by contrasting "intersubjectivity" and "transsubjectivity": "According to the standpoint of intersubjectivity, the perspective of human agents is constitutive of the validity and meaning of their interactions, whereas the standpoint of transsubjectivity locates this validity and meaning in a source external to the shared perspectives of social agents, in the standpoint of a thinker-observer" (*Critique, Norm, and Utopia*, p. 90). Because of his transsubjective perspective, "Hegel is led to deny the 'otherness' constitutive of the perspectives of the first and second person" (p. 95). The multiple perspectives of actual historical agents become the march of logic. Benhabib spells the ethical/political danger of Hegel's use of third-person accounts: "The well-known authoritarianism of Hegel's theory of the state, therefore, is not a matter of mere political preference. It is perfectly consistent with a transsubjective ideal of freedom which assigns insight into the meaning and validity of individuals' activities of a 'third' who observes and comprehends, while excluding the standpoint of intersubjectivity" (p. 98).

Marx reworks this Hegelian legacy by making the third-person explanation not the realization of *Geist* but the material force of capitalism that shapes intersubjective relations. Marx also reorients Hegel's retrospective role for philosophy, summed up by his famous remark that "the Owl of Minerva spreads its wings only with the falling of dusk" (Hegel, *Philosophy of Right*, p. 13), into a prospective utopian one. Marx will turn this subject toward the future, so that what is happening behind the backs of agents can be appropriated by them. This future reconciliation means the end of the need for a third-person perspective that can reveal false consciousness, and it means the emergence of transparent society. Until that time, however, we find two perspectives: the perspective of the historical actors and the explanatory perspective offered by the systemic account of capital available to the narrator.[5]

The other great attempt to combine explanation and understanding in the study of culture is Freud's psychoanalytic theory. He redescribes the contents of consciousness in terms of psychic mechanisms rather than historical forces. Although Freud's goal is not social transformation, many theorists, such as those in the Frankfurt School, put Marx and Freud together into critical theory. As Habermas says, "Psychoanalytic therapy is not based, like somatic medicine, which is 'causal' in a narrower sense, on making use of known causal connections. Rather, it owes its efficacy to overcoming connections themselves" (*Knowledge and Human Interests*, p. 271).

Nietzsche offers a deep critique of the legacies of Kant, Hegel and Marx, and yet he does not work from a scientific model as Freud does. He stands at right angles to the ethical/political histories we tell ourselves. Against the notion of developing tradition, Nietzsche initiates genealogical inquiries that unmask the philosophical categories of ethical/political self-understanding such as the "will" and the "moral." "Willing seems to me above all something *complicated*, something that is a unit only as a word" (*Beyond Good and Evil*, p. 25). Subject and object are not unities but coverups for complex psychic and historical forces: "We seek a doer for every event . . . A thing is the sum of its effects" (*The Will to*

---

[5] See Benhabib (*Critique, Norm, and Utopia*, pp. 125–26) for a discussion of the conflict between the perspective of capital and of the proletariat. "What is missing in Marx is the mediation between these two points of view" (p. 126).

Power, p. 551). Unlike Hegel, Nietzsche finds no unifying *Geist* working behind the backs of agents to bring about the unity of community and freedom; instead, he finds the will-to-power at work behind mystifying ideals of the Enlightenment and Christianity: "Life itself is *essentially* appropriation, injury, overpowering of what is alien and weaker ... 'Exploitation' does not belong to a corrupt or imperfect and primitive society: it belongs to the essence of what lives, as a basic organic function; it is a consequence of the will to power, which is after all the will to life" (*Beyond Good and Evil*, p. 203). The cunning of reason is replaced by the cunning of contingency. Where Hegel and Marx employ third-person accounts to explain the misguided and confused self-understandings of historical actors, Nietzsche seeks to unmask both agents and explainers, both understanding and explanation. The will-to-truth that characterizes the explainers and philosophical culture is itself a sign of the impoverished character of modernity.

The problem of explanation and understanding is given its most influential hermeneutical formulation by Heidegger in *Being and Time*. Heidegger seeks to revise the way we think about ourselves and the world. One of his central claims is that understanding is not just one kind of knowing – as opposed to explaining. Rather, understanding is the power to grasp one's own possibilities for being within the context of the everyday world. All explanatory, scientific culture is derivative of this primordial sense of understanding that makes us who we are. Scientific methods encourage us to step back and examine objects, to sever them from their living contexts, which we already understand before attempting to isolate objects. For Heidegger, subject and object emerge together within the horizon of cultural practices that make up our pre-understandings. The epistemological paradigm of subject against object is replaced by a hermeneutic circle (*Being and Time*, p. 194). In his later writings, Heidegger abandons the philosophical anthropology of *Being and Time* for a deeper critique of Western ontology, a critique that links the objectification of Being into entities with the placement of "man" and his interests at the center of philosophy. In this view, we try to get clear and distinct ideas about the entities in the world so that we can control them for our use. Heidegger calls this objectifying, calculative thinking *Gestell*. This critique of modern culture has been the source of complex dispute, which far transcends this elementary exposition.[6] His shallow notion of history, his transcendental account of what it means to be a human being, his dismissal of democratic institutions, and his focus on authenticity rather than intersubjectivity are crucial philosophical problems.

In *Truth and Method*, Hans-Georg Gadamer develops a dialogical hermeneutics that revises Heidegger's understanding of subjectivity and history. Like Heidegger, Gadamer argues against the subject/object methodologies that inform history and the other social sciences. For Gadamer, however, the subject is not thrown in search of authenticity in the midst of the "idle talk" of modern culture (*Being and Time*) nor is the history of Western thought the story of the rise of *Gestell*. Gadamer's subject is embedded in an historical tradition that is continually reproduced (*Truth and Method*, p. 293) through a dialogue between past and present. There is no cunning of reason driving the development of tradition, no infinite perspective that transcends the continuous re-appropriations of tradition, in which the present re-understands itself, the past, and the future. Language is the historical medium in which we finite beings live, a medium that heals the Kantian splits among epistemology, ethics, and aesthetics and that delivers us from subject-centered reason. Yet Gadamer's dialogical account drives out what Marx's and Freud's third-person accounts seek to bring to the foreground – the forces that twist and contort cultural dialogue but are never thematized.[7] Moreover, his notion of tradition overlooks the plural and conflictual nature of culture.

In the 1960s, the Freudian and Marxist projects grafted the structural explanations of linguistics (Saussure) onto their causal explanations (Lacan and Althusser are the best examples). Structural explanations of language seek to map out the rules and processes by which linguistic units are articulated and combined. In structuralism and poststructuralism, the purpose of this graft was

[6] Heidegger says, "That period we call modern . . . is defined by the fact that man becomes the center and measure of all beings. Man is the *subjectum*, that which lies at the bottom of all beings, that is, in modern terms, at the bottom of all objectification and representation" (Cited in Habermas, *The Philosophical Discourse of Modernity*, p. 33). Heidegger's alternative to calculative thinking is poetic thinking, in which "man is not the lord of beings" but "the shepherd of beings" ("Letter on Humanism," p. 239). On the Heidegger controversy, see Victor Farias, *Heidegger and Nazism* and Richard Wolin, *The Politics of Being*.
[7] See his famous debate with Habermas collected in *The Hermeneutic Tradition*, eds. Gayle L. Ormiston and Alan D. Schrift.

to replace "understanding" – a concept that was overloaded with the humanistic vocabulary of hermeneutics and phenomenology – with an anti-humanistic system that explored the conditions that made speech possible.[8] In this way, structuralists and poststructuralists could complicate or eliminate Marxism's causal account and still explain (unmask) the subject's self-understandings. Poststructuralism does not give up interest in force for an interest in structure; instead, it replaces Marx's causal explanation with Nietzsche's genealogy of power, which makes force coextensive with language and not external to it. Instead of seeking an explanation for our self-deceptions in economic forces or in the complex interplay of psychic mechanisms, poststructuralists, like Nietzsche, propose an invisible story of power that is buried so deeply in language and history that we cannot overcome it.

However, not all theorists follow Saussure's structural explanation, which excludes the agent's self-understanding, or Nietzsche's evaporation of causality into a vague ontology of power. Habermas's reconstructive linguistic project seeks to uncover the implicit know-how that speakers activate in their discourse. Unlike Saussure's concern with signs and with *la langue*, Habermas focuses on pragmatics – that is, with speakers, speech acts, referents, etc. Moreover, he ties this structural explanation to causal explanations as well – e.g., the ways that capitalism distorts speech. Although Habermas does not seek to bypass the agent's understanding in the way structuralism and poststructuralism do, he resists giving historical self-understanding the privileged status that separates it from the methods of science, as Gadamer does,[9] for such a view is underwritten by the presumption of consensus among all participants in the tradition. That is, to use a famous Gadamerian phrase, historically effective consciousness "is inescapably more being than consciousness" (*Philosophical Hermeneutics*, p. 38). For Habermas, such a philosophy provides no way of criticizing the domination, exclusion, and violence that is embedded in tradition. For him, critical theory requires the social scientific resources of explanation – accounts of the development

---

[8] See Jonathan Culler's "Beyond Interpretation" for an example of this anti-hermeneutic impulse and Paul Ricoeur's "What Is a Text?" for the unification of structural explanation and interpretation.

[9] See Richard Bernstein's *Beyond Objectivism and Relativism* and Joel Weinsheimer's *Gadamer's Hermeneutics*, for a critique of Gadamer's limited, positivistic view of science.

of the individual and modern society – as well as the hermeneutics of understanding. As we will see, Habermas uses reconstructive theory to create an idealized space of critique within his theory of communication action.

In all of these reworkings of the problematic of explanation and understanding, there are two key difficulties: the interpreter's own understanding and the dialogues between this understanding and the misguided (or at least different) understanding of those who are being studied. In all cases, the agent (including another theorist) is spoken about from a cultural space that is not victimized by the same vocabularies, even if the agent is also addressed – e.g., when an analyst speaks to an analysand or an intellectual speaks to workers' movements. The interpreter cannot simply explain in a positivist way without appealing to meanings and ideals that are shared with the reader/listener. The explainer may use a third-person vocabulary to account for views he/she wants to discredit but must implicitly, if not explicitly, use a first-/second-person vocabulary in directing this account to an audience. Kant's two realms of theory and practice are reworked in terms of hermeneutics of critique and utopia. Genealogies and explanations are ways of speaking that give distanced redescriptions of our dialogical positions. Airtight determinism (or oppression) is foreclosed because explanation is part of cultural hermeneutics and not outside of it. If we were completely coopted, we would not be able to talk about it. Thus, what I mean by the problem of "the interpreter's own understanding" comes down to two questions: How does the theorist account for this critical understanding? Toward what better future is this critique directed? Although the nature of this account in contemporary theory varies, as we will see, all such accounts bring with them a dialogical problem: How do those people whose self-understandings are redescribed by third-person accounts respond to having their desires and commitments unmasked? This question concerns linguistic as well as ethical/political and emotional issues. How can people talk who have different and usually incommensurate vocabularies? A good example of this dialogical difficulty emerges in the last paragraph of Terry Eagleton's well-known *Literary Theory*. "We know that the lion is stronger than the lion tamer and so does the lion tamer. The problem is that the lion does not know it" (p. 217). There are three different subjects here, each of whom speaks a different language. "We" apparently stands for Marxist intellectuals who share an understanding of how and why others are in the grip of ideology and where we need to go. The lion (the oppressed) and the lion tamer (the oppressors) are locked into different ideological positions that make each other's self-understanding as well as "our" self-understanding inaccessible to them.[10]

In the next section, I begin by laying out the problematics proposed by Derrida, Foucault, and Lyotard – the word (sign), the practice, and the sentence, respectively – and show their power to disclose the shape and force of ideology in ways that are not available through other means, including Habermas's critical pragmatics. At the same time, I'll show the mystification in their claim to have broken with the hermeneutic circle. Their theories can be complemented with a hermeneutic view of subjectivity so that poststructuralist theories become options in the interpretive repertory. My goal is not to offer a comprehensive analysis and critique of all the poststructuralists' moves, for this has now been done by several astute commentators.[11] Instead, I will limit myself to poststructuralism's failure to account for agency and to its refusal to provide ethical/political contexts for its critiques. This narrow focus will give me the argumentative space to move critical dialogue to the next level without getting bogged down in lengthy discussion.

I will then look at the Marxist tradition and Habermas's critical theory, both of which try to retain a complementary relationship between explanatory (third-person accounts of subjects) and hermeneutic stories (first-person/second-person accounts). Habermas abandons the utopian claim of Marxism by developing a philosophy of language that makes liberation internal to language itself. In this way, Habermas tries to escape from the conflicts of cultural values and differences and to offer only a set of formal procedural guidelines for the way conflicts should be discussed. Not only does this effort fail, but it once again forces out of consideration the kinds of cultural practices that can nourish the

---

[10] See John McGowan's commentary (*Postmodernism and Its Critics*, p. 165) on this passage.
[11] See Manfred Frank's *What Is Neostructuralism?*, Peter Dews's *Logics of Disintegration*, Richard Bernstein's *The New Constellation*, as well as McGowan's *Postmodernism and Its Critics*.

present and inform the future. Since Habermas makes major changes in the Marxist program, I will examine the work of Fredric Jameson and Edward Said. Jameson, perhaps the most utopian Marxist theorist, to show how his model offers only an elaborate critique of industrial society but no recuperation of cultural practices to nourish the present. Instead, his utopia is an appeal to a cultural memory of desire before the constraints of capitalism. Said claims to have gone beyond the limits of poststructuralism and Marxism; however, by refusing to situate himself in any ethical/political traditions, he is forced to tack on rather than account for the ideals to which he appeals.

Thus, the purpose of this chapter is not simply to argue for the logical necessity of agency, for the closing hermeneutic circle, but to show the need for enriching it. My critique is not simply theoretical but ethical, political and axiological; both Habermas and the poststructuralists are axiological ascetics who are reticent about utopia and the role of language in articulating it. Poststructuralists rest their case on an ethics of difference and a politics of negative liberty, while Habermas wants to factor out the particularities of different forms of life in constructing a formal rationality. (Jameson is no ascetic, but for him a better future is not yet visible.) In the rest of the chapter, I will be sorting out these competing problematics for the subject by seeing if they account for both the oppression and the agency of textual subjects.[12] Since stories of oppression and stories of agency are imbricated, we cannot read one dimension of the story without the other. That is, a theory that insists on either the progressive achievements of autonomy or the withering genealogy of subjection avoids the ambiguity of cultural history, in which cultural values that we esteem today (e.g., equality, autonomy, or justice) are historically bound up with practices we seek to overcome, such as racism, sexism, and reification. It is the work of a democratic hermeneutics to expose these histories and to recount how these values can be retrieved and reconfigured so as to inform future action.[13]

---

[12] See Anthony Cascardi, *The Subject of Modernity*, for an excellent account of the multiple discourses of modernity, an account that explicitly distances itself from the reductiveness of philosophical stories, such as Habermas's.

[13] Thus, exposing the sexism in Kant's work – see for example Jane Flax's "Is Enlightenment Emancipatory?" – would require an historical account of what makes this critique possible, an account that would have to retrieve some aspect of the Enlightenment project.

Third-person stories of culture: the poststructuralists and Barbara Smith

Poststructuralists work from Nietzsche and Heidegger to develop their own distinctive third-person accounts of the subject. Foucault's genealogies are written from a problematic that displaces human agency into disciplinary practices: "The subject who knows, the objects to be known and the modalities of knowledge must be regarded as so many effects of these fundamental implications of power-knowledge and their historical transformations" (*Language, Counter-Memory, Practice*, pp. 27–28). If Foucault rewrites intentional actions in the larger space of disciplinary practices, then Derrida's reversals and paleonomies displace meaning "before" – in the logical, not temporal sense – it can even be taken up by the subject: "Subjectivity – like objectivity – is an effect of *différance*, an effect inscribed in a system of *différance*" (*Positions*, p. 28). Derrida's deconstructions – whether the issue is the binary opposition, the inside versus the outside, or the graft – always operate on the boundaries of the differential articulation of the sign.[14] I do not mean that Derrida simply focuses on the role of words in culture – e.g., Raymond Williams's *Keywords* – but that his problematic is the concept and its other ("Deconstruction and the Other," pp. 110–11). He breaks down the semantic containment of concepts, reads against familiar historical embeddings to show how their articulations are not natural or logical but arbitrary and ideological. He places neither himself nor the text under consideration in larger ontological categories – background, lifeworld, web of beliefs – even though they are implicit. The sentence, in contrast to the other two problematics, reserves a place for the subject. In Lyotard, this subject position is determined by various discursive structures, such as language games, genres of discourse, etc.: "Our 'intentions' are tensions to link [sentences] in a certain way that genres of discourse exercise on the senders, receivers, referents, and meanings. We think that we want to persuade, seduce,

---

14 See Eve Tavor Bannet's *Structuralism and the Logic of Dissent*, for an analysis of how all of Derrida's moves are based on the sign. In his exchange with Derrida in Paris in 1981, Gadamer picks up on the difference between Derrida's problematic of the sign and his own idea of dialogue but misses Derrida's point about why deconstructive critique is not reducible to dialogue: "It seems to me I go beyond Derrida's deconstruction, since a word exists only in conversation and never exists there as an isolated word but as the totality of a way of accounting by means of speaking and answering" ("Destruction and Deconstruction," p. 112).

convince ... but this is because a certain genre of discourse – dialectic, erotic, didactic – imposes itself on 'our' sentence and on 'us' its mode of linkage" (*Le Différend*, p. 197). Hence, even though Lyotard makes subjectivity an issue, he does so only to knock down the strawperson of consciousness that uses language to express a private, prelinguistic intention. Poststructuralist operations do not establish an explanatory space outside the self-understandings of the agents; instead, they follow structuralism in seeking to displace the vocabularies of these self-understandings by opening up contradictions and gaps. Hermeneutics, in their view, packs too many presuppositions about pre-understandings and consensus into its dialogical account of culture.

What can we say of these decentered claims? First, they do not account for the agency of their own statements. Like statements that maintain the truth of relativism, statements that assert that we are simply constructed and not constructing are self-refuting ("performative contradictions" in Habermas's phrase[15]). This immanent critique is important for the crack it offers in poststructuralist self-presentations, but it is hardly grounds for dismissing the productiveness of their anti-hermeneutic problematics. Habermas, like Karl-Otto Apel, fills his theory of communication so full of necessary presuppositions that he drives out critiques of our linguistic embeddedness, as we will see later in the chapter. We can thus say that poststructuralists do not escape the hermeneutic circle; instead, they ignore the consequences for their own texts of their theories of the constructed subject. Derrida is the best at trying to avoid this, since he claims that neologisms such as *différance* are the conditions of possibility of construction and unraveling.[16] Moreover, both his open-ended ontology of dissemination and his discussion of strategies of reversal and intervention

---

[15] Habermas's most recent formulation of the idea taken from Jaakko Hintikka and Karl-Otto Apel appears in *Moral Consciousness and Communicative Action*.

[16] In *The Tain of the Mirror*, Rodolphe Gasche defends this Derridean practice, while Rorty rightly questions this move: "Since that for which the conditions of possibility are sought is always *everything* that any previous philosopher has envisaged – the whole range of what has been discussed up to now – anybody is at liberty to identify any ingenious gimmick that he dreams up as a 'condition of possibility'" (*Essays on Heidegger and Others*, p. 123). I do not deny that Derrida's critique has force, but I, like Rorty, question Derrida's transcendental appeal as a means of escaping attack by others. For a powerful political interpretation of the problematic of the sign, see Gregory S. Jay, "Values and Deconstructions," chapter 1 of *America the Scrivener*, pp. 31–80.

show that he thematizes the possibility of action. However, he gives no account of subjectivity and language to enable this action. The observer's point of view is employed but never accounted for. In a parallel fashion, Hubert Dreyfus's claim that Foucault moves "beyond hermeneutics" because he abandons the hermeneutics of suspicion that relies on a "true deepest meaning for a surface behavior" ("Beyond Hermeneutics," p. 80) turns out to be simply an appeal to a deeper layer of meaning: "Foucault seeks to demonstrate that the deeper meaning that authority directs the participants to uncover in his practices itself hides another, more important meaning which is not directly available to the participants" (p. 80). In unmasking the self-understanding of agents through the cunning of contingency, poststructuralists depend on certain implicit linguistic, ethical, and political understandings that are never thematized. While Habermas exaggerates the nature of these understandings, poststructuralists avoid speaking of them.

What is preserved by such reticence about agency or the ethical/political resources that make it possible is precisely what Derrida, Foucault, and Lyotard try to subvert – that is, the privileging of the epistemological over the ethical. The reasoning works like this: because all identities are the factitious products of power that cover over the truth of being (dissemination in Derrida, the space between sentences in Lyotard, the unthought in Foucault), liberty and truth come together. We *ought* to concern ourselves with the epistemological enterprise of subversion rather than theorize how such a subversive action is possible or how language and value might connect in a positive way. Ought is derived from is. Each of these theories gets its authority from its claim to truth, and each is totalizing. By "claim to truth," I mean that they assert that their conclusions are necessary, that their positions are forced on them rather than that they are deliberative options within a field of possibilities. Moreover, each is totalizing. This may seem like a strange charge to make against thinkers who are committed to breaking capitalist and Marxist totalities, and they do offer problematics designed to block and break down traditional hermeneutical or dialectical routes. Nonetheless, their critiques are made through a single fundamental unit, an implicit transcendental argument, that excludes alternatives. Transcendental arguments, as Charles Taylor says, "start from some feature of our experience which they claim to be indubitable and beyond cavil. They then move to a stronger conclusion, one concerning the nature of the subject or his position in the world" ("The Validity of Transcendental Arguments," p. 151). Poststructuralists do not claim that their way is one way of reading and that there are other alternatives; instead, each theorist claims that his theory is incommensurate with those of others. Lacking a common ground, poststructuralist debates are not arguments but exchanges in which each problematic reformulates the claims of the opponent in terms of his/her own problematic. This totalization produces not only incommensurability but also their "rigor." The price is a dangerous ontological terrorism, in which fidelity to a deep transcendental truth makes dialogue impossible or even unethical.

Thus, what is crucial to the poststructuralist view of the subject is not just its linguistic configuration but also its shaping force – that is, power. Poststructuralists develop their idea of power from Nietzsche, whose *Genealogy of Morals* inaugurates a tradition in which narratives of power unmask narratives of value. They not only follow this lead, they raise the stakes. For them, the discursive is the oppressive so that linguistic structures are not enabling but ensnaring. Gadamer, Habermas, and the poststructuralists all agree that the subject is embedded in historical processes, but what these processes are is radically different for each. Unlike Gadamer, with his notion of the tradition, or Habermas, with his division into lifeworld and system, poststructuralists assume that all constructions are oppressive, that goodness can be found only in the ruptures and fissures of power structures. They offer no alternative narratives of value. This is true not only of Foucault,[17] as is well known, but Derrida as well: "The repression at the origin of meaning is an irreducible violence" ("Afterword," p. 150). The legibility of textual structures does not come from the norms available to the agents or the continuity of tradition, as hermeneutics would read them, but from "stratifications that are already differential and of very great stability with regard to the relation of

---

[17] Foucault says, "I think to imagine another system is to extend our participation in the present system" (*Language, Counter-Memory, Practice*, p. 230). He wants to set up utopia as an uncritical wish-fulfillment to which he opposes heteropias (*The Order of Things*, xviii). I see no reason to strip all utopian thinking of its critical dimension and to identify critique with disruption. My critique does not apply to Foucault's late work – which begins with the second volume of the *History of Sexuality*.

forces and all the hierarchies they suppose and put into practice" (p. 144).

Lyotard, Foucault, and Derrida get their bite by exposing the networks of power and making an implicit appeal to negative freedom.[18] Three short quotations will serve to illustrate this point. Foucault says in "What Is Enlightenment?": "The point, in brief, is to transform the critique conducted in the form of necessary limitation into a critique that takes the form of a possible transgression." This permits us to "separate out, from the contingency that made us what we are, the possibility of no longer being, doing, or thinking what we are, do or think ... It [this kind of critique] is seeking to give new impetus, as far and wide as possible to the undefined work of freedom" (*The Foucault Reader*, p. 45). In *The Postmodern Condition*, Lyotard seeks to create "a politics that would respect both the desire for justice and the desire for the unknown" (p. 67). He carries this out in *Le Différend* by valorizing what is silenced by discourse – the *différends* – and what transcends discourse – the sublime. Derrida speaks of the liberating possibilities of dissemination: "I would like to believe in the multiplicity of sexually marked voices. I would like to believe in the mass, this undeterminable number of blended voices, this mobile of non-identified sexual marks whose choreography can carry, divide, multiply the body of each 'individual' whether he be classified 'man' or 'woman' according to the criteria of usage" ("Choreographies," p. 76). In all three citations we see utopian energy that insists on escaping all representation. There are several problems with this common strategy. The first is raised nicely by Nancy Fraser, "Why is struggle preferable to submission? Why ought domination to be resisted? Only with the introduction of normative notions could he [Foucault] begin to answer such questions, ... tell us what is wrong with the modern power/ knowledge regime and why we ought to oppose it" (*Unruly Practices*, p. 29). How do we adjudicate among competing *différends* or exclusions? Are they all bad? The second problem is related to the first: there is no theoretical account of the agent who recognizes

[18] See Charles Taylor's "What's Wrong with Negative Freedom?" for a discussion of this distinction and a call to develop a notion of positive freedom. See McGowan, *Postmodernism and Its Critics*, pp. 89–144, for a discussion of negative freedom in Derrida and Foucault. McGowan says, "The oddity of postmodern thought is that it has clung to a liberal image of negative freedom, even while demolishing the self that could embody that freedom" (p. 211).

or acts against oppression. Hence, negative freedom and an untheorized notion of agency work together. The reason post-structuralists do not invoke utopian criteria is that they want to avoid the Marxist dialectic of ideology and utopia in which history is viewed as the self-realization of humanity. Such a theory makes presuppositions about human nature and emancipation that are themselves oppressive. I would go further than Fraser and say that the subject of poststructuralism is at issue. Lastly, poststructuralism does not say what resources are to be drawn on to sustain us in the present or to guide us toward this future. It is precisely this longing for "total revolution," to borrow Bernard Yack's phrase, that disempowers us in the present. If the past and the present offer no resources, and no improvement on the present is imaginable before the demise of capitalism, logocentric thinking, and the technologies of the self, then the cultural agenda is handed over to the right. Even "local, strategic" work requires guidance and justification from ethical/political ideals.[19]

A good example of how this revolutionary purity appears in criticism can be seen in a debate in *Critical Inquiry* over Spike Lee's *Do the Right Thing*. In "The Violence of Public Art: *Do the Right Thing*," W.J.T. Mitchell puts Lee's movie in the context of a *"critical* public art that is frank about the contradictions and violence encoded in its own situation, one that dares to awaken a public sphere of resistance, struggle, and dialogue" (p. 898). In his response to Mitchell ("Spike Lee, Corporate Populist") Jerome Christensen will have no recuperation of works infiltrated by commercialism; he attacks Mitchell's interpretation and reads Spike Lee's position in the film as part of "corporate populism." "The apotheosis of Lee's 'personal responsibility' is not Brechtian but Reaganite" (p. 589). I do not wish to get into the details of interpretation of the film or of Spike Lee's involvement with Nike. My point is that Christensen avoids specifying the site from which he reads the film and Lee's career exactly like the poststructuralist views I have been criticizing, and this site is at such a distance from the present that Lee and Reagan appear as political brothers. Mitchell, in a spirited retort ("Seeing *Do the Right Thing*"), puts his

---

[19] I am referring to Foucault's opposition between the specific intellectual, who works on a particular social issue, and the universal intellectual, such as Marx, Freud, or Habermas, who proposes a grand theory. See *Power/Knowledge*, pp. 126–33.

finger on the neo-Romantic premise that informs Christensen's essay: "Romantic criticism resists corporate populism by prefiguring a future that is the true one – that new one we cannot picture" (p. 608). The assumption that informs Christensen's essay and poststructuralism is phrased nicely by Rorty, "Our imagination and will are so limited by the socialization we have received that we are unable even to propose an alternative to the society we have now" (*Contingency, Irony, and Solidarity*, p. 64).

Since those who operate with poststructuralist premises refuse to recuperate any ethical/political traditions, they are forced to engage in contradictions in order to meet the demands for identity and value made by the dominated or excluded. The best example of this dilemma is "strategic essentialism," and the most extensive treatment of it is Diana Fuss's *Essentially Speaking*. I will focus on her discussion of Luce Irigaray's so-called "essentialist" redescriptions of women's bodies. Here is a representative passage cited by Fuss.

Woman's autoeroticism is very different from man's. In order to touch himself, man needs an instrument: his hand, a woman's body, language ... And this self-caressing requires at least a minimum of activity. As for woman, she touches herself in and of herself without any mediation, and before there is any way to distinguish activity from passivity. Woman 'touches herself' all the time, and moreover no one can forbid her to do so, for her genitals are formed of two lips in continuous contact. Thus, within herself, she is already two – but not divisible into one(s) – that caress each other. (cited in *Essentially Speaking*, p. 58)

Fuss defends Irigaray's "essentialism" by saying that "the point, for Irigaray, of defining women from an essentialist standpoint is not to imprison women within their bodies but to rescue them from enculturating definitions by men" (p. 63). I wholeheartedly agree with this defense of the new self-understanding that Irigaray offers but reject Fuss's shallow characterization of Irigaray's texts as an example of "strategic essentialism." This phrase means that women's redescriptions of themselves have no epistemological worth but only a political one. Epistemological claims about relational identity can only be articulated in a third-person constructivist vocabulary and can never be appropriated by the first-/second-person vocabularies of the subject. The constructivist problematic ignores the history of women's achievements, reducing them to another chapter in the saga of logocentrism. The poststructuralist premise permits women to say only that they are oppressed; they cannot invoke their own traditions or ideals.

We can see the problems this position creates in Fuss's text, for first- and second-person vocabularies resurface without a theoretical place. First, we can see the political vacuum that constructivism creates. Fuss says, "When put into practice by the dispossessed themselves, essentialism can be powerfully displacing and disruptive" (p. 32). Why is disruption *per se* good? How do "we" know when and how to operate strategically and on what grounds? To what end is this displacement put? For whom and by whom? Second, we see the rhetoric of intentionality and agency creep back into her discussion of judgment: "This, to me, signals an exciting way to rethink the problem of essentialism; it represents an approach which *evaluates the motivations behind the deployments of essentialism* rather than prematurely dismissing it as an unfathomable vestige of patriarchy (itself an essentialist category)" (p. 32, my emphasis). Without a recuperation of democratic ideals and of agency, there is not place for such evaluations.

Another important theorist who seeks to make a third-person constructivist account consistent with agency is Judith Butler. She claims that her "critique of the subject is not a negation or repudiation of the subject, but, rather, a way of interrogating its construction as a pregiven or foundationalist premise" ("Contingent Foundations," p. 42). Butler is suspicious of a vocabulary that merely "situates the self,"[20] because she fears that this formulation gives the self a kind of prediscursive unity or privilege outside the system of power: "The 'I' is not situated; the 'I,' this 'I,' is constituted by these positions" (p. 42). Butler's point is well taken insofar as one takes a vocabulary for the self in the way she describes. However, the notion of a linguistically embedded subject requires not simply a third-person vocabulary of its genealogical constitution but the dialogical vocabulary of its agency in, not outside, language. When Butler moves from this constructivist formulation to agency, she tries to steer between the foundationalist idea that the subject is a ground and the constructivist

[20] The reference is to Seyla Benhabib's work *Situating the Self*, which Butler criticizes. See the debate among Benhabib, Butler, Fraser, and Drucilla Cornell in *Feminist Contentions: A Philosophical Exchange*.

notion that it is an effect: "The subject is neither a ground nor a product, but the permanent possibility of certain resignifying mechanisms of power, but which is power's own possibility of being reworked" (p. 47). The problem is that Butler does not characterize this possibility. As Nancy Fraser says, Butler assumes we have critical capacities but never says where they come from ("False Antitheses" (1995), pp. 66–67). Moreover, Butler does not give a shape to these acts of resignification since she eschews invoking any values or norms, except negative liberty and difference. In brief, Butler tries to smudge the difference between the explanatory moment of critique, in which the self-understanding of the agent is unmasked, and the utopian moment in which agency is recuperated. Hence, she loses the capacity to thematize the aspects of cultural history she wants to attack from those she wants to recover: "If performativity is construed as that power of discourse to produce effects through reiteration, how are we to understand the limits of such production, the constraints under which production occurs?" (*Bodies that Matter*, p. 20). "Effects" has the anti-humanistic dimension of the third-person account that seeks characterizations divested of their axiological character. This is a useful moment of distanciation that must be cashed out hermeneutically by a "we." Butler puts this hermeneutic vocabulary in her sentence – "we" and "understand" – but she never says how she makes the move from "production" and "performativity" to this "we." My position is that no single vocabulary should try to do all the work of explaining how we are constructed and articulating our hopes. A democratic hermeneutics needs to be able to lay out the historical resources that make these stories possible. For Butler, the claim that there is no space of critique outside power means that all value terms are so complicitous with a kind of cultural mystification she wants to unmask that they must be avoided: "Power pervades the very conceptual apparatus that seeks to negotiate its terms, including the subject position of the critic" ("Contingent Foundations," p. 39). But the presence of power in all ethical/political terms does not mean that all ethical/political vocabularies are worthless.

Thus, I agree with Habermas's charge that these thinkers "can and want to give no account of their own position" (*The Philosophical Discourse of Modernity*, p. 336). However, unlike Habermas and many other critical theorists,[21] I am not willing to dismiss the poststructuralists' critique, since we can cash out their readings by closing the hermeneutic circle, by accounting for the constructing as well as the constructed subject. At the same time, we can hold on to the poststructuralist insight that previous ways of closing the hermeneutic circle have been ethno/androcentric and that any closing should be tentative and problematic. Another way of approaching the tension between first-/second-person and third-person accounts of the subject is to ask why Habermas is willing to offer a hermeneutic complement to research in the social sciences that takes only the point of view of the observer (that speaks only of what forces operate behind the backs of participants) and not do the same for poststructuralism? The reason is that poststructuralism – unlike social scientific theories that approach language behavioristically in terms of systems of rationality – offers linguistic problematics that challenge hermeneutics instead of ignoring it, problematics that fracture the site of reason and block the research routes of a sociology of knowledge. Poststructuralist readings show patterns in language that cut across intentional structures, but they do not connect these patterns to extralinguistic explanations but only a nebulous ontology of power.

Poststructuralism is suspicious of the hermeneutics of suspicion proposed by Marx and Freud because of the assumptions these theories make about human development. They do not liberate us from capitalist culture but merely package us in different ways that must also be examined. As John Rajchman puts it in his defense of Foucault against Habermas, "He [Foucault] does not ask how our sexual desires incurred an alienation and a mystification; he asks how practices to discover the truth about ourselves ever became part of our experience of sexuality" (*Michel Foucault*, p. 92). Habermas's response to this position is that such theories must be refuted rather than complemented, which is my position. I will

---

[21] The response to Derrida and Lyotard is more hostile than it is to Foucault. In addition to Habermas, see Thomas McCarthy, "The Politics of the Ineffable: Derrida's Deconstruction" and Nancy Fraser, "The French Derrideans," in *Unruly Practices*. Derrida admits that he "never succeeded in directly relating deconstruction to existing political codes and programs . . . I try where I can to act politically while recognizing that such action remains incommensurate with my intellectual project of deconstruction" ("Deconstruction and the Other," pp. 119–20.) In my view, Derrida's theory of the sign makes a commitment to anything more than an ethics of difference and a politics of negative liberty impossible.

develop my argument in two steps. First, I will look at justifications for poststructuralists' refusal to participate in existing dialogical structures and then examine how Habermas limits the role of language in his critique and effaces linguistic difference. During the course of this analysis, I will prepare the way for a new hermeneutic space that puts us in a dialogical relationship with both sides.

Foucault addresses the issue of hermeneutics in justifying the absence of not only "I" but "we" in his texts. "The problem is, precisely, to decide if it is actually suitable to place oneself within a 'we' in order to assert the principles one recognizes and the values one accepts; or if it is not, rather, necessary to make the future formation of a 'we' possible, by elaborating the question. Because it seems to me that the 'we' must not be previous to the question; it can only be the result – and the temporary result – of the question as it is posed in the new terms in which one formulates it" (*The Foucault Reader*, p. 385). This is part of Foucault's preference for analyzing in terms of practices instead of beliefs, the latter of which participate in a philosophy of consciousness. Such a move is fine for a third-person account, but not when someone asks "you" a question, as the quotation illustrates. He sets up a false opposition between placing "oneself within a 'we'" and the creation of a "we" so as to block the possibility of transformation by a "we" that is not coopted by the present system. Foucault wants to avoid the space of questioning that traditional hermeneutics imposes by using a theory that makes room only for a constructed subject and then leaving out the part of the hermeneutic circle that accounts for his own discourse and the background practices that make it possible. Hence, I prefer to say that he implicitly calls for a revision, not an abandonment, of hermeneutics, even though he offers no positive version.

In the same way, Derrida refuses to accept the position assigned to him in the institution of philosophical debate when he responds to Searle in a way that unmasks the ideological charge of the latter's supposedly neutral theoretical vocabulary.[22] Derrida's critiques have a transcendental and an empirical dimension. The empirical dimension admits improvement in the theory under consideration. In Searle's case, for example, we could come up with a new taxonomy that did not make the same distinction

---

[22] Derrida's texts on speech-act theory are collected in *Limited Inc.*, while the key texts from Searle are *Speech Acts* and *Expression and Meaning*.

between fictional and nonfictional statements that Derrida criticizes. (Derrida, of course, never proposes such a revision.) The transcendental dimension of Derrida's critique blocks such a revision since it is part of a linguistic ontology that is expressed through the well-known neologisms such as *différance* and iterability: "iterability blurs a priori the dividing line that passes between ... opposed terms" ("Limited Inc.," p. 210). These terms are "nonconcepts" that are covered over by logocentrism. This "covering over" is not entirely successful, and we see the effects of *différance* through the aporias of discourse. These rhetorical effects work through power ("There is never anything called power or force, but only differences of power and force" ["Afterword," p. 149]), but they are not reducible to power either. The disseminating power of language can never be contained; this is its ontological status. We are never completely in or out of reason but both at once. Derrida does not deny that there is "relative specificity of the effects of consciousness, of the effects of speech" (*Margins of Philosophy*, p. 327). That is, saying that people can follow directions to the post office does not refute his claim about the dissemination of meaning. He is trying to drive a critical space into the excessively grand hermeneutic notion of "understanding." Hence, Derrida does not offer arguments for his claims but reads key signs in ways that unravel them. The impossibility of closure becomes the possibility of renewal: "everything becomes possible against the language-police; for example, 'literature' or 'revolutions' that as yet have no model. Everything is possible except for an exhaustive typology that would claim to limit the powers of graft or of fiction" ("Limited Inc., p. 243). By working on the borders of signs rather than at the level of intentionality, where signs are synthesized into sentences, Derrida shows how the presuppositions work in professional "dialogue" and exposes how otherness emerges within individuals and not just between them. He defines deconstruction as "a positive response to an alterity which necessarily calls, summons or motivates it." This "other opposes self identity ... [that] precedes philosophy and necessarily invokes and provokes the subject before any genuine questioning" ("Deconstruction and the Other," p. 118). Indeed, the ethical strength of deconstruction comes from its ability to "listen" and find gaps at levels that are covered over not only by humanist assumptions about communication but also by theories based on the notion of "webs of holistic belief" such as those proposed by Habermas, Davidson, Rorty, and Gadamer, despite their differences.[23]

Otherness emerges not in the stories the marginalized are able to tell but in the rearticulation of discursive fractures in existing languages. Thus, Gayatri Spivak's Derridean analysis of colonial discourse shows that the "subaltern cannot speak," for Derrida's critique does not demarcate marginalized voices. He "does not invoke 'letting the other(s) speak for himself' but rather invokes an 'appeal' to or 'call' to the 'quite-other' (tout-autre as opposed to a self-consolidating other)" ("Can the Subaltern Speak?," p. 294). This idea of the "other" is an ethical possibility that is consistent with the politics of total revolution, since the other is excluded by the present discursive system and appeals to a "you" who is also not coopted by the system. What makes poststructuralist writing both so suggestive and so disconcerting is that it collapses the two moments of critique, ideology and utopia, into a single discursive thread that "exposes" the presuppositions of the text under consideration without thematizing either the background that makes such a critique possible or the ends toward which the critique is directed. Both elements are "implicit," since without this background their work would be unintelligible and without an appeal to norms it would have no bite. The complicity between the presupposed practices and the proposed utopia is what poststructuralists want to expose in others, so it is not surprising that they omit this in their own work.

The problems of insisting on a third-person view of the subject that fractures its hermeneutic and ethical integrity emerge in Barbara Smith's *Contingencies of Value*. In this book she employs a functional/systemic model drawn from sociology (especially from Bourdieu's work) to examine axiological theories of the past and present. Her thesis is that "all value is radically contingent, being neither a fixed attribute, an inherent quality, or an objective property of things, but, rather, an effect of multiple, continuously changing, and continuously interacting variables . . . that is, value is the product of the dynamics of a system, specifically an economic system" (p. 30). Smith's theory of contingency vitiates all attempts to give value an absolute ground. The continuities that seem to belie contingency are not the result of reason or truth but of complex

---

[23] I discuss Derrida's relationship to Rorty's holism in chapter 2.

systemic movements animated by the desire for survival. Her goal is not to create new norms but to criticize theories that provide "two different kinds of explanation for human preferences – one for canonical tastes and the stability of preferences (convergence on an objective norm, the intrinsic value of certain objects) and another for deviant tastes and the mutability of preferences" (p. 39). Even though her model departs from those of poststructuralism, she joins them in three ways: (1) in failing to offer a hermeneutic complement to her anti-hermeneutic, third-person account; (2) in assuming that her theory is incommensurate with theories of her contemporaries; (3) and in tying her theory only to an ethics/politics of difference that offers no account of cultural resources.

We can clarify Smith's approach by comparing it to Foucault's. What distinguishes Smith's view is that she refuses the ontology of power; she breaks with the textual model and uses the function as the minimal unit; she invokes Darwinian metaphors of "survival" and "self-preservation" to replace power; and she abandons the critical, utopian dimension of Foucault. Although Smith assumes the third-person point of view, she is careful not to deny agency: "The current value of a work ... is by no means independent of *authorial* design, labor and skill" (p. 48); however, she rewrites in terms of functions the language through which authors act and constitute themselves. Unlike poststructuralist critiques that work through an immanent critique of such languages – that is, disclosure of their internal inconsistencies – Smith offers a revision. She justifies this redescription of their agency in a different language by saying that "the traditional discourse of value – including a number of terms I have used here, such as 'subject,' 'object' ... reflects an arbitrary arresting, segmentation, and hypostasization of the continuous process of our interactions with our environments or what could also be described as the continuous interplay among multiple configurable systems." Smith wants to root out hermeneutic vocabulary such as "belief" and "community" used by Rorty and other nonfoundationalists because they "obscure the dynamics of value" (p. 31): "An *ethnos* or tribe ... would not be constituted ... of those who share *beliefs* but, rather, of those who share situations and conditions and therefore, also share histories and economies, and accordingly, have developed, over time, more or less congruent routines and patterns of behavior, and therefore, engage in mutually consequential interactive practices" (p. 169).

In brief, a group is never what its members believe it to be but only what a sociologist armed with this model can discern. Here we see the objectivist, positivistic dimension of social theory that refuses to thematize its own norms, that refuses a dialogical exchange between the language of community under investigation and the language of the investigating community. She offers an account of the "processes of evaluation" that tells us what the movements of subjectivity "really" look like: "Throughout our lives, we perform a continuous succession of what are, in effect, rapid-fire cost-benefit analyses" (p. 42). "The feedback loop of differential consequences – that is, the mechanism whereby the different consequences of different actions ... produce in agents a tendency to repeat, modify, or avoid those actions in the future – operates to adjust actions to the conditions in which they are practiced." (p. 163). Since this is what is going on behind our backs, Smith suggests that it would be therapeutic for us to think of ourselves in these terms, to make our self-understandings approach our explanations and purge ourselves of the mystifying vocabularies of ethics. However, Smith never says what an axiological choice or commitment looks like from the "inside," (from the point of view of a participant). What does it look like to live through a functionalist vocabulary? If she adopts the therapeutic goal of Wittgenstein and Rorty that seeks to rid us of obfuscatory vocabularies, she offers no justification for her vocabulary, no meta-theoretical argument against competing nonfoundationalist problematics.

When she discusses possible objections from others, we see the incommensurability thesis emerge: "What is inconsistent with her theory," says Smith, characterizing the debate from the point of view of an observer, "is their theory; what is inconsistent with her practice is their description of her theory" (p. 151). This familiar move in contemporary theory makes dialogue impossible; one can only redescribe others in one's own terms. Smith tries to obviate the need for a meta-theoretical argument by saying that there are no direct political consequences in her theory, that there may be fascists, liberals, or radicals who think through her model. However, her view of human nature, which she describes as "scrappiness" (p. 148) has obvious political consequences, as the long-standing arguments between Marxists and liberals on this issue make clear.[24]

---

[24] See Albrecht Wellmer's "Models of Freedom," for a discussion of the relationship between views of freedom and understandings of human nature.

Without a meta-theoretical argument, she can unmask but go no further: "The fact that Homer, Dante, and Shakespeare do not figure in the personal economy of these people [those who are not "among the orthodoxly educated population of the West"] ... might properly be taken as qualifying the claims of transcendent, universal value made for such works" (p. 53). Fair enough. But this is where the question begins, not where it ends. What kinds of critics/citizens does a democratic society seek to produce? What positive reasons for reading these or any works can be proposed? To answer this, we have to leave a functionalist frame and speak about what languages we want to use to constitute the world, what norms or other guides can inform our decisions, and what resources we can rehabilitate from the past.

Thus, Smith's functionalist critique of axiological theory follows poststructuralism in its failure to offer a first-/second-person or hermeneutic account of the dynamics of language and value and in its failure to acknowledge this shortcoming. Like the poststructuralists, she can unmask values, but she cannot account for her own voice or how her theory helps answer axiological issues of the present. This omission is directly connected to the incommensurability claim made by all of them. If they all rightly expose what remains hidden in glib appeals to "the shared background" against which differences appear, they lose a great deal by failing to connect their critique to the shared concepts they want to retain or rework. That is, there is an inevitable route through hermeneutics in order to reach the space where meaning can be reconfigured into their critical modes. As Derrida says in response to McClintock and Nixon's criticism of his essay "Racism's Last Word": "The text of an appeal obeys certain rules; it has its grammar, its rhetoric, its pragmatics ... [A]s you did not take these rules into account, you quite simply *did not read* my text in the most elementary and quasi-grammatical sense of what is called *reading*" ("But Beyond ...," p. 356). However, Derrida passes through this horizon of understanding only to reinscribe it in a critical rather than constructive manner. Are all constructions equally oppressive under the leveling eyes of difference, in any of the senses used by the theorists we have discussed? If positive constructions are not consistent with Derrida's disseminating ontology, then why do we have to remain within such a problematic and not see it as just one of several theoretical options that can help bring out the textual possibilities we want? Current debate precludes such a move because each theorist seeks to trump the other's problematic. If all these theorists expose a liberal humanist theory of meaning and value, their critiques rejoin liberal humanism in its inability to talk about ethical goods other than freedom and justice. I am not calling for dogmatism about what the good life is; rather, I am calling for a theory that will enable us to speculate about good lives and not just about concrete oppression and abstract liberty. We can realize such a project by revising hermeneutics. Before doing this, however, we need to look at the tradition that complements the explanatory accounts of social sciences with the hermeneutic accounts of agents' self-understandings, Marxism and Critical Theory.

The failures of Marxism and Critical Theory: Jameson, Said, and Habermas

Although Jameson's elaborate hermeneutics dialectically appropriates for Marxism everything from Northrop Frye to the poststructuralists, he takes the standard Marxist position on ethics. In this view, past ethical systems are denounced as ideological mystifications of class interests in the name of an ethics of liberation that can be realized in a utopia.[25] Indeed, for Jameson it is not logocentrism or the metaphysics of presence but politics that is the most prominent ideological barrier in the present: "Not metaphysics but ethics is the informing ideology of the binary opposition; and we have forgotten the thrust of Nietzsche's thought and lost everything scandalous and virulent about it if we cannot understand how it is ethics itself which is the ideological vehicle and the legitimation of concrete structures of power and domination" (*The Political Unconscious*, p. 114). Jameson carries his important challenge to ethics so far as to make all ethical categories and practices incapable of recuperation: "In our time, ethics, wherever it makes its reappearance, may be taken as the sign of an intent to mystify, and in particular to replace the more complex and ambivalent judgements of a more properly political and dialectical perspective with the more comfortable simplifications of a binary myth" (cited in Cornel West, *Postmodernism Politics*, p. 143).

---

[25] See Steven Lukes, *Marxism and Morality*.

What makes Jameson's critique and utopia possible is a
two-pronged hermeneutical reading of history, prongs that Perry
Anderson calls two types of causality: "the permanent oscillation,
the potential disjuncture in Marx's own writings between his
ascription of the primary motor of historical change to the
contradiction between the forces of production and the relations of
production, on the one hand . . . and to the class struggle, on the
other . . ." (cited in Alex Callinocos, *Making History*, p. 3). Marxists
influenced by structuralism and poststructuralism – e.g., Althusser
and Jameson – have reworked and complicated the base/super-
structure opposition so as to make the notion of cause disappear;[26]
however, these elaborations neglect the causality of human agents
to concentrate on portraits of our ideological embedding. We find
no map of the possibilities of the present or past nor of the aims of
transformation. That is, Marxism does not spell out, as Steven
Lukes says, "What the morality of emancipation implies for the
future constitution and organization of society" (*Marxism and
Morality*, pp. 45–46). This failure may be phrased hermeneutically
as a refusal to recuperate elements from the past that sustain us in
the present and that concretize future possibilities. This weakness
is crucial since a society needs to "know, or at least have good
reason to believe, that the 'new society,' latent in the old, will take a
form that is emancipatory . . . [that] justif[ies] their support for the
proletariat's struggle" (p. 42).

Jameson takes aim at this problem in *The Political Unconscious*,
where he claims that Marxism "can no longer be content with its
demystifying vocation to unmask and to demonstrate the ways in
which a cultural artifact fulfills a specific ideological mission . . . It
must not cease to practice this essentially negative hermeneutic
function . . . but must also seek . . . to project its simultaneously
Utopian power as the symbolic affirmation of a specific historical
and class form of collective unity" (p. 291). However, he says he is
not up to the task, for he warns the reader not to "expect anything
like that exploratory project of what a vital emergent political
culture should be" (p. 10). Hence, his materialist dialectic – the
"rewriting of a given text in terms of a particular master code" and

[26] Jameson says, "Fundamental realities are somehow unrepresentable or, to use
the Althusserian phrase, are something like an absent cause . . . Yet this absent
cause can find figures through which it can express itself in distorted symbolic
ways" (*Postmodernism*, p. 411).

the "evaluation of such codes or, in other words, of the 'methods' of approaches current in American literary and cultural study today" (p. 10) – leads only to a critique and not a recuperation. In a later essay, Jameson insists again on the urgency and impossibility of utopian thinking: "What is wanted, then, is the reinvention for late industrial society of a new form of the utopian project, about which I have suggested elsewhere that its most judicious beginning might lie in a self-punishing enumeration of all the blocks that make the reimagining of utopia today a difficult, if not to say well-nigh impossible task" ("On Habits of the Heart," p. 111). The reason this task is so difficult is the same one offered by poststructuralists: We are so infiltrated by corrupt forces that we cannot imagine an alternative that does not reproduce them. Jameson seems to abandon Marx's view of rationality and Gramsci's reconciliation of Marxism with a concept of tradition for the Weberian nightmare inherited by Adorno and extended by Foucault. Even though Jameson differs from Foucault in affirming the liberatory possibilities of desire, Jameson locates his utopia in the desire for freedom available in the collective memory of prefeudal society: "The primary energy of revolutionary activity derives from this memory of prehistoric happiness which the individual can regain only through its externalization, through its reestablishment for society as a whole" (*Marxism and Form*, pp. 113–14). Such a prehistoric memory provides no guidelines for sorting out cultural history so we must be content with empty formulations that speak only of negative freedom, of freedom from oppression but not positive freedom, "History is what hurts, it is what refuses desire and what sets limits to individual and collective praxis" (*The Political Unconscious*, p. 102).

The result is that Jameson dismisses ethics and the ethical significance of literature since they must wait for political change: "The proposition that in our time politics and political questions have superseded ethical or moral ones implies a complete transformation of society" (*Ideologies of Theory*, pp. 123–24). For him, ethical acts emerge in "those situations alone in which individuals face each other as conscious and responsible or rational agents." Since modern literature offers "situations that are far more complex than this, where an individual or character is not faced with an impersonal relationship, which is an ethical choice, but rather with a relationship to some determining force vaster than the self or any individual, that is, with society itself, or with politics and the movement of history ... We have left ethical content and ethical criticism behind for a literature and criticism of a more political or psychological cast" (*Ideologies of Theory*, p. 124). Will there ever be such a moment? And what is supposed to sustain us in the meantime? Hence, Jameson says that the ethical ideas in George Eliot's *Middlemarch* are to be understood as symptoms of a social situation that calls for "the supplement or corrective of the doctrine in question" (p. 125). Yes, but what kind of supplement? Do we have to have a full-blown utopia in order to recuperate Eliot? Are all cultural products after the rise of capitalism hopelessly ruined and without value in the present?[27] In response to questioning on totality, Jameson acknowledges that his focus does not substitute "for the politics of new social movements." However, he sets this question aside for the larger game of a total transformation that he cannot articulate, "The question is how to think those local struggles, involving specific and often different groups, within some common project ... [W]ithout some notion of a total transformation of society and without the sense that the immediate project is a figure for that total transformation, so that everybody has a stake in the particular struggle, the success of any local struggle is doomed, limited to reform" ("Discussion of 'Cognitive Mapping,'" p. 360). I would reverse the question: Without a way to theorize reform, one cannot theorize revolution. Indeed, Jameson's utopianism not only impoverishes the local ethical and political debates of today but leaves no place for them in the future. As Mary Dietz says, "Once freedom is achieved, they [Marxists] seem to say politics ends or becomes little more than what Marx himself termed 'the administration of things' ... [W]hat emerges is a picture of economic, not political, freedom and a society of autonomous fulfilled beings, not a polity of citizens. As a result a whole complex of vital political questions is sidestepped or ignored: What is political freedom? What does it mean to be a citizen?" ("Context is All," pp. 70–71). Cornel West offers an important corrective to Jameson's evasions

---

[27] Philip Goldstein says, "Jameson's pursuit of a utopian realm beyond the ideological or instrumental shows an ultimate indifference to practical action" ("The Politics of Fredric Jameson's Literary Theory," p. 257). Jameson recognizes how overwhelming a deterministic theory can be (*Postmodernism*, pp. 5–6) but does not apply it to himself.

by talking about the recuperative dimension that Marxist theory needs: "The Marxist aim is to discern an evolving and developing Sittlichkeit in the womb of capitalist society, a Sittlichkeit whose negative idea is to resist all forms of reification and exploitation and whose positive ideals are social freedom and class equality" (*Postmodernism and Politics*, p. 137). These ideals become the guide for "transforming present practices – the remaining life – against the backdrop of previous discursive and political practices, against the dead past" (p. 138). West criticizes Jameson's utopianism since it "rests neither on specifiable historical forces potentially capable of actualizing it or on the notion that every conceivable historical force embodies it" (p. 140). The former has already been illustrated; the latter appears most clearly in the following passage: "The preceding analysis entitles us to conclude that all class consciousness of whatever type is Utopian insofar as it expresses the unity of a collectivity; yet it must be added that this proposition is an allegorical one. The achieved collectivity or organic group of whatever kind – oppressors fully as much as oppressed – is Utopian not in itself, but only insofar as all such collectivities are themselves *figures* for the ultimate concrete collective life of an achieved Utopian or classless society" (Jameson, *The Political Unconscious*, pp. 290–91, cited in West, *Postmodernism and Politics*, p. 140).

In Jameson's recent work on postmodernism, we find a similar difficulty, since all his efforts are devoted to explaining the decentered and dominated subject. He retells his tale of alienation in which "the truth of experience no longer coincides with the place in which it takes place. The truth of that limited daily experience of London lies ... bound up with the whole colonial system of the British Empire that determines the very quality of the individual's subjective life" (*Postmodernism*, p. 411). If modernism tried "to square this circle and to invent new and elaborate formal strategies for overcoming this dilemma" (p. 411), postmodernism shows how this problem is exacerbated: "If this is so for the age of imperialism, how much more must it hold for our own moment, the moment of multinational network, or what Mandel calls 'late capitalism'" (p. 412). Hence, for Jameson the "spatial peculiarities of postmodernism" are "symptoms and expressions of a new and historically original dilemma, one that involves our insertion as individual subjects into a multidimensional set of radically discontinuous realities, whose frames range from the still surviving spaces of bourgeois private life all the way to the unimaginable decentering of global capital itself" (p. 413). Hence, we have to come up with an explanatory structure, which Jameson calls "cognitive mapping," a structure that will "enable a situational representation on the part of the individual subject to that vaster and properly unrepresentable totality which is the ensemble of society's structure as a whole" (p. 51). Jameson's Marxism offers an alternative explanatory structure to poststructuralism, but it shares the quest for total revolution that can only unmask the struggles of the past, map the emptiness of the present, and gesture toward an inarticulate future. My own political position on the question of total revolution is phrased well by Chantal Mouffe: "If the Left is to learn from the tragic experiences of totalitarianism, it has to adopt a different attitude towards liberal democracy and recognize its strengths as well as its shortcomings" (*Radical Democracy*, p. 1). Hence, critique "does not imply the rejection of liberal democracy and its replacement by a completely new form of society as the traditional idea of revolution entailed, but a radicalization of the modern democratic tradition" (p. 1).

Edward Said tries to recuperate insights of poststructuralism and Marxism for engaged criticism while avoiding their Eurocentrism and determinism. He breaks with poststructuralists by connecting his hermeneutics to the Marxist project of ideology critique and utopian projection. In his critique, he wants to expose the ideologies of Western imperialism and of those cultures that fought against it. These ideologies have prevented us from seeing how power and cultural identity work together to carve up the world into competing islands. In his utopian dimension, he hopes to reconnect these islands by retelling their stories in a way that recognizes both Western culture and the marginalized cultures of the Third World. Said builds his idea of community on empirical and utopian claims. The empirical claim concerns the interconnectedness of the world's experience (*Culture and Imperialism*, p. xx). At the utopian level, he wants "to bind the European as well as the native together in a new non-adversarial community of awareness and anti-imperialism" (p. 274). He seeks to develop an alternative to the anti-humanistic problematics of Foucault and Derrida that have been influential in the postcolonial work of Gayatri Spivak and Homi Bhabha. Said rejects Spivak's thesis that imperial discourse completely coopts the native subject into complicity with his/her own oppression. As Benita Parry says, "In Said's account, signs of counter-hegemonic opposition are located not within the interstices of the dominant discourse or the ruptures of the imperialist representation [that is, the way poststructuralist theories locate opposition] but in acts and articulations of native defiance" ("Overlapping Territories," p. 36).

The problem is that Said never talks about the ethical/political location from which he tells these stories. He views cultural positioning only negatively, as if he is so afraid of being coopted, of reducing the complexities of the past and the possibilities of the future by using gross categories of self-understanding that he gives no positive vocabulary to describe his theoretical location. "Culture" and "tradition" are defined only negatively as entrapment (*Culture and Imperialism*, pp. 15–16).[28] Said insists on his rootlessness but appeals to humanistic and democratic values: "For in the main . . . criticism must think of itself as life-enhancing and constitutively opposed to every form of tyranny, domination, and abuse; its social goals are noncoercive knowledge produced in the interests of human freedom" (*The World, the Text, and the Critic*, p. 29). He recognizes that these values put him at odds with Foucault and in line with the cultural criticism of Noam Chomsky: "I've always felt that one in fact could incorporate both of them [Foucault and Chomsky]" (Imre Salusinszky, "Interview with Edward Said," p. 134). But Said never tells the story of how one can "incorporate both." The result is that he tacks on the notion of "community" as an ideal.

Said tries to achieve such community through contrapuntalism, a technique that brings together stories that imperialist and nationalist narratives have isolated: "We must be able to think through and interpret together experiences that are discrepant, each with its particular agenda and pace of development, its own

---

28 As Catherine Gallagher says, "He notes that knowledge is always bounded by place but insists that there is an epistemologically privileged locus of displacement called exile" ("Politics, the Profession, and the Critic," p. 37). Said cites T.S. Eliot's idealist, elitist notion of tradition (*Culture and Imperialism*, pp. 4–5) in order to show how such ideas are precisely what he wants to unmask. The theory of tradition that he cites favorably (pp. 32–34) is the one proposed by Terence Ranger and Eric Hobsbawm in *The Invention of Tradition*. This work considers tradition only as a patchwork of rationalization, a factitious product of power, not a resource.

internal formations, its internal coherence and system of external relationships" (*Culture and Imperialism*, p. 32). He offers no help, however, on how to think through these stories, only the hope that juxtaposing incommensurate stories will produce political change: "My interpretative political aim (in the broadest sense) [is] to make concurrent those views and experiences that are ideologically and culturally close to each other and that attempt to distance and suppress other views and experiences" (p. 33). By refusing to recuperate any traditions, he deprives his notion of community of any concreteness.[29] Said is eloquent on his empirical positionality – that is, his upbringing in Palestine, Egypt, and America – but he says little about how he situates his thought in any traditions. Community is not a utopia but a regulative ideal that is not connected to any ethical/political traditions, and I use this Kantian term to emphasize how Said's "community" is deracinated from historical traditions. The traditions with which he identifies, the resistance writings of Frantz Fanon and C.L.R. James, are praised because they take contrapuntal views of history and because they employ "nomadic, migratory, and anti-narrative energy." What is important is heterogeneity *per se* rather than the argumentative direction provided by their texts. This deracination is facilitated by the location of his critique at the meta-philosophical level. "Imperialism," "resistance," and "contrapuntalism" are meta-theoretical terms that factor out all aspects of culture except identity and difference. The value of the meta-theoretical term "contrapuntalism" has to be cashed out in first-order values and stories that inform the shapes of our existing cultural dialogues. Without a gesture of recuperation, the ideals that inform the critique of imperialism simply drop from the sky.

The work of Jürgen Habermas revives not only a good deal of the Marxist project but also the ethical/political project of modernity initiated by Kant and Hegel. What is crucial from my perspective is that he affirms the ideals of the Enlightenment against the interpretation loosely shared by Weber, Adorno, Jameson and

---

[29] Said claims that he is not doing a wholesale critique of Western culture or the cultures of resistance; however, he never does any recuperation. In his reading of Jane Austen, he says, "Yes, Austen belonged to a slave-owning society, but do we therefore jettison her novels as so many trivial exercises in aesthetic frumpery? Not at all, I would argue" (*Culture and Imperialism*, p. 96). But what values from Austen's work can be recuperated for Said's project? We never find out.

poststructuralists, in which Enlightenment reason is reduced to instrumental reason that engulfs and defoliates all modern society. Habermas concedes that instrumental reason has taken over much of modern life, the part governed by what he calls "the system," and that instrumental reason is tied both to a bankrupt philosophy of consciousness (a subject-centered view) and to the operations of capitalism. Habermas insists, however, that this is not the whole story. There is a space in modern society that sustains anti-instrumental cultural practices, a space he calls "the lifeworld." As Thomas McCarthy says, "He stands with Marx in regarding them [the processes of rationalization] as due not to rationalization as such but to the peculiar nature of capitalist modernization" (*Ideals and Illusions*, p. 152). Although I agree with Habermas's effort to recuperate aspects of modernity – specifically, autonomy, recognition, ethical reflexivity, and the public sphere, which I will take up in chapters 2 and 3 – my focus here will be on my disagreement with his attempt to defend the existence of these cultural resources through a narrow and tendentious philosophy of language that not only is easily undermined but that also gives a poor account of the resources of the very lifeworld for which he wants to argue. The core thesis of his alternative view of reason is that "the use of language with an orientation to reaching understanding is the original mode of language use, upon which indirect understanding, giving something to understand or letting something be understood, and the instrumental use of language in general, are parasitic" (*The Theory of Communicative Action*, vol. I, p. 288). The priority of this communicative use of language is the key to Habermas's philosophical project because it enables him to make a scientific claim that communicative discourse is fundamental and liberating. He thus can avoid the normative and utopian claims that it should be given priority, claims that Habermas fears can only be relativistic rather than universal. As David Rasmussen says, "What may not be immediately apparent in Habermas's program . . . is that there is a certain kind of agenda that seems to be endorsed – i.e., egalitarian, universal rights, radical democracy . . . presented under the rubric of reconstructive science, the claims of which are read out of a philosophy of language" (*Reading Habermas*, pp. 3–4). The reason he is forced to make his philosophy of language so narrow is that he not only wants to show that there is a space for communicative reason but that his pragmatics provides a formal model for universal reason that can overcome cultural relativism.

Habermas goes back to Kant for his idea of morality as universality. Habermas fears that without such a meta-ethical principle to trump the ethical practices of different cultures the claims of democratic values will be reduced to "our preferences." However, rather than making morality hinge on the universalizable maxims of the categorical imperative, on the thought experiment of the isolated subject, as Kant does, he wants to make universality intersubjective. For Kant, the principle governing the generation of moral maxims is that of noncontradiction. For Habermas, the test is agreement. Habermas feels that he has handled Hegel's objections to Kant because mutual recognition and needs are given a place in moral discourse. At the same time, this Hegelian enrichment is divorced from Hegel's transsubjective understanding of culture and history. "The unbridgeable gap Kant saw between the intelligible and the empirical becomes, in discourse ethics, a mere tension manifesting itself in everyday communication as the factual force of counterfactual presuppositions" (*Moral Consciousness*, p. 203). By trying to pack all of these ideals into a scientific truth about language – rather than making normative and utopian appeals to certain kinds of linguistic, ethical, and political practices – Habermas severely limits the role of language in culture and weakens some of his strong arguments against the critics of modernity.[30]

I will not lay out Habermas's theory of language, which others have already done, but instead will examine some of his assumptions about linguistic practices and linguistic competence that reduce the role of language in critical theory. Habermas does not use the idea of linguistic practice *per se* but two global characterizations: "lifeworld," adapted from Husserl, and "background," which he borrows from Searle. "Insofar as speakers and hearers straightforwardly achieve a mutual understanding about something in the

---

[30] The focal point for critiques of Habermas's theory of language is his reworking of the communicative and instrumental uses of language to fit Austin's distinction between illocutionary and perlocutionary acts, respectively: "As the meaning of what is said is constitutive for illocutionary acts, the intention of the agent is constitutive for teleological actions" (*The Theory of Communicative Action*, vol. I, p. 289). Jonathan Culler's critique cuts to deep problems: "Many illocutionary acts seem primarily designed to produce certain effects rather than to bring about understanding" ("Communicative Competence and Normative Force," p. 136).

world, they move within the horizon of their common lifeworld; this remains in the background of the participants – as intuitively known, unproblematic, unanalyzable, holistic background" (*The Philosophical Discourse of Modernity*, p. 298).[31] This background can be studied by the reconstructive sciences so that "the pretheoretical grasp of rules on the part of competently speaking, acting, and knowing subjects" (p. 298) can be made explicit. Reconstruction seeks to unpack and map the subject's pretheoretical know-how: "Starting primarily from the intuitive knowledge of competent subjects – competent in terms of judgment, action, and language – and secondarily from systematic knowledge handed down by culture, the reconstructive sciences explain the presumably universal bases of rational experience and judgment, as well as of action and linguistic communication" (*Moral Consciousness*, pp. 15–16). Reconstruction is thus not an interpretation of the speaker's discourse but a neo-Kantian investigation into the conditions of the possibility of speaking. "Background" provides commensurability among practices, so that the diverse particular histories and actualities of these practices fall into a horizon of unity. This unity is the basis for a subject of competence as defender of claims: "Rationality is understood to be a disposition of speaking and acting subjects that is expressed in modes of behavior for which there are good reasons or grounds" (*The Theory of Communicative Action*, vol. 1, p. 22). As opposed to strategic action, communicative action is the "medium through which the lifeworld is reproduced" (*The Philosophical Discourse of Modernity*, p. 299). The lifeworld and communicative reason provide an alternative space to the systems of instrumental reason (*The Theory of Communicative Action*, vol. 1, p. 34). Moreover, this background is revealed only through the unit of the sentence, since this is the unity in which validity claims can be made. Commensurability is crucial for Habermas, since, unlike Davidson and Rorty, he seeks not only to refute radical skepticism or otherness but to lay the basis for universal reason through a formal pragmatics that permits us to discuss claims to truth, truthfulness, and right independently of their cultural context. By using a formal approach, Habermas seeks to retain the power of critique while avoiding dogmatism and relativism. Only

---

[31] Habermas says elsewhere, "The lifeworld is bounded by the totality of interpretation presupposed by the members as background knowledge" (*The Theory of Communicative Action*, vol. 1, p. 13).

with a shared background do these claims make sense, since his counterfactual, ideal-speech situation for moral discourse – a situation in which all parties have the right to make and criticize claims and in which all parties share common interests – "cannot judge the value of competing forms of life" ("Reply to My Critics," p. 227).[32] "Background" and "lifeworld" coincide with "form of life," and all these terms seek the objectivity of a neutral description, a description sanctioned by theoretical necessity and not axiology.

But let's say the forms of life are within and not just between societies? If so, then the formal approach begins to break down. Mary Louise Pratt shows the troublesome effects produced by the unified views of language and community that lie behind the work of Saussure, Chomsky, and the pragmatic theorists: "The distance between langue and parole, competence and performance is the distance between the homogeneity of the imagined community and fractured reality of linguistic experience in modern stratified societies" ("Linguistic Utopias," p. 51). Lyotard phrases this assumption by saying that such theories presuppose "a language that is naturally at peace with itself" (*Le Différend*, pp. 199–200). For Lyotard, language is a discursive battle, in which one type of discourse can silence or oppress another: "A *différend* takes place between two parties when the 'settlement' of the conflict that opposes them is made in the idiom of one while the injury from which the other suffers does not signify in that idiom" (pp. 24–25). By locating conflict in language itself rather than between competing claims by subjects, Lyotard emphasizes the ways that linguistic practices situate subjectivity. For Habermas, linguistic practices permit us to make claims but they do not become modes of being that shape what we are and that exclude alternative shapes. It is this sense of exclusion that gives norms and practices an "oppressive" dimension which is coextensive with their enabling dimension, even when power is not a factor. Habermas tries to block out the force and shape of practices by assuming that such conflicts take place only between but not within "forms of life." As Benhabib

---

[32] Habermas also uses the Wittgensteinian phrase "forms of life" to mean difference within lifeworlds: "Forms of life comprise not only institutions that come under the aspect of justice, but language games, historical configurations of habitual practices, group memberships, cultural patterns of interpretation, forms of socialisation, competencies, attitudes and so forth" ("Reply to My Critics," p. 262). He acknowledges that "any universalistic morality is dependent upon a form of life that meets it halfway" (*Moral Consciousness*, p. 207).

notes, "Discourse [Habermas's term for ideal dialogue] arises when the intersubjectivity of ethical life is endangered; but the very project of discursive argumentation presupposes the ongoing validity of a reconciled subjectivity" (*Critique, Norm, and Utopia*, p. 321). The issue is not whether we need shared concepts to talk at all – the typical example for these arguments is with an alien culture – but which concepts are engaged in a given situation and how they work. In order to make such analysis, we need linguistic problematics that operate at levels other than the sentence and that theorize the shaping force of practices. In an effort to answer the totalizing claims made by the Frankfurt School and the poststructuralists, in which modernity is reduced to instrumental reason or a network of power, Habermas seeks an equally grand response. In doing so, he limits critique to counterfactual thought-experiments and drives out deep theories of internalization such as poststructuralism, which thematizes our constructedness against the grain of the lifeworld.

We can see how much work Habermas's notion of the "lifeworld" must do to contain linguistic diversity by examining his typologies of discourse. If Habermas follows Weber in dividing knowledge into spheres with specialized vocabularies, he sees these areas as unified within themselves and against the background of "intramundance learning processes" (*Philosophical Discourse of Modernity*, p. 339). In the same way, values are distinguished from other validity claims because they are "located within the horizon of the lifeworld of a particular group or culture" and thus "do not count as universal" (*Theory of Communicative Action*, vol. 1, p. 42). The critique of values "presupposes a shared preunderstanding among participants in the argument, a preunderstanding that is not at their disposal but *constitutes* [my emphasis] and at the same time circumscribes the domain of the thematized validity claims" (p. 42). The constitutive is opposed to the descriptive dimension of language and then is sequestered from the major validity claims. Habermas's theory of language is connected to his wish not simply to keep instrumental questions separate from communicative ones but to keep questions of the good life separate from morality. "Participants in processes of self-clarification cannot distance themselves from the life-histories and forms in life in which they actually find themselves. Moral-practical discourse, by contrast, requires a break with all of the unquestioned truths of an established, concrete ethical life" (*Justification and Application*, p. 12). However, it is precisely this constitutive dimension of language that is connected to our deepest commitments, our "strong evaluations," in Charles Taylor's phrase, as we shall see in chapter 3.[33]

Habermas employs a parallel opposition between the "problem-solving function" and the "world-disclosing function" of language. He consigns the work of Heidegger and Derrida to the "poetic world-disclosing function of language" (*The Philosophical Discourse of Modernity*, p. 204). According to Habermas, Derrida ignores "the fact that everyday communicative practice makes learning processes possible (thanks to built-in idealizations) in relation to which the world-disclosive force of interpreting language has in turn to prove its worth" (p. 205). The "everyday" lifeworld becomes the center around which difference must cluster, and this assumption is just what Derrida is interested in exposing. This is not to say that all discourses are the same – which is how Habermas reads Derrida's view.[34] I would agree with Habermas that Derrida's problematic of the sign can only deconstruct rather than construct typologies of linguistic practices and that such typologies are crucial. (Derrida's view of language is not too grand, but too impoverished. It is not world-disclosing enough to articulate social shapes.) However, any such typology needs to abandon the "everyday" as a meta-type that provides a common core for all types. The need for idealization does not require such a massive presupposition. Habermas's distinction between the everyday and the literary genres of discourse – influenced by Weber and the Frankfurt School arguments about the autonomy of art – collapses the issue of the institution of art with the problem of language and ignores the collapse of the opposition between literary and nonliterary language that is now a commonplace among literary theorists. (See, for example, Terry Eagleton's *Literary Theory*.[35])

---

[33] See Taylor's *Human Agency and Language*. Habermas acknowledges the importance of such evaluations for ethical questions but keeps them separate from moral ones. See *Justification and Application*, pp. 1–17, 69–76, for his discussion.

[34] Habermas says, "One cannot, like Derrida, conclude from the unavoidably rhetorical character of *every* kind of language, including philosophical language, that it is all one and the same – that the categories of everyday life and literature, science and fiction, poetry and philosophy collapse into each other" (*Autonomy and Solidarity*, pp. 161–62).

[35] The question is not whether "poetic or fictional communication is parasitical on the communication which takes place in everyday practice," as Allen Wood says ("Habermas's Defense of Rationalism," p. 156), but how we characterize the

The fact that literary texts do not refer to "real" events does not make them discontinuous with "everyday language." Literary stories, like historical ones, can challenge, revise, or confirm the linguistic practices through which we constitute ourselves. The separation of the aesthetic sphere from the cognitive and the moral spheres that Kant initiates is characteristic of a particular line of criticism that culminates in literary modernism, whose moment has long passed. Moreover, Habermas' charge that Derrida ignores accepted conventions of discourse is misguided. Derrida admits that "no research is possible in a community ... without the prior search for minimal consensus" ("Afterword," p. 146). He says, "Formalisation is a fruitful, useful activity ... So the effort towards formalisation of such codes is indispensable" even if such a project "cannot be completed" ("Some Questions and Responses," p. 252). Derrida does not ignore these idealizations but explores them with a theory of the sign that exposes difficulties with the particular idealizations at issue. Thomas McCarthy puts the opposition between Habermas and Derrida nicely, though he draws a different conclusion than I do: "Are the idealizations built into language more adequately conceived as pragmatic presuppositions of communicative interaction or as a kind of structural lure that has ceaselessly to be resisted? (Or perhaps as both?)" (*Ideals and Illusions*, p. 231). The answer is that we need a theoretical space that can entertain both perspectives. In order for Habermas to keep his two forms of self-reflection distinct – "reflection upon the condition of potential abilities of a knowing, speaking and acting subject as such" and "reflection upon unconsciously produced constraints to which a determinate subject (or group of subjects ...) succumbs in the process of self-formation" ("A Postscript to Knowledge," p. 182) – he must keep these anonymous background rules free from hermeneutics and make them as transcendental as possible. Certainly, some presuppositions are necessary but this necessity does not mean that these presuppositions are neutral; nor does it tell us how these presuppositions are formulated or which ones are at work in a particular situation. Both Habermas

discourse of everyday life. Part of the problem with Wood's and Habermas's discussion of this issue is that they rely on Jonathan Culler's limited reading of the Searle/Derrida debate and that their interest is in philosophy and social science, not in the philosophical exploration of the way the language of stories provides modes of critique and insight.

and Derrida take an all-or-nothing view, which keeps the entire issue of pragmatics encrusted in the issue of closure and nonclosure. If Derrida never announces the criteria of his critique, Habermas tries to cloak axiology in necessity and reconstruction in order to avoid placing the question in the space of a democratic hermeneutics. The result is that neither helps us much in reforming the present. Habermas places social critique in the narrow confines of a linguistic formalism that helps sort out oppressive or instrumental relationships but does not show how to rework the past for the future. Derrida cannot discriminate nourishing from coercive cultural practices but can only show the exclusionary nature of them all and point toward a vacuous alternative in which difference floats freely.

Hence, if reconstruction is hermeneutic, it is also utopian. The development of a theory of competence itself is not simply a reconstruction of what speakers must assume but of what they ought to assume. If a theory of competence is to avoid Gadamer's assumption that consensus is given in being, then this theory must include an explanatory dimension – critical models for clarification and demystification that are used to break up holistic structures. When we invoke these explanatory models is a function not just of our misunderstanding but of what we hope for (and hence also of what we want to show up). That is why we tend to explain our enemies and speak to our friends – that is, our enemies do not simply disagree with us; they are laboring under an illusion. (The difference between Jameson's discussion of Marxists and non-Marxists and Rorty's discussion of pragmatists and foundationalists provides good illustrations of how explanation is selectively invoked to expose one's enemies.) These third-person accounts break with our existing dialogical vocabularies and urge us to revise our self-understandings. This utopia cannot be limited to Habermas's etiolated formal requirements of the ideal speech situation and his procedural ideal nor the poststructuralist appeal to negative freedom.

Habermas's debate with Derrida over the role of idealization obscures what is a crucial problem in both linguistic theories – the failure to theorize the powers of language, powers that appear in the work of many writers, from Paul Ricoeur and Charles Taylor to Ralph Ellison and Toni Morrison. (I will develop these dimensions of language in chapters 2–5.) Habermas never considers the worlds proposed by texts, worlds that offer ethical and political critiques available to many forms of analysis, not just poststructuralism. Novels provide the kind of thematization that Benhabib calls for in her revision of Habermas's communicative ethics to include a utopian dimension: "The requirement that needs and their interpretations become the focus of discursive argumentation has the consequence that those traditions, and practices, the semantic content of which define the good life and happiness, are thematized" (*Critique, Norm, and Utopia*, p. 336). When these needs are thematized, they will not only invade claims to truth or rightness but show how reductive it is to speak of the complex relationships among language, value, and subjectivity as "claims."

Clearly, a hermeneutics that can address these issues must discard some of Gadamer's assumptions, from his well-known failure to thematize issues of domination to his ontological underwriting of the idea of play.[36] What marginal texts ask us cannot be answered within the tradition but only by a break with the tradition. Holism's claim that there are no "radical" breaks in our beliefs, since such breaks would be unintelligible, does not account for the ethical and ontological force of the change that women, African Americans, and other groups have discussed in their stories of discovery of critical awareness, in which they narrate the excavation of their internalization of tradition's judgments and establish new self-understandings. The critique by Marxists and poststructuralists of the conservatism of Heideggerian and Gadamerian hermeneutics points vividly to this failure; however, this critique leaves out the need for a new hermeneutics that works at smaller levels than the "tradition" and that gives attention to the normative and axiological assumptions that are buried in any problematic. In this way, islands of community and difference can be theorized. That is, the fragmentation of poststructuralism can be brought into new wholes that force us to examine the differences in holistic practices. Ethical judgment is

---

[36] See Robin Schott's "Whose Home Is It Anyway?" for an excellent critique of Gadamer, particularly the connection of the ontological and the normative: "Ontology for Gadamer clearly does have normative implications, since he speaks of those who refuse to abandon themselves fully to the play. Therefore, differences in human identity (such as gender) may become normatively inscribed into interpretations of being" (p. 204). This critique of Gadamer does not leave his project in ruins, however; see, for example, Mae Gwendolyn Henderson's appropriation of Gadamer and Bakhtin in "Speaking in Tongues."

not cast into "decisionism," in which the subject finds him-self/herself confronted with incommensurate possibilities and no criteria so that he/she simply leaps in one direction or another.[37] Rather, the subject participates in and is informed by a variety of texts and contexts. At the same time, the critical possibilities for repartitioning and rethinking commitments keeps the embodied self, which is advanced not only by feminists such as Carol Gilligan but also by communitarians like Charles Taylor, Alasdair MacIntyre, and Michael Sandel, from being an imprisoned one. Benhabib phrases this concern well, "whereas communitarians emphasize the situated of the disembodied self in a network of relations and narratives, feminists also begin with the situated self but view the renegotiation of our psychosexual identities, and their autonomous reconstitution by individuals as essential to women's and human liberation" ("Beyond the Politics of Gender," pp. 12–13). What saves hermeneutics from conservatism is the utopian dimension that first emerges not in explanation or understanding but in application – i.e., in the ways the text speaks to our present and future possibilities – for it is here that the categories of self-constitution are not endorsed or even accepted as given.

The conclusion to be drawn from this analysis is that the incommensurability of the various problematics we have seen can be bridged provided we do not totalize them (that is, make them nonnegotiable truths about what being is). What permits us to overcome this impasse is the assumption that the incommensura-bility is not radical unintelligibility. As Richard Bernstein says, "The very rationale for introducing the notion of incommensurability is to clarify what is involved when we do compare rival paradigms" (*Beyond Objectivism*, p. 82). Indeed, all the participants share many assumptions – e.g., that subject and world emerge from a space of linguistic practice. No one advocates a neo-Cartesian view. The question is how to theorize the subject's historical embeddedness, and all of the thinkers we have examined come up with too grand an answer. While Habermas and Gadamer try to make the

---

[37] In *Human Agency and Language*, Taylor provides an example of "decisionism" through a discussion of Sartre's portrayal of a man torn between fighting for the French Resistance and staying home to care for his ailing mother. Taylor criticizes Sartre's characterization of this dilemma, in which the man can only throw himself in one direction or the other, as a flawed model of ethical reflection.

hermeneutic circle too small by packing in assumptions of common ground, the poststructuralists try to avoid the circle altogether. Both try to escape the inevitable productive tension between third-person accounts and dialogical accounts of the subject, which I will develop in chapter 3. For the moment, we can say that poststructuralist problematics need to be read as ethical and political challenges to the way the hermeneutic circle has been closed – to the ways in which speakers, their objects and their languages have been constructed – rather than as insuperable logical or ethical/political obstacles to its closing. Poststructuralism, like Smith's functionalism, reveals ways of fracturing unity and revealing unsuspected coercion as well as gaps of opportunity. Hermeneutics has been too narrowly conceived, not just because it ignores material features of history but also because it lacks a vocabulary for articulating differences within a culture and between cultures. If poststructuralism exposes differences in what we took to be unities, hermeneutics needs a vocabulary to bring these third-person insights into a language of participants so that complex islands of similarities and difference can be negotiated. Each of these problematics has strengths and weaknesses; the choice among them needs to be made by utopian thinking that does not eliminate the resources of the past, rupture all ties with the present, or rest content with an affirmation of difference and diversity.

If I am arguing for a space of deliberation that is not entirely structured by the totalizing claims of the theorists discussed in this chapter, what kinds of considerations can inform it? The answer will come in the next two chapters. This chapter has been devoted to a meta-theoretical critique of how contemporary theories foreclose important aspects of democratic subjectivity. I have not fully disclosed the theory that drives this meta-critique but am using the meta-theoretical analysis to identify our theoretical needs. Chapter 2 will shift the focus of the meta-theoretical analysis to the liberal/communitarian debate in order to bring forward connections among language, ethics, and politics that are not made available in the arguments examined in chapter 1. In chapter 3, I will advance my theory of how stories of agency and stories of oppression can work together and use this theory to read (first-order criticism) particular texts.

2

Language, ethics, and subjectivity in the liberal/communitarian debate

> The strong textualist simply asks himself the same question about a text which the engineer asks about a puzzling physical object: how shall I describe this in order to get what I want?
>
> Richard Rorty, *Consequences of Pragmatism*

> There ... is a deep incompatibility between the standpoint of any rational tradition of enquiry and the dominant modes of contemporary teaching, discussion and debate.
>
> Alasdair MacIntyre, *Three Rival Versions of Moral Enquiry*

In chapter 1, I argued for breaking the poststructuralist genealogies of power and for exploring ethical and cultural resources in ways that Habermas's universalizing reconstructive science does not permit. If poststructuralism shows how cultural differences have been suppressed, it provides no way of articulating the ethical goods of alternative cultures or of deliberating about these conflicting goods. This chapter takes up these two problems. I use the phrase "ethical goods," which will seem bizarre to literary critics, precisely to force the problem of value out of the impoverished vocabulary of literary theory toward ethical theory. I will bring the concerns of ethical theory into the interests of literary theory by connecting ethics to the philosophy of language and hence to textual practices. In this way, I will heal the split noted by Martha Nussbaum between Anglo-American ethical theory and literary theory – see the Introduction – and show how a politics of difference does not have poststructuralism as its only resource. My means of development will be through the linguistic philosophies of Richard Rorty and Alasdair MacIntyre, who are good representatives of the debate between liberals and communitarians over the good life and the self.[1]

---

[1] The bibliography of the debate is enormous. There are two recent collections of essays that give a good sampling of views: *Liberalism and the Moral Life*, ed. Nancy

Before examining their works, however, we need a brief characterization of liberalism and communitarianism. As a point of departure, we can say that liberalism stands for autonomy, rights, the separation of public and private, and the priority of justice over the good; that is, a liberal regime must be neutral with regard to conceptions of the good. The oppressions and conflicts that emerged in pre-modern attempts to establish a common good – e.g., religious wars – teach us that the good life should be a private, not a public, matter. As John Rawls says, "Political liberalism assumes that, for political purposes, a plurality of reasonable yet incompatible comprehensive doctrines is the normal result of the exercise of human reason within the framework of the free institutions of a constitutional regime" (*Political Liberalism*, p. xvi). Like poststructuralism, liberal theory is more eloquent in saying what it is against – e.g., monarchies, aristocracies, dogmatic conceptions of the good, etc. – than what it is for. In this view, to borrow an example from Michael Sandel, free speech can be defended as a right but not on the grounds that a life informed by political debate is worthier than one that is not (Introduction, *Liberalism and Its Critics*, p. 4). Society in the liberal conception is an aggregate of individuals who negotiate interests through the regulative idea of a social contract, not a community defined by constitutive goods. Consequently, there is a concern with distributive justice and procedural correctness rather than with conflicts about good lives. The priority of justice brings with it a certain view of the self, a self that can step back from itself and the world and make choices. As Sandel says, "As the priority of justice arose from the need to distinguish the standard of appraisal from the society being appraised, the priority of the self arises from the parallel need to distinguish the subject from its situation" (*Liberalism and the Limits of Justice*, p. 20). This self is based on Kantian efforts to define an individual's dignity and freedom independently of social context and of an individual's or group's needs and desires, to keep the issues of morality and the good life separate. If Habermas seeks Kantian universality through an ideal speech

Rosenblum, and *Liberalism and the Good*, ed. R. Bruce Douglass et al. See also Stephen Mulhall and Adam Swift's book-length survey and assessment of the debate, *Liberals and Communitarians*. There are many issues in the debate that are not relevant to my focus on language, the self, and the good life – e.g., affirmative action. At the end of the chapter and in the Conclusion, I will look at the need to rework this debate.

situation, Rawls employs the regulative ideal of the original position, in which the subject of justice is deprived of any knowledge about his/her own self.[2] Political liberalism aspires to be a "freestanding" conception of justice rather than a comprehensive moral doctrine that is tied to any beliefs about human nature or ethics, for such comprehensive doctrines lead to tyranny (*Political Liberalism*, pp. 86–87).[3]

Although this liberal conception of the self is precisely the kind that poststructuralist and Marxist theories attack for ideological and epistemological reasons, communitarians offer a different critique. They raise issues about the embeddedness of self, the good life, the rationality of traditions, and the community. Communitarians are concerned that liberalism's misguided view of autonomy and right is producing a fragmented and sterile political culture dominated by procedures and distributive justice. Individuals' ethical horizons are informed principally by a desire to be left alone (negative liberty) so they can pursue a life defined by the economic and spiritual acquisitions of the self. (Communitarians often say that the liberal self is not only ethically inadequate but incoherent, and hence they join Marxists.) Communitarians want to restore civic republicanism to public life so that citizens can identify with a common good. As Chantal Mouffe puts it, "This tradition . . . affirms in its political discourse that true human realization is only possible when one acts as a citizen of a free and self-governing political community" (*The Return of the*

---

[2] Sandel's critique of John Rawls, the preeminent liberal theorist, in *Liberalism and the Limits of Justice*, has been the focal point of much of the argument. I rely on the Sandel/Rawls opposition here because it concerns the relationship of ethics and the self. I must massively simplify very complex issues for the sake of economy. Rawls's *Theory of Justice* works from a Kantian framework while trying to jettison Kant's metaphysics. Rawls's liberal self of justice is not a transcendental being but a being shaped by two basic conditions that characterize the "original position." The first is that the self lies behind a "veil of ignorance" so that it knows nothing about its own sex, class, intelligence, etc. The only knowledge available to this self is knowledge of "primary goods" – that is, goods such as rights, liberties, income that everyone wants. Rawls calls this "the thin theory of the good," since it gives people enough in common to start negotiations about justice but does not make such a large presupposition about the good that alternative views are crowded out. Rawls has changed his view in recent years, adopting a more communitarian than Kantian justification for liberalism – e.g., *Political Liberalism* – that has complicated the debate.

[3] The work of Chantal Mouffe (*Radical Democracy* and *The Return of the Political*), Stephen Salkever ("Lopp'd and Bound" and *Finding the Mean*), and William Galston (*Liberal Purposes*) on the liberal/communitarian debate and on democracy is important here. I discuss them later.

Political, p. 24). The communitarian critique is made by reworking a premodern philosophy or culture, and the most popular is Aristotle's. Sandel's *Liberalism and the Limits of Justice*, which offers a critical reading of Rawls's work, is one of the key communitarian texts: "Justice as fairness fails to take seriously our commonality. In regarding the bounds of the self as prior, fixed once and for all, it relegates our commonality to an aspect of the good, and the good to a mere contingency, a product of indiscriminate wants and desires 'not relevant from a moral standpoint'" (p. 174). Such a view of the self makes autonomy a decontextualized formal assumption rather than an achievement tied to specific kinds of cultural nourishment: "By putting the self beyond the reach of politics, it [liberalism] makes human agency an article of faith rather than an object of continuing attention and concern, a premise of politics rather than its precarious achievement" (p. 183). Communitarians, particularly neo-Aristotelian ones such as Alasdair MacIntyre and Robert Bellah, focus their attention on the virtues of particular cultures, especially literary cultures, as Bellah's work on American culture shows (*Habits of the Heart* and *The Good Society*). Liberals, in turn, attack these projects as throwbacks to pre-modern, oppressive states, where dogmatic views of the good life forced the views of the majority or the powerful on minorities, where liberties and rights had no place, and where cultural diversity was not an issue. Literary theorists give this fascinating debate little play, because they think that liberalism is dead and that communitarianism makes the conservative move of putting ethics ahead of politics, of going back to a discredited humanism.

This neglect is unfortunate, since the debate is relevant to literary disputes, such as Gerald Graff's proposal "to teach the conflicts," discussed in the Introduction. For example, when Graff feels obliged to back away from his leftist agenda, accept pluralism, and make his goal for students an awareness of the conflicts, he is acting on the liberal insight that it is both difficult and wrong to impose a rich and dogmatic view of the good on students: "Speaking as a leftist, I too find it tempting to try to turn the curriculum into an instrument of social transformation. But I doubt whether the curriculum (as opposed to my particular courses) can or should become an extension of the politics of the left" ("Teach the Conflicts," p. 70). Graff focuses on the "can" –

that is, too many disagree to make such an agenda possible – rather than the "should"; and consequently his suggestion to teach the conflicts avoids thematizing the ethical and political context in which the conflicts are presented. Graff leaves the question in an unmanageable form: Either we simply present conflicts or we indoctrinate students. Here is precisely where the critiques of pluralism as false neutrality stumble. Of course, there is no way that a state or a curriculum can be ethically and politically neutral, that democracy can avoid imposing a certain shape to life even if this shape is indeterminate. The question is where to go from here. We can avoid ricocheting between neutrality (relativism) and dogmatism by specifying the ethical/political goods of liberal democracy through an historical argument – something that liberal theory does not do well – so that positive democratic values are privileged and given context. Teachers and students will then be able to move from the recognition of difference to reflection on ways that democratically biased institutions have, and can handle difference. Before addressing this problem – to which I will return at the end of the chapter and in the Conclusion – we need an initiation into the debate.

MacIntyre's communitarian argument is important for my purposes, because it is an argument, first of all, for an alternative way of thinking about the language in which political and ethical debates are cast. From a political point of view, MacIntyre is not as good a representative of the communitarian position as are Michael Walzer or Sandel. However, my interest is not primarily in political theory but in the connections among philosophies of language, subjectivity, and ethics. MacIntyre's principal contribution is the meta-theoretical point that contemporary thinkers ignore tradition-based views of rationality and language. His work is important for a politics of difference precisely because he brings out how modern and postmodern theories evaporate the linguistic and ethical density embedded in the languages of rival traditions. In place of these theories, he offers a rich, positive conception of the dynamics of language and ethics. The major shortcoming of his work is his dismissal of the achievements of modernity, his failure to bring the tradition-based rationality into a dialogue with democratic institutions and sophisticated, critical recuperations of the liberal project. In short, his work offers ethical insights that require a political reconstruction and contextualization.

I use the work of Richard Rorty as my central example of liberalism for many reasons. First, with the publication of *Contingency, Irony, and Solidarity* (1989), Rorty presents a nonfoundationalist philosophy of language that becomes the guiding thread for his theory of the self and for his political vision. No other liberal theorist does this in such a comprehensive way, though many develop liberal political theory in much more detail and with greater sophistication (e.g., Rawls, Ronald Dworkin, Will Kymlicka). His work permits me to develop the connection between linguistics and ethics/politics from chapter 1 – a connection that Rorty's readers ignore for the most part[4] – and to defuse the transcendental argument or immanent critiques against the subject of liberalism mounted by poststructuralism and communitarians. The debate can thus move to another level.

In addition to the meta-philosophical thread that continues the focus of chapter 1, I will concentrate on supplementing the third-person, second-order accounts of language and subjectivity with a first-order account so that we have not only a constructed but a constructing subject whose ontology is informed not simply by epistemology but by ethics and politics. In contrasting MacIntyre's problematic of tradition with Rorty's linguistic holism, I argue for theoretical flexibility that all parties to the dispute ignore and that is important for a politics of difference. My development falls into four parts: (1) Rorty's view of meta-philosophy and its relationship to histories of philosophy; (2) the connection of his meta-philosophical linguistic claim to his understanding of subjectivity and ethics/politics; (3) MacIntyre's competing problematic of tradition-based inquiry with its understanding of language and ethics; (4) a summing up of the dilemmas of the first two chapters in which I recast the communitarian/liberal debate in a more productive form than Rorty and MacIntyre phrase it and show how this recasting helps address the failures of the theories discussed in chapter 1.

---

[4] The cohesiveness of Rorty's theory has not been discussed by his critics, who praise his critique of the foundationalist tradition in analytic philosophy and challenge his defense of ethnocentric liberalism. See Nancy Fraser's "Solidarity or Singularity: Richard Rorty between Romanticism and Technocracy," *Unruly Practices*, pp. 93–112, Thomas McCarthy's "Private Irony and Public Decency" and Cornel West's "The Politics of American Neo-Pragmatism," in *Keeping Faith*.

Histories of philosophy

A crucial question for Rorty is how one reads the history of philosophy, and he outlines his view in "The Historiography of Philosophy: Four Genres." Rorty begins with two different types of reconstruction – historical and rational. The former seeks to reconstruct the historical situation as the agent would understand it, as he/she would represent it to his/her contemporaries; the latter tries to make thinkers of the past participants in the questions of the present, so we try to make up "what an ideally reasonable and educable Aristotle could be brought to accept" (p. 51). The third genre, "doxography," is the old-fashioned kind of history that seeks to tell one story about philosophy (or literary history). It takes a contemporary problem that is judged to be important – theory of meaning in philosophy, or paradoxical figures, closure, rhetorical subversion in literature – and uses this to interrogate texts. Doxography "is the attempt to impose a problematic on a canon drawn up without reference to that problematic, or, conversely, to impose a canon on a problematic constructed without reference to that canon" (p. 62). Rorty's lesson here is not just about the bias of a given set of criteria but about the absence of self-consciousness concerning the relationship of the problematic to the canon and the call to thematize the relationship of theory to value. The fourth genre is *Geistesgeschichte*, which probes the problematics rather than the problems that inform philosophical questions – for example, "Why should anyone have made this question of ___central to his thought?" (p. 57). This last type involves an argument about what philosophy is, not about "particular solutions to philosophical problems" (p. 57). The practitioners of this type include Hegel, Nietzsche, Heidegger, and Derrida. Rorty's call to thematize the relationship of problematics to canons and histories is important for literary theorists and critics, whose unthematized commitment to a single problematic is used to interpret and valorize certain groups of texts.[5]

Rorty works primarily in the second and fourth types. In the latter, he takes the anthropological view of the meta-philosopher toward philosophical issues – e.g., foundations of the subject – that

---

[5] The relationship between critical problematic and canon is well known in some areas – e.g., the poets that New Criticism discusses and its concern with irony and paradox – but not so well in others – e.g., deconstruction. I discuss the relationship of problematic and canon further in chapter 5.

he wants to dismiss. This does not involve a hermeneutic dialogue with the issues that the texts themselves present but a genealogical investigation of the conditions that produce the questions. These genealogies, which are, of course, informed by his pragmatism, ask questions of this type, "'What sort of people see these problems?' and 'What vocabulary, what image of man, would produce these problems?'" (*Consequences of Pragmatism*, p. xxxiii). Rorty uses these kinds of questions and the portraits they evoke to offer a third-person critique (as his explanations) rather than using the explanations of social science in the manner of Habermas or Marxists. He is suspicious of any grand claims about social or historical necessities that can separate truth and ideology. When he writes in the second type, he shows how William James, Dewey, Wittgenstein and others were asking the right questions – that is, the same questions that he is asking – despite some occasional lapses. These authors he seeks to "understand" rather than explain. The purpose informing these readings has only the negative goal of urging us to abandon hope of finding something outside of our own desires. Pragmatists are "interested not so much in what's out there in the world, in what happened in history, as in what we can get out of nature and history for our own use" (*Philosophy and the Mirror of Nature*, p. 359).

For those who write in the *Geistesgeschichte* genre – Hegel, Nietzsche, Heidegger, Derrida, and Rorty himself – there is "the temptation of thinking that once you have found a way to subsume your predecessors under a general idea you have thereby done something more than found a redescription of them" – that is, that "none of the descriptions that applied to them applies to you – that you are separated from them by an abyss" (Rorty, *Contingency, Irony, and Solidarity*, p. 107). One of the great phrases of mystification in such a view is "conditions of possibility," which, for Rorty, is a poetic rather than an argumentative concept: "Since that for which the conditions of possibility are sought is always *everything* that any previous philosopher has envisaged – the whole range of what has been discussed up to now – anybody is at liberty to identify any ingenious gimmick that he dreams up as a 'condition of possibility'" (*Essays on Heidegger and Others*, p. 123). These "gimmicks" often produce fascinating re-readings of the history of philosophy, but that is all they should claim to be doing. Heidegger falls into this trap, even though he is aware of the difficulty of the "ironist theorist" – that is, the attempt to be the last philosopher, "to write something which will make it impossible for one to be redescribed except in one's own terms" (Rorty, *Contingency, Irony, and Solidarity*, p. 106). Rorty urges that we give up the theoretical dimension and write only in an ironic manner that acknowledges the contingency of language, self, and community. The problem here is that Rorty gives a poor account of his own work. He is not offering a first-order account of his life but a new problematic for understanding contemporary philosophical issues and the history of philosophy. The fact that he uses "more useful" rather than "true" as a justification for this view does not mean that it is not a theory.

This contingency means that our current philosophical, scientific, or literary paradigms, just like the ones that preceded them, were not brought about by using criteria for the comparison and assessment of competing paradigms: "Europe did not *decide* to accept the idiom of Romantic poetry, or of socialist politics, or of Galilean mechanics. That sort of shift was no more an act of will than it was a result of argument. Rather, Europe gradually lost the habit of using certain words and gradually acquired the habit of using others" (p. 6). Rorty is here arguing against an account of history that is written from inside the intentions of the historical actors as well as against a Hegelian story about the cunning of reason doing its necessary work behind the backs of agents. But the failure of these two approaches does not mean that we are not involved in arguments about how to understand our relationship to the past. Here, Rorty's admirable self-consciousness disappears behind a troubling rhetorical structure that appears throughout his text: He sets up a rationalist or foundationalist position and then offers a suggestive debunking formula that he does not develop. This tactic is particularly troubling when the first half is a strawperson rather than another nonfoundationalist position. The effect is to displace a more challenging question at the next level in which all interlocutors are presumed to have read Kuhn. That is, he not only refuses to leave the meta-philosophical level of problematics but assumes that his problematic is so different from others that no debate is possible. A similar formulation appears at the beginning of *Contingency, Irony, and Solidarity*, where he says that he will "show how a recognition of that contingency [of language] leads to a recognition of the contingency of conscience and how both recognitions lead to a picture of intellectual and moral progress as a history of useful metaphors rather than of increasing understanding of how things really are" (p. 9). However, the debate about history is no longer cast in these easy terms between realists and figuralists. The reason Rorty employs this strategy is that he wants to set up a site of writing in a language game that is incommensurate with positions in contemporary debate. Incommensurability will justify his attempt to "show up" rather than argue against these positions since argument can take place only within and not between language games: "Conforming to my own precepts, I am not going to offer arguments against the vocabulary I want to replace. I am going to try to make the vocabulary I favor look more attractive by showing how it may be used to describe a variety of topics" (p. 9). This move requires him to exaggerate his differences from rival views, often by simplifying them into a global "foundationalism." I will discuss what he means by "argument" and "redescription" in the next section, but first we need to see how he reworks the tradition.

Rorty's history of philosophy does not seek to deconstruct the tradition but to overcome it. His response to those he calls "intuitive realists" (Nagel and Cavell) is not to deny that we have intuitions "to the effect that 'truth is more than assertability'"; rather, "the pragmatist is urging that we do our best to stop having such intuitions, that we develop a new intellectual tradition" (*Consequences of Pragmatism*, pp. xxix-xxx). Such a development requires that we prune the language of the tradition as well as create new languages. We get some sense of this project through the terms he offers in place of the traditional vocabulary: "normal/abnormal" (*Philosophy and the Mirror of Nature*, pp. 320, 365), "inquiry/conversation" (p. 371), "conforming to the canons of rationality/muddling through" ("A Reply to Dreyfus and Taylor," p. 39), "corresponding/coping" (p. 39), "categories and principles/advantages and disadvantages" (*Consequences of Pragmatism*, p. 168). Notice the absence of the words "reference," "representation," "truth," "being," and "subject" even as foils. For Rorty, this traditional vocabulary does not need to be deconstructed but avoided. Indeed, he laments that "it is as important for the deconstructors as for the realists to think that metaphysics – that genre of literature which attempted to create unique, total, closed vocabularies – is very important" (*Essays on Heidegger and Others*, p. 105).

We can see how he rewrites traditional questions by looking at his remarks on two perennial issues: the ontology of the human and the interpretation of the text. Ontological questions need to be rewritten: "There is no inference from 'I can get what I want out of X by thinking of it as Y' to 'X is in itself a Y'" ("A Reply to Dreyfus and Taylor," p. 43). Rorty closes off the possibility of a nonfoundationalist ontology by adding "in itself," by making his opponent's position more rigorous than it has to be. Questions about "what" something is do not disappear once one accepts his premise that both subject and object emerge from a holistic network of belief. Yet, Rorty wants to drop ontological questions and replace them with moral/political ones: "There is no ontological break between human and nonhuman but only (to put it in somewhat misleading Kantian terms) a moral break" (p. 46). Shifting "attention from 'the demands of the object' to the demands of the purpose which a particular inquiry is supposed to serve . . . modulate[s] philosophical debate from a methodologico-ontological key into an ethico-political key" (*Objectivity, Relativism, and Truth*, p. 110). In the view I will develop later, ontology is not simply a methodological issue but precisely an ethical/political one. Rorty's willingness to speak "loosely" about ethics but not about ontology is part of his fear of the return of the tradition; however, this fear is itself an attachment, since it makes the old assumption about the priority of epistemology to ethics. As Charles Taylor says, "The great vice of the tradition is that it allows epistemology to command ontology" ("Rorty in the Epistemological Tradition," p. 264). Rorty's peculiar variation on this tradition is to say that he is not making a claim to truth when he criticizes others but only saying that his way is "useful" and theirs is out of date, not false.[6]

---

[6] It is not that Rorty thinks that we cannot refer to things, though he prefers "aboutness" to "reference": "For 'aboutness' is not a matter of pointing outside the web. Rather, we use 'about' as a way of directing attention to the beliefs which are relevant to the justification of other beliefs, not as a way of directing attention to nonbeliefs" (*Objectivity, Relativism, and Truth*, p. 97). I leave aside here the strawperson strategy – who still thinks that assertions do locate a world of things outside beliefs – to focus on the meta-philosophical issue. That is, the citation above accounts for reference within webs of belief, but it does not make a truth claim about "webs of belief" as problematic as opposed to alternative views. Rorty cannot make such a claim if his problematic is incommensurate with others as he says; hence, he falls back on "usefulness."

With regard to texts, Rorty rewrites the standard question in the same way. The "object" of concern, the text, like the human, dissolves, so that we return to the phrase that is the touchstone for all inquiry: "what I [we] want": "The critic asks neither the author nor the text about their intentions but simply beats the text into the shape which will serve his own purposes ... [F]rom a full-fledged pragmatist point of view, there is no interesting difference between tables and texts, between protons and poems. To a pragmatist, these are all just permanent possibilities for use" (*Consequences of Pragmatism*, pp. 152–53). Indeed, whether the issue is truth, aesthetics, or ethics, the way to proceed is to ask ourselves this question: "The question of what propositions to assert, which pictures to look at, what narratives to listen to ... are all questions about what will help us get us what we want" (p. xliii). What leads Rorty to repeat the phrase "what we want," as if it ended rather than began a debate? Why should our hermeneutical interrogation of and by past traditions be reduced to this decontextualized formula? In a recent essay on Heidegger, Rorty offers a meta-philosophical historical clarification. He agrees with Heidegger's claim that "if you begin with Plato's motives and assumptions you will end up with some form of pragmatism" (*Essays on Heidegger and Others*, p. 27). Unlike Heidegger, he thinks that "pragmatism is a good place to end up" (p. 27). From the time of the Greeks, "we have been asking ourselves the question: what must we and the universe be like if we are going to get the sort of certainty, clarity, and evidence Plato told us we ought to have?" (p. 29). However, the history of philosophy shows that "the only thing we can be certain about is what we want" (p. 29). Rorty's phrase is a meta-philosophical statement, not a first-order statement and it is a phrase that communitarians would contest. To clarify the nature of Rorty's meta-philosophical problematic and to develop its relationship to ethics/politics, we need to look at how he connects language and subjectivity.

Language, ethics, and subjectivity

Rorty defines pragmatism as a "doctrine [in which] there are no constraints on inquiry save conversational ones – no wholesale constraints derived from the nature of objects, or the mind, or of language, but only those retail constraints provided by the remarks of fellow-inquirers" (*Consequences of Pragmatism*, p. 165).

Although he argues for the liberation of our "conversations" from foundationalist concerns with truth and representation, he does not think of language in the same way as Habermas and the poststructuralists do.

Rorty develops his view of language through the work of Donald Davidson. For Davidson, truth concerns the internal coherence of belief rather than reference to a nonlinguistic reality. As Rorty puts it, "Nothing counts as justification unless by reference to what we already accept, and there is no way to get outside our beliefs and our language so as to find some test other than coherence" (*Philosophy and the Mirror of Nature*, p. 178).[7] Both Davidson and Rorty accept Quine's point that analytic philosophy has been on the wrong track by working with isolated sentences rather than with a holistic network of beliefs.[8] Holism should lead us to abandon the scheme/content epistemological model, since this model perpetuates the view that competing conceptual schemes organize the world differently. No conceptual scheme that is intelligible to us can also be radically different from ours. This means that we and the people we can talk to must be, for the most part, right. As Davidson puts it, "Someone with a (more or less) coherent set of beliefs has a reason to suppose his beliefs are not mistaken in the main" ("A Coherence Theory of Truth and Knowledge," p. 314). Davidson and Rorty avoid solipsism by maintaining the distinction between causality and truth. "We need to make a distinction between the claim that the world is out there and the claim that truth is out there ... To say that truth is not out there is simply to say where there are no sentences there is no truth ... The world is out there, but descriptions of the world are not" (Rorty, *Contingency, Irony, and Solidarity*, pp. 4–5). This move permits Davidson/Rorty to say that sensations can cause beliefs but that "a causal explanation of a belief does not show how or why the belief is justified" (Davidson, "A Coherence Theory of Truth and Knowledge," p. 311). This split between causality and language is immediately healed, since only the misguided scheme/content view could lead us to imagine any radically

---

[7] This passage is cited by Davidson with approval in "A Coherence Theory of Truth and Knowledge," p. 310.

[8] For a discussion of the development of holism and the problems it was supposed to correct, see Milton Munitz, *Contemporary Analytic Philosophy*, especially pp. 357–58.

divergent alternatives: "We must, in the plainest and method-
ologically basic cases, take the objects of a belief to be the causes of
that belief. And what we, as interpreters, take them to be is what
they in fact are. Communication begins where causes converge:
your utterance means what mine does if belief in its truth is
systematically caused by the same events and objects" (pp.
317–18). Since this position places conflicts among beliefs within
and between holistic systems rather than between subject and
object, we should expect some theory of discursive confrontation,
of the dynamics of the reweaving of webs of belief, but we get very
little. The best example of what Rorty and Davidson do offer
appears in their discussions of metaphor.

Davidson denies that metaphor is an issue of words, of tensions
between literal and figurative meaning; instead, he claims that
metaphor "belongs exclusively to the domain of use" and that
"the meanings of the words remain what they ordinarily are"
(*Inquiries into Truth and Interpretation*, p. 247). These aberrant uses
are off the semantic chart. They produce "effects," such as
catching our attention or offering an alternative conceptual web;
however, these "effects" are not part of the metaphor: "The
common error is to fasten on the contents of the thoughts a
metaphor provokes and to read these contents into the metaphor
itself" (p. 261). Davidson thus assimilates metaphor (language)
into other disruptive behaviors: "Joke or dream or metaphor can,
like a picture or a bump on the head, make us appreciate some fact
– but not by standing for, or expressing, the fact" (p. 262). Rorty
subscribes to Davidson's view, which he characterizes as follows:
"Tossing a metaphor into a conversation is like suddenly breaking
off the conversation long enough to make a face, or pulling a
photograph out of your pocket and displaying it" (*Contingency,
Irony, and Solidarity*, p. 18). Thus, language that falls outside the
language game in play at the moment has a causal, rather than a
persuasive or argumentative, effect: "New metaphors are causes,
but not reasons for changes in belief" (p. 50). Metaphor is thus not
an issue of words or sentences but of language games, in which
metaphoric use is so unfamiliar that it fits no language game (p.
18). Thus, a behavioristic account of metaphor simply labels it
"unusual," "unpredictable." Rorty limits his theory of metaphor
to epochal shifts in paradigms of thought – e.g., Copernican,
Newtonian – but he offers no account for less grandiose uses of

75

metaphor. Rorty rightly distinguishes between reasons within a language game and reasons for using a language (p. 48); however, he seems to consider discursive conflict within a language game as too pedestrian to merit comment, while conflict between even local games cannot be accounted for at all.[9] This refusal to get "inside" a language game that is shared by anyone else parallels what we saw in the section in this chapter on the history of philosophy, where he remains at the meta-philosophical level.

Rorty's commitment to the incommensurability of different language games leads him to reject argument as a discursive strategy. Interesting philosophy "is implicitly or explicitly a contest between an entrenched vocabulary which has become a nuisance and a half-formed vocabulary which vaguely promises great things" (p. 9). Argument is fine for parliamentary politics or normal science, but not for radical change in politics, science, or philosophy (p. 9). He refuses to argue for his position since the post-philosophical critic "cannot argue without turning himself into a metaphysician, one more claimant to the title of primal deepest vocabulary" (*Essays on Heidegger and Others*, p. 101). The key here is what Rorty means by "argument." "Argumentation requires that the same vocabulary be used in premises and conclusions – that both be part of the same language-game" (p. 125). This means that Hegel, Heidegger, and Derrida are not arguers, not "rigorous" philosophers: "I object to the idea that one can be 'rigorous' if one's procedure consists in inventing new words for what one is pleased to call 'conditions of possibility' rather than playing sentences using old words off against each other. The latter activity is what I take to constitute argumentation" (p. 124). Argumentation can take place only where the "logical space remains fixed" (p. 94) not between language games.[10] "The ironist's unit of persuasion is vocabulary, not the proposition" (*Contingency, Irony, and Solidarity*, p. 78), and the goal of persuasion is not to convince interlocutors "that their propositions are false but that their languages [are] obsolete" (p. 78).

Despite his critique of argument, Rorty does not see himself as

---

[9] I cannot address the complex debate on metaphor here. For a detailed critique of Davidson that follows the same line as my discussion, see Ian Hacking, "The Parody of Conversation" and "Styles of Scientific Reasoning."

[10] In "Inquiry as Recontextualization," in *Objectivity, Relativism, and Truth*, Rorty employs a similar opposition between inference and imagination, rationality and "something else" to characterize his division of contexts.

entirely in agreement with Derrida, and Rorty's effort to clarify their differences reveals a good deal about his linguistic philosophy. For example, he warns us against the famous phrase "il n'y pas de hors texte": "taken in a weakly literal-minded sense, this claim is just one more metaphysical thesis" (*Consequences of Pragmatism*, p. 154). Rorty laments the moments that Derrida offers theses and arguments, particularly about language, for these passages have led commentators such as Rodolphe Gasché to lay out Derridean principles, such as: "Concepts and discursive totalities are already cracked and fissured by necessary contradictions and heterogeneities" (cited in Rorty, *Essays on Heidegger and Others*, p. 126). Such a reading locks Derrida into a metaphysical position that withers the critical force of his work. At the same time, by reducing his work to neologistic theses about the conditions of possibility, Derrida's defenders insulate his work from critique.

Rorty disputes the claims of Jonathan Culler, Christopher Norris, and Gasche that Derrida is a "rigorous" philosopher: "The result of genuinely original thought, on my view, is not so much to refute or subvert our previous beliefs as to help us forget them. I take refutation to be a mark of unoriginality, and I value Derrida's originality too much to praise him on those terms" (*Essays on Heidegger and Others*, p. 121). Rorty discusses the difference in their problematics by contrasting the word with the proposition, not with his own problematic of the language game. He says that Derrida's work would count as argumentative "if one had a conception of argument as subpropositional – one which allowed the unit of argumentation to be the word rather than the sentence" – that is, the idea that "there is a 'movement of the concept' for the philosopher to follow, not reducible to the reweaving of a web of belief by playing beliefs off each other" (p. 126). Derrida does not place himself or the text under consideration in larger ontological categories – background, lifeworld, web of beliefs – even though they are implicit. The omission of this "context" has resulted in considerable confusion concerning his work, and this omission no doubt contributes to Rorty's conflation of two issues: that argument has to be phrased in a proposition or sentence and that all linguistic forces must operate at the level of the sentence. Deconstruction shows how certain terms are privileged in the construction of signs and how these terms infect a variety of discourses. Rorty is correct to point out that Derrida neglects other levels of linguistic analysis, but he is wrong to deny linguistic forces at the subpropositional level and hence wrong to deny the critical power of deconstruction. Moreover, by limiting his notion of the proposition to the way it is presented in analytic philosophy rather than exploring the pragmatics of the sentence, which we find in the work of Lyotard, Benveniste, and others, Rorty misses an opportunity here to offer a critique of Derrida. For Rorty, the problematic of the sentence is just a way of acknowledging that attacks on Derrida by those in the Anglo-American tradition, such as John Searle, have a point, but that this point has nothing to do with what Derrida's writing is really about.

With this reading, Rorty makes Derrida part of the group who wants to see language as a medium rather than as a tool. For Rorty, language is not a mediator between self and world or an autonomous force but simply one kind of behavior: "The activity of uttering sentences is one of the things people do in order to cope with the environment. The Deweyan notion of language as a tool rather than picture is right as far as it goes." Of course, he goes on to make the standard disclaimer – that we should not take this to mean that "there is some way of breaking out of language in order to compare it with something else" (*Consequences of Pragmatism*, pp. xviii-xix) – but he does not discuss how this disclaimer challenges the tool metaphor or what other metaphors for language might be appropriate. The objection is merely something that the tool-user should keep in mind. The tool metaphor avoids the pernicious idea "that there is a core self which can look at, decide among, use, and express itself by means of such beliefs and desires" (*Contingency, Irony, and Solidarity*, p. 10) or a preexisting world waiting for articulation. This characterization holds for the representationalist tradition but not for Derrida, who would agree with Rorty's view that the self and world emerge through vocabularies rather than are "expressed" or "represented" by them. Rorty's real complaint against Derrida is not that language is a medium but that Derrida makes language an agent. For Rorty, the concept "does not go to pieces; rather, we set it aside and replace it with something else" (*Essays on Heidegger and Others*, p. 126). The repeated phrase "what we want" would seem to reinstate the valuing and epistemic subject, whose self-consciousness masters knowledge and assigns value; however, he claims that this "we" has accepted the deconstructive critique and hence feels no need for "double writing": "Most contemporary intellectuals live in a culture which is self-consciously without archai, without telos, without theology, teleology, or ontology. So it is not clear that we need a 'new sort of writing' in order to think what 'the structured genealogy of philosophy's concepts' . . . has been able to dissimulate or forbid" (pp. 100–01). Giving agency to language challenges Rorty's tool metaphor and his behaviorism. Rorty wants causes outside language so that the interface between coherence and causality replaces the one between representation and object.

Rorty's position on language creates a number of problems. First, it leaves untouched the question of whether the change he is offering is so radically incommensurate that it justifies ignoring argument. He allies himself with a host of others (e.g., Gadamer, Sartre, Dewey and Derrida) who share his nonfoundationalism and then "redescribes" those who continue to seek grounds; however, he does not argue with those he identifies as participants in his language game and with whom he could – in his own terms – have an argument. For example, the move noted above of replacing "true" with "obsolete" – which is his way of putting his claim "under erasure," of trying to criticize without making a truth claim – could, and should, be defended against counterarguments by those who share his Davidsonian assumptions. Instead, he simply points out their residual attachments to ontology or epistemology. He characterizes the kinds of language games played by the redescribers only negatively as nonargumentative. Hence, all violations of language games – whether Derridean, Hegelian, or Lyotardian – are lumped together: "The method is to redescribe lots and lots of things in new ways, until you have created a pattern of linguistic behavior which will tempt the rising generation to adopt it . . . This sort of philosophy does not work piece by piece . . . Rather, it works holistically and pragmatically. It says things like 'try thinking of it this way'" (*Contingency, Irony, and Solidarity*, p. 9). Thus, Rorty's "we" emerges in opposition to foundationalists in analytic philosophy and includes a group of profoundly different authors who share a very thin notion of nonfoundationalism. This horizon of solidarity, which is underwritten by linguistic holism, puts problems of subjectivity, desire, intentionality, and reference – which could be raised in his recurrent phrase ("what we want") – out of play, since "we" share a common language that makes "our" differences on these issues insignificant. Rorty's solution simply displaces these problems rather than providing a problematic for their discussion, since almost no one Rorty includes in his "we" would accept his characterization of his/her position. Thus, it is not surprising that even sympathetic critics such as Richard Bernstein find Rorty's formulations frustratingly vague: "Aren't these substantive philosophical issues that need to be defended?" (*Beyond Objectivism*, p. 201).

Secondly, the holistic Davidsonian definition he is giving to "language game" cannot embrace the various kinds of discourse that appear in arguments and also provide criteria for what is in or out of bounds. Wittgenstein, whom he invokes throughout, insists on the multiplicity of language games that appear in texts. The debate is no longer formulated in terms of the opposition between those who study sentences in isolation and those who invoke webs of belief; rather, the problem is how to articulate these webs. As Nancy Fraser says of Rorty's appeal to solidarity with a unified community, "Why assume a quasi-Durkheimian view according to which society is integrated by way of single monolithic and all-encompassing solidarity? Why not rather assume a quasi-Marxist view according to which modern capitalist societies contain a plurality of overlapping and competing solidarities" (*Unruly Practices*, p. 98). Rorty focuses on the problem of translation between alien cultures, the locus of the debate in the Quinian tradition, and assimilates it too easily to domestic disputes. It is one thing to say that we could not understand a language that is completely unintelligible in our own and quite another to say that differences among various kinds of language games, sentences, or genres of discourse are insignificant. Important linguistic differences do not just arise between cultures but within living rooms.[11] As we'll see with MacIntyre's analysis, there are deep linguistic and ethical incommensurabilities among the various canonized traditions that Rorty includes in his "we." Thus, one does not have to accept the scheme/content opposition in order to have a critical vocabulary that can distinguish different kinds of discourse and linguistic practices. When he is criticizing attempts to ground solidarity on "human nature" or an "ur-language," Rorty recognizes the need for "thick descriptions of the private and idiosyncratic"

---

[11] See chapter 6 of my *Realism and the Drama of Reference*.

that can "sensitize one to the pain of those who do not speak our language" (*Contingency, Irony, and Solidarity*, p. 94). However, he only refers us to examples rather than characterizing their discourse. His chapters on literary figures in *Contingency, Irony, and Solidarity* (Proust, Nabokov, and Orwell) are thematic rather than linguistic. When Henry Staten charges that he provides no means of making stylistic distinctions among authors, Rorty answers that "such a worry seems as unnecessary as the metaphysicians' worry that the failure of causal theory of reference will make it impossible to distinguish physics and politics" (Staten, "Rorty's Circumvention of Derrida," 464). His holism thus permits him to identify "argument" with the misguided foundationalist claim that having "a neutral ground" (Rorty, *Essay on Heidegger and Others*, p. 121) is a prerequisite for attacking an opponent and that a knockdown foundationalist proof is the only reason to undertake an argument: "The trouble with arguments against the use of a familiar and time-honoured vocabulary is that they are expected to be phrased in that very vocabulary. They are expected to show that central elements in that vocabulary are 'inconsistent in their own terms' or that they 'deconstruct themselves.' But that can *never* be shown" (*Contingency, Irony, and Solidarity*, p. 8).[12] Rorty puts the emphasis on "never," but for me, the key is "shown." That is, the only one way to make a point in argument is foundationalist demonstration; since this is not possible, there is no point in arguing. "Argument" is not a complex discursive concept whose textual variety needs to be studied; rather, it is a style of writing that needs to be dropped, for all arguments "are always parasitic upon, and abbreviations for, claims that a better vocabulary is available" (p. 9). For Rorty, either we play the argumentative game of analytic philosophy or we do not; and if we do not and opt for the "redescription of vocabularies," then there is no critical terminology to describe our textual strategies, only the meta-philosophical claim that the self is a holistic web of beliefs. (Even such limited distinctions as those proposed by narratology are never mentioned.) Rorty's valorization of "redescription" justifies the reading strategy that we saw earlier, in which the critic simply "beats the text into the shape which will serve his own purposes" (*Consequences of Pragmatism*, p. 152). Since the critic's language game and the text's language

---

[12] Rorty is very loose with his terminology, as he slips among "language game," "vocabulary," and "holism.'

game are incommensurate, the critic is not only at liberty to say anything he/she wants but avoids bad faith by using an openly aggressive metaphor to describe his/her relationship to the text. The metaphor implies that epistemological foundations are, and should be, the only constraints on or considerations about how we read or behave.

In the same way that his linguistic theory is used to authorize rather than thematize a view of interpretation, this theory is used to underwrite ethical/political views. Perhaps the most obvious cases appear in "Solidarity or Objectivity?" and "Postmodernist Bourgeois Liberalism" (*Objectivity, Relativism, and Truth*), in which he argues against those who seek to ground human solidarity in moral universality, objectivity, or transcultural rationality – that is, those in the liberal analytic tradition (e.g. Putnam, Rawls, Dworkin) – and maintains that ethical questions, like all others, emerge within a historically specific culture. When it comes to distinguishing "the sort of individual conscience we respect from the sort we condemn as 'fanatical,'" all we can appeal to is "the tradition of a particular community, the consensus of a particular culture" (*Objectivity, Relativism, and Truth*, p. 176). Rorty wants to drop any rationalistic justification of the Enlightenment views about human nature (e.g., moral faculty) and about universal rights and make the priority of justice a contingent historical matter of our tradition. (He says this is a plausible reading of Rawls's recent work, where the Kantian emphasis of *A Theory of Justice* is downplayed in favor of Hegelian and Deweyan elements.) Rorty strips liberalism of its epistemological and ethical foundationalism so that its democratic resources are not tied to its metaphysics; this is an important move that I endorse. However, his presentation of these resources is limited, and the source of these limitations can often be assigned to his views of language. What is important in these essays is not his proposition that all discourse is positional, which is not controversial, but the political and ethical conclusion he draws from this. Rorty tells us, for instance, that "to be ethnocentric is to divide the human race into the people to whom one must justify one's beliefs and the others" (p. 30). Thus, attempts to explain cruelty are better when they focus on a society's terms of identification rather than on moral universals such as "inhumanity," or "hardness of heart," or "lack of a sense of human solidarity." "The point of these examples is that our sense of solidarity is strongest when those with whom solidarity is expressed are thought of as 'one of us,' where 'us' means something smaller and more local than the human race" (*Contingency, Irony, and Solidarity*, p. 191). But why is the vague notion of identification – how much do people need to share in order to say "we'? What are they sharing? – the only alternative to universals? What drives and underwrites this "ethical holism" is his linguistic holism: "Within a language game, within a set of agreements about what is possible and important, we can usefully distinguish reasons for belief from causes for belief which are not reasons . . . However, once we raise the question of how we get from one vocabulary to another, from one dominant metaphoric to another, the distinction between reasons and causes begins to lose its utility" (p. 48). Here, the "we" is produced by his abstract view of the self that embraces all conflicting positions in a democratic culture. Theories that show attention to the other are not simply ethically misguided but epistemologically misguided, since we cannot understand radical otherness. Rorty pays no attention to the way language has created "others" inside, as well as outside, the West, which is the focus of poststructuralist thought; nor does he discuss Western traditions that urge responsibility for people with whom we share little common culture. Moreover, he does not examine the ethical significance of the changes dialogue can produce within or between cultures. He does call for an ever-expanding inclusiveness through new descriptions of those omitted from a democratic politics but leaves out the problem of self-representation for those outside the dominant vocabularies. Rorty ignores how language and the subject of liberalism are implicated in these omissions. Furthermore, he asserts, rather than defends, the position that liberal institutions are for the most part right, and in doing so, he implicitly echoes his Davidsonian point that it is impossible to conceive of massive error (critique). "I think that contemporary liberal society already contains the institutions for its own improvement ... Indeed, my hunch is that Western social and political thought has had the last conceptual revolution it needs" (p. 63).

The capacity of Rorty's holism for reducing difference within and between communities and disciplines is never brought out so clearly as in these passages. By remaining at the meta-philosophical level in which his adversary is a universalist or essentialist, he can play the epistemological role of routing out error, while avoiding questions about how we draw lines between "dominant meta-phorics" and about the role of ethical vocabularies in shaping these alternative communities. From this Olympian view, all the forces that traverse and fragment the culture can be enclosed in the name "West." The text of the West and its other, the problem of the "inside and outside" of the West, the cultural and economic powers at work in dialogues with the other and with ourselves as other, are reduced to the epistemological maxim that radical difference is unintelligible.

When the issue is an internal dispute within the West or within a political community, Rorty replaces the distinction between "we/they" with the distinction between public and private, between "we" and "I." Rorty makes the linguistic basis of the latter distinction explicit: "The vocabulary of self-creation is necessarily private, unshared, unsuited to argument," whereas "the vocabulary of justice is necessarily public and shared, a medium for argumen-tative exchange" (p. xiv). Thus, texts fall out into those that "help us become autonomous" and those that "help us become less cruel" (p. 141). Rorty links this linguistic distinction to the liberal priority of justice over the good.[13] He wants to drop any rationalist justification based on human nature or universal rights and make the priority of justice a contingent matter of our tradition (*Objectivity, Relativism, and Truth*, pp. 177–96). (He thinks Rawls's recent work makes this correction.)[14] Rorty also agrees with Rawls's two-part definition of the self, one for justice (public) and one for the good (private), a definition that Sandel phrases as follows, "I am not merely the passive receptacle of the accumulated aims, attributes, and purposes thrown up by experience, not simply a product of the

---

[13] Rorty cites approvingly Rawls's formulation that "no general moral conception can provide the basis for a public conception of justice in modern democratic society ... [S]uch a conception must allow for a diversity of doctrines and plurality of conflicting, and indeed incommensurable conceptions of the good affirmed by the members of existing democratic societies" (*Objectivity, Relativism, and Truth*, p. 179).

[14] He accepts Rawls's recent articulation of the priority of justice since Rawls appeals "to our history and traditions embedded in our public life" (*Objectivity, Relativism, and Truth*, p. 185) rather than relying on the Kantian arguments used in *A Theory of Justice*. In my view, Rawls's recent work drops the foundationalist vocabulary but blocks the articulation of conflict. Liberalism seeks to contain conflict by establishing a moral center, or, in Rawls's words, a "neutral ground, given the fact of pluralism" (*Political Liberalism*, p. 192). Rorty gives this strategy a linguistic cast with his theory of holism.

vagaries of circumstance, but always, irreducibly, an active, willing agent, distinguishable from my surroundings and capable of choice" (*Liberalism and the Limits of Justice*, p. 19). How does Rorty square such a view with his own embedded contingent subject? "Rawls is not interested in conditions for the identity of the self, but only in conditions for citizenship in a liberal society" (*Objectivity, Relativism, and Truth*, p. 189). In short, Rorty is saying that Rawls's willingness to make justice a contingent, ethnocentric commitment of "our tradition" enables us to throw out not just Rawls's language of the self but all first-order claims about the self, since this historical premise permits all such language to be rewritten in terms of Rorty's definition of the self as a "contingent web of beliefs." The only conception of the self that justice needs is the meta-philosophical one. The self and the good take a back seat to the meta-philosophical subject and its meta-value justice. Rorty offers no first-order account of the goods that are to be adjudicated, since for this we need a corresponding theory of self and value and not just a meta-account. Sandel says, "Like the primacy of justice, the priority of the right over the good appears initially as a first-order claim, in opposition to utilitarian doctrine, but comes ultimately to assume a certain meta-ethical status as well, particularly when Rawls argues more generally for deontological ethical theories as opposed to teleological ones" (*Liberalism and the Limits of Justice*, p. 17).

The absence of a first-order account of self and value contributes to the impoverished formulation of liberal justice into terms of banal argument and cruelty, a formulation that does not capture the liberal sense of justice as we see it in Rawls or Habermas. Rorty claims that he and Habermas are in political agreement, despite Habermas's "misguided" attempt to distinguish "subject-centered" from "communicative reason": "A liberal society is one which is content to call 'true' (or 'just' or 'right') whatever the outcome of undistorted communication happens to be" (*Contingency, Irony, and Solidarity*, p. 67). Thomas McCarthy strongly protests this identification: "Rorty takes himself to be in agreement with Habermas on political matters, but the whole point of Habermas's *Theory of Communicative Action* is to show how capitalism undermined democracy" ("Ironist Theory as a Vocation," p. 654). I agree with McCarthy that Rorty does not "take seriously the fact that processes of individuation are interwoven with processes of socialization" (p. 650). Rorty's focus on meta-philosophical critique leaves out many other stories, particularly the social and political ones that concern Habermas. However, what underwrites Rorty's omissions and their ethical and political justifications is what he shares with Habermas: a simplified view of language, in which the opposition between center and margin, the everyday and the deviant, plays an overwhelming role in their trivialization of the conflicts of multiple identities and virtues in society. If Rorty and Habermas disagree about the importance of these "deviant" vocabularies, they agree about keeping them off the agenda of the public sphere.

Rorty makes an even grander redescription of Continental thinkers than he does with Rawls, for he consigns the work of Heidegger, Derrida, Nietzsche, and others to the private realm of the individual's search for autonomy rather than to the public sphere: "I agree with Habermas that as public philosophers they [Nietzsche, Heidegger, Derrida] are at best useless and at worst dangerous, but I want to insist on the role they and others like them can play in accommodating the ironist's *private* sense of identity to her liberal hopes" (*Contingency, Irony, and Solidarity*, p. 68). Rorty makes theory itself part of the public realm of banal argument, not as the space of political innovation that can challenge the boundaries of public and private: "The later Derrida privatizes his philosophical thinking, and thereby breaks down the tension between ironism and theorizing. He simply drops theory – the attempt to see his predecessors steadily and whole – in favor of fantasizing about these predecessors, playing with them, giving free rein to the trains of associations they produce. There is no moral to these fantasies, nor any public (pedagogic or political) use to be made of them; but, for Derrida's readers, they may be exemplary – suggestions of the sort of thing one might do, a sort of thing rarely done before" (p. 125). The value of Derrida's texts is reduced to the utility of their "deviance" for private life. Rorty uses the public/private distinction to isolate those who invent "new vocabularies" from ethical/political assessment and to keep public life vacuous: "*Privatize* [Rorty's emphasis] the Nietzchean–Sartrean–Foucauldian attempt at authenticity and purity in order to prevent yourself from slipping into a political attitude which will lead you to think that there is some social goal more important than avoiding cruelty" (p. 65).

It is precisely public and shared vocabularies that carry historical oppression and that need to be challenged. Aren't new vocabularies, new stories, one of the principal means by which a society becomes "less cruel"? Moreover, justice cannot always be separated into distinctive vocabularies and virtues as MacIntyre shows; indeed justice can be reconceived through a politics of difference such as Iris Young's: "The repoliticization of public life does not require the creation of a unified public realm in which citizens leave behind their particular group affiliations, histories, and needs to discuss a mythical 'common good.' In a society differentiated by social groups, occupations, political positions, differences of privilege and oppression ... the perception of anything like a common good can only be an *outcome* of public interaction that expresses rather than submerges particularities" (*Justice and the Politics of Difference*, p. 119). Certainly, not all "deviant" vocabularies are politically significant, but "deviance" *per se* can hardly be a criterion for the public relevance of a particular discourse. The connection between Rorty's linguistic holism, instrumentalism, and politics is pointedly phrased by Nancy Fraser: "Rorty homogenizes social space, assuming that there are no deep cleavages capable of generating conflicting solidarities and opposing we's. It follows from this absence of fundamental social antagonisms that politics is a matter of everyone pulling together to solve a common set of problems. Thus, social engineering can replace social struggle" (*Unruly Practices*, pp. 314–15). Rorty's philosophy of language remains the same in his Romantic moments (private) and his Deweyan (public) ones. Only the ends change. When he identifies with strong poets, he does not espouse a Romantic philosophy of language but emphasizes innovation independently of social connection. In his Deweyan moments, innovation is put in the service of society. "Whereas Heidegger thinks of the social world as existing for the sake of the poet and the thinker, the pragmatist thinks of it the other way round. For Dewey as for Hegel, the point of individual human greatness is its contribution to social freedom" (*Essays on Heidegger and Others*, p. 18).

Of course, we should not try to make writers whose subject is autonomy and writers whose subject is justice "speak a single language" (*Contingency, Irony, and Solidarity*, p. xv); at the same time, we should not segregate them in such a facile way. Isn't autonomy also a public matter, one of the virtues of citizenship in a liberal democracy, a virtue developed in part by education? Moreover, autonomy itself is not just about the liberty to create vocabularies that can establish one's uniqueness. Autonomy in a democracy means that the capacities for mutual recognition and articulation in both public and private life are nourished. Understanding existing vocabularies and making innovations are important to both spheres. Rorty takes an abstract, theoretical liberal position that makes virtue and goodness merely private matters that ("if we take care of political freedom, truth and goodness will take care of themselves" [p. 84]) do not need to be characterized. Since I will address the controversial questions of autonomy and the distinction between public and private later, I will limit myself to three additional points: (1) that he fails to account for the institutionalization of the private that is exposed not only by Foucault but by the history of women's writing under liberal democracies, in which we see not only the issues of power and autonomy but also the connection of linguistic innovation to solidarity;[15] (2) that his thematic discussion of writers (Nabokov for the private and Orwell for the public) fails in part because it tries to decide these issues from the distant view of meta-theory and vague thematic commentary rather than with a first-order account of subjectivity and ethics; (3) that the liberal idea of giving different views for the public and private self needs to be reworked in response to challenges by communitarians and radicals.

Thus, Rorty's position on the subject is ambiguous. On the one hand, he talks easily about what "we" have learned and mastered; on the other, he never offers an inside view of the self. Instead, he speaks of "a web of beliefs without a center," which is a second-order, third-person account. As Habermas says, "Rorty absolutizes the perspective of the observer" ("Questions and Counter-Questions," p. 195). Rorty avoids theorizing the self from the inside because the history of such efforts has been connected to foundationalist enterprises. Nonetheless, his problematic ("webs of belief") is compatible with a much richer first-person account than the tool-using subject he proposes. Rorty tries to make the connection between his meta-philosophical theory and his first-order

---

[15] The development of Adrienne Rich's poetry thematizes the inseparability of the public and the private. In addition to Fraser, see McCarthy's "Private Irony and Public Decency" for an excellent discussion of the relationship of the public/private distinction to twentieth-century philosophy and Rorty's work.

theory seem inevitable. By breaking this connection, I will force the theoretical controversy out of the meta-philosophical level, where Rorty likes to keep it, and offer an alternative view of language, subjectivity, and value. Moreover, this view will provide a space to thematize the philosophical differences between Rorty and the poststructuralists. Rorty accepts the contingent, historically situated subject only as a meta-philosophical premise that permits the subject to sit comfortably in its institutions. On the other hand, the utopian desires in poststructuralist texts seek forms that are so radically discontinuous with the present that they cannot be formulated. If Rorty has made a case for agency and for meta-philosophical reflection, he has not given us a way to characterize the ethical dimensions of these agents. To develop these dimensions, we need to look at the work of Alasdair MacIntyre, who not only offers a first-/second-person account of the subject but who also embeds this subject in the ethical substance of tradition. We will then be ready to bring our narratives of agency and hope into a dialogue with our narratives of determination so that the space of subjectivity is as an ideological space that requires both critique and recuperation.

The virtues of traditions

Alasdair MacIntyre's concern is not residual foundationalism but the debased and confused ethical understanding in modernity. In *After Virtue* and *Whose Justice? Which Rationality?*, he calls up the image of a fragmented ethical world that current philosophies neither explain nor rectify. We have a society of isolated individuals who are patched together from the moral fragments of a past they do not understand. Ethical issues are seen as matters of feeling or individual interpretation rather than as rational arguments. When MacIntyre seeks a culprit for this ethical fragmentation, he points a finger at the Enlightenment's attempt to separate the principles of reason from the particularities of tradition. This effort not only failed but deprived us of an important insight that we need to recover – "a conception of the rational as embodied in a tradition" (*Whose Justice?*, p. 7).

MacIntyre is not merely denouncing the foundationalist enterprise of the Enlightenment and its successors – in this he joins a host of nonfoundationalists who all too often are content with debunking;

what he is claiming to do is to offer a distinct alternative from those who celebrate modernity's fragmentation as emancipation from traditional modes of thought. MacIntyre follows Weber, Habermas, and the poststructuralists in criticizing the way that instrumental rationality has invaded modern life. Unlike the poststructuralists, MacIntyre does not locate the source of this problem in the oppressiveness of language or disciplinary practices. Unlike Habermas, MacIntyre does not look to a procedural ideal of communicative rationality but to a reconstruction of historical debates within and between traditions.

MacIntyre begins by focusing on modernity's view of moral agency, which he defines as the "capacity of the self to evade any necessary identification with any contingent state of affairs ... To be a moral agent is, on this view, precisely to be able to stand back from any and every situation in which one is involved, from any and every characteristic that one may possess, and to pass judgment on it from a purely universal and abstract point of view that is totally detached from all social particularity" (*After Virtue*, pp. 31–32). What MacIntyre has in mind here is, first, the Kantian/Rawlsian self, which is abstracted from the ends that defined pre-modern, teleological ideas of the self (the good life). We will recall that for Rawls, "a moral person is a subject with ends he has chosen, and his fundamental preference is for conditions that enable him to frame a mode of life that expresses his nature as a free and equal rational being as fully as circumstances permit" (Rawls, cited in Sandel, *Liberalism and the Limits of Justice*, p. 22). However, MacIntyre's stakes go far beyond Rawlsian liberalism; liberalism, for MacIntyre, is not a political position but a *Weltanschauung* that includes Barthes and Derrida, as well as Rawls and Rorty: "The democratized self which has no necessary social content and no necessary social identity can be anything, can assume any role or take any point of view, because it is in itself nothing" (*After Virtue*, p. 32). Thus, MacIntyre has his sights directly on Rorty's disengaged, instrumental self-creator. A subject who frames a life only in terms of "what he/she wants" reveals a poverty that is coextensive with its liberty. For MacIntyre, modern and postmodern philosophers remain unaware of their loss and incoherence, and *After Virtue* tries to make us understand both through its historical account of how we got into this situation and through its development of a neo-Aristotelian alternative. Like

Rorty, MacIntyre seeks historical precursors who sketch the outlines of his problematic; however, MacIntyre seeks these precursors in the pre-modern world, before tradition-based inquiry was displaced by the narrow epistemological obsessions of modernity. He reconstructs the dynamic arguments among pre-moderns to show how they contrast with the shallow discussions in contemporary ethics.

Unfortunately, MacIntyre's stories in *After Virtue* and *Whose Justice? Which Rationality* never negotiate how his ideas on tradition and virtue will find a place in pluralistic, democratic societies. In *After Virtue*, he frames our alternatives as Aristotle or Nietzsche – that is, either we try to vindicate Aristotle's practical reason in small communities or we hand ourselves over to Nietzsche's announcement of the death of reason. This failure has led some readers to dismiss his project as a simply nostalgic exercise, as a call to go back to the model of the Greek polis, where communitarian ideals authorized and even depended on slavery and the oppression of women. MacIntyre's failure to critique (with democratic ideals) the traditions he recuperates is a serious shortcoming but not a devastating one. His work needs to be read as a contribution to the ethical/political dilemmas of modernity and postmodernity, not as an escape from them. As Richard Bernstein says, "The problem today is how we can live with the conflict and tension between the 'truth' implicit in the tradition of the virtues and the 'truth' of the Enlightenment" ("Nietzsche or Aristotle?," p. 140).[16]

What does MacIntyre contribute to our understanding of these dilemmas? First, his approach yields a distinctly different conception of subjectivity than the previous theorists, including Rorty. While he shares Rorty's emphasis on the first-/second-person, MacIntyre rejects the instrumental vocabulary of pragmatism. For MacIntyre, the starting point for thinking about language, ethics, and subjectivity is not epistemological grounding or the discrimination of commonplace versus deviant vocabularies but the understanding of action. To understand an action, we have no choice but to invoke

---

[16] In his review of *Whose Justice? Which Rationality?*, Charles Larmore points out MacIntyre's implicit modernity: "His outlook is not a return to the past, but an innovation, and a distinctively modern one at that," even though MacIntyre himself ignores his modernity ("Review," p. 440). Larmore calls this MacIntyre's "buried commitment to modernity" (p. 442). For a reading of MacIntyre that sees him as simply a throwback, see Stephen Holmes, *The Anatomy of Antiliberalism*, chapter 4.

the intentions of the agent in question and the setting in which the action takes place.[17] MacIntyre takes aim at behaviorism (and any other third-person account of the subject), which seeks only a predictive characterization of action from the outside. He gives the following example: "For if someone's primary intention is to put the garden in before winter and it is only incidentally the case that in so doing he is taking exercise and pleasing his wife, we have one type of behavior to be explained; but if the agent's primary intention is to please his wife by taking exercise, we have quite another type of behavior to be explained" (*After Virtue*, p. 206). These intentions are not private or freely invented, for "we cannot characterize intentions independently of the settings which make those intentions intelligible both to agents themselves and to others" (p. 206). Settings may be as broad and stable as institutions or as local as practices, but the key is that they have histories, histories "within which the histories of individual agents not only are, but have to be, situated" (p. 206) in order to be intelligible.

"Practice" is a key term for MacIntyre, and he defines it as follows, "any coherent and complex . . . activity with standards of excellence which are appropriate to, and partially definitive of, that form of activity, with the result that human powers to achieve excellence, and human conceptions of the ends and goods involved, are systematically extended" (p. 187). Practices include such activities as farming, architecture, portrait painting, and running a household, and they involve two kinds of goods: internal (e.g., insight, pleasure) and external (e.g., prestige and money). Attaining the internal goods requires that one submit to the rules of the practice; indeed, these rules structure action so that they may be called constitutive – for example, a move in chess or the act of promising in speech-act theory. In turn, these rules place the individual in a social context and an historical tradition. By distinguishing internal and external goods, MacIntyre is challenging the liberal conception of self, whose private dimension is filled with its own wishes and whose public dimension is emptied of all specific content.[18] In neither case is the self situated within a

---

[17] MacIntyre describes this well: "Unless we begin by a characterization of a society in its own terms, we shall be unable to identify the matter that requires explanation. Attention to intentions, motives, and reasons must precede attention to causes" ("The Idea of Social Science," p. 223).

[18] Sandel discusses the difference between the liberal subject of the good and the liberal subject of justice. The subject of the good is often utilitarian: "The

practice and a tradition; thus, the liberal self has no access to internal goods. Rorty's notion of redescription fits MacIntyre's characterization very well, since it levels all cultural practices by making the subject an empty tool-user in search of vocabularies. Thus, Rorty says that one "read[s] history, novels, or treatises on moral philosophy as a way of getting additional suggestions of how to describe (and change) oneself in the future" (*Essays on Heidegger and Others*, p. 155). Rorty makes the neo-Enlightenment move from "there are no objects outside linguistic practices" to "distinctions among linguistic practices have no force if they are deprived of foundationalist objects."

With "intention," and "setting" comes a third inevitable term for understanding human action: "narrative," "the basic and essential genre for the characterization of human actions" (MacIntyre, *After Virtue*, p. 208). That is, human actions are "enacted narratives" (p. 211). In this way, we reflect on "what causal efficacy the agent's intentions had" (p. 208). Life does not have narrative order imposed upon it in his view; rather, "stories are lived before they are told" (p. 212). Although MacIntyre's principal interlocutors are those who think that "stories are not lived but told" (Louis Mink, cited in MacIntyre, *After Virtue*, p. 212) and atomistic theorists of action, his point comes back to ethics: "In what does the unity of an individual life consist? The answer is that its unity is the unity of a narrative embodied in a single life. To ask what is the good for me? is to ask how best I might live out that unity and bring it to completion" (p. 218). However, MacIntyre does not go on to link this narrative unity to an Aristotelian teleology for "man"; instead, he gives a remarkably individualistic formulation: "The good life for man is the life spent in seeking the good life for man" (p. 219).[19]

With action comes character, and character plays a key role in MacIntyre's reading of culture, for it "morally legitimates a mode of social existence" (p. 29). The link between practices and

principle for an individual is to achieve as far as possible his own welfare, his own system of desires" (Rawls, *A Theory of Justice*, p. 23, cited in Sandel, *Liberalism and the Limits of Justice*, p. 160).

[19] I will return to problems in this formulation at the end of the chapter and to issues of narrative in chapters 4 and 5. Bernstein notes that MacIntyre's ideas of practice and narrative do not exclude liberal and even radical notions of culture: "MacIntyre and Nietzsche look like close companions. For Nietzsche himself portrays for us a variety of practices, their internal goods, and what is required to excel in these practices" ("Nietzsche or Aristotle?," p. 126).

characters is provided by virtues – that is, "those dispositions which will not only sustain practices and enable us to achieve the goods internal to practices, but which sustain us in the relevant quest for the good" (p. 219). Because modern culture has evaporated an understanding of action within a tradition, modern characters are devoted to the acquisition and manipulation of external goods. Its representative characters are the manager, the therapist, and the aesthete. The manager represents "the obliteration of the distinction between manipulative and nonmanipulative social relations; the therapist represents the same obliteration in the private sphere" (p. 30). The aesthete takes an ironic distance from traditions and devotes himself/herself to collecting experience in pursuit of an individualist aestheticism.[20]

What does MacIntyre add that the other theorists examined so far do not? All of them pass through MacIntyre's key terms – intention, narrative, and practice – that is, they accept in part MacIntyre's argument for the intelligibility of human action. Yet, they do not accept his attention to the integrity of the language of self-understanding or his call to situate their own discourse in such a framework or to acknowledge their own intentionality in unmasking the intentions of others. As MacIntyre says of Nietzsche's and Foucault's genealogies, "The function of genealogy as emancipatory from deception and self-deception thus requires the identity and continuity of the self that was deceived and the self that is and is to be . . . For if this genealogist is inescapably one who disowns part of his or her own past, then the genealogist's narrative presupposes enough unity, continuity, and identity to make such disowning possible" (*Three Rival Versions of Moral Enquiry*, p. 214).[21] In addition, MacIntyre is the only philosopher

[20] Rorty, who fits MacIntyre's idea of the aesthete very well, characterizes his goal for the private, as opposed to the public self, as a quest for self-enlargement: "The desire to enlarge oneself is the desire to give oneself over entirely to curiosity, to end by having envisaged all the possibilities of the past and the future" (*Essays on Heidegger and Others*, p. 154). Rorty does not think MacIntyre's three characters of modernity should be regretted. If we content "ourselves with narrative tailored ad hoc to the contingencies of individual lives, then we may welcome a Baconian culture dominated by 'the Rich Aesthete, the Manager, and the Therapist' – not necessarily as the final goal of human progress, but at least as a considerable improvement on cultures dominated by, for example, the Warrior or the Priest" (p. 161).

[21] MacIntyre says of Rorty's *Philosophy and the Mirror of Nature*: "His dismissal of 'objective' or 'rational' standards emerges from the writing of genealogical history, as do all the most compelling such dismissals, Nietzsche's for example.

examined thus far who reconstructs cultural issues at the level of argument among traditions and individuals. He also offers only an idealistic treatment of language that ignores the dynamics of domination.

In *After Virtue*, MacIntyre develops his problematic in three stages, the practice, the narrative order of a single life, and the tradition, and the last is the most important. His notion of the tradition is not only the linchpin of his argument in *After Virtue* but the crux of the meta-theoretical position he defends in his subsequent books: "A living tradition ... is a historically extended, socially embodied argument, and an argument precisely in part about the goods which constitute the tradition" (p. 222). In this view of reason, we find "a conception according to which the standards of rational justification themselves emerge from and are part of a history in which they are vindicated by the way in which they transcend the limitations and provide remedies for the defects of their predecessors within the history of that same tradition" (*Whose Justice?*, p. 7). A tradition justifies itself by narrating "how the argument has gone so far" (p. 8) in these particular historical circumstances. For MacIntyre, traditions do not ossify or universalize their presuppositions but remain contingent, open-ended, and revisable: "Only those whose tradition allows for the possibility of its hegemony being put in question can have rational warrant for asserting such a hegemony" (p. 388). This position seems to share much with Rorty's; indeed, the formulation is obviously a modern reconstruction of tradition, since pre-modern traditions never phrased their own vulnerability in these terms. However, while Rorty emphasizes innovation through the breakdown of argument, MacIntyre makes argument crucial. For MacIntyre, reason has many shapes that need to be mapped, while Rorty prefers to forget about "reason" and to talk about the commonplace and the deviant. MacIntyre's subject – to use a term he eschews – is embedded in a rich context that is not simply unmasked but is fleshed out in terms of the self-understandings of the participants. Dialogue about a tradition is not done in the third-person vocabulary of poststructuralism or sociology; nor does it fall out into the

But at once the question arises of whether he has written a history that is in fact true, and to investigate that question requires implicit or explicit references to standards of objectivity and rationality of just the kind that the initial genealogical investigation was designed to discredit" ("Philosophy, 'Other' Disciplines," p. 138).

proto-pragmatists and unrepentant foundationalists of Rorty's stories. Instead, we find attention to the first-person vocabulary of participants. While Rorty and the poststructuralists are quick to distance themselves from the Enlightenment's reason in most respects, they still see pre-Enlightenment traditions as traps whose grip on us we have to acknowledge even as we struggle to get beyond them.

We can see this shallow understanding of the tradition in Rawls's and Rorty's recent responses to communitarians, "Justice as Fairness: Political not Metaphysical" and "The Priority of Democracy to Philosophy" (in *Objectivity, Relativism, and Truth*) respectively, where they adopt the word "tradition." The word "tradition" in Rorty and the recent Rawls serves as a replacement term for "foundation," as an ultimate term used to end debate about epistemological grounding; however, neither Rorty nor Rawls uses "tradition" as a problematic that itself can help us enrich our ethical self-understandings – e.g., how does the distinctiveness of African American cultural traditions challenge the thin theory of the good and the neutrality of the public sphere? – and help us dialogue about its limits. Rorty takes the following quotation from Rawls as his guide: "What justifies a conception of justice is not its being true to an order antecedent to and given to us, but its congruence with our deeper understanding of ourselves and our aspirations, and our realization that, given our history and the traditions embedded in our public life, it is the most reasonable doctrine for us" (Rawls, cited in Rorty, *Objectivity, Relativism, and Truth*, p. 185). Rorty puts the word "tradition" in a context where it makes no sense to defend it. To those who already are in it, a tradition is too obvious or too deep a presupposition to be discussed. To those who hold positions that are incommensurate with it, there is no way to defend it.

This denial of tradition-based reason whether in the name of postmodern liberalism or genealogical unmasking is what, in MacIntyre's view, unifies the problematics of modernity. MacIntyre offers a meta-theoretical claim against these readings: "The conclusion to which the argument so far has led is not only that it is out of the debates, conflicts, and enquiry of socially embodied, historically contingent traditions that contentions regarding practical rationality and justice are advanced, modified, abandoned, or replaced, but that there is no other way to engage in the formulation, elaboration, rational justification, and criticism of accounts of practical rationality and justice except from within some one particular tradition" (*Whose Justice?*, p. 350).

Because of this conclusion, MacIntyre gives a different position to philosophy than do the moderns. Philosophy in his view "gives organized expression to concepts and theories already embodied in forms of practice and types of community" (p. 390).[22] The principles of such an inquiry are "justified insofar as in the history of this tradition they have, by surviving the process of dialectical questioning, vindicated themselves as superior to their historical predecessors" (p. 360). But how do they arrive at solutions for a crisis? Solutions must meet three criteria: (1) they must solve "problems which had previously proved intractable in a systematic and coherent way"; (2) they "must also provide an explanation of just what it was which rendered the tradition, before it had acquired these new resources, sterile and incoherent or both"; (3) the first two tasks must show "some fundamental continuity of the new conceptual and theoretical structures with the shared beliefs in terms of which the tradition of enquiry had been defined up to this point" (p. 362). This solution "enables adherents of a tradition of enquiry to rewrite its history in a more insightful way" (p. 363). The result is that some parts of this particular tradition or a rival tradition are discredited. The fact that there are many traditions does not produce relativism or perspectivism, because "the multiplicity of traditions does not afford a multiplicity of perspectives among which we can move, but a multiplicity of antagonistic commitments, between which only conflict, rational or nonrational, is possible. Perspectivism, like relativism, is a doctrine only possible for those who regard themselves as outsiders, as uncommitted or rather as committed only to acting a succession of temporary parts" (p. 368). MacIntyre explicitly opposes his conception of historical argument to Hegel's. MacIntyre's tradition includes no teleology, Absolute Subject, or totalized account of history: "Traditions are always and ineradicably to some degree local, informed by particularities of language and social and

---

[22] MacIntyre disagrees with Rorty about the history of philosophy and the relationship of philosophy to social practice: "It is false that philosophy has *ever* been a genuinely unitary form of enquiry in the way that Rorty's account requires; and it is false that philosophy itself engendered the central philosophical problems with which Rorty is concerned" ("Philosophy, 'Other' Disciplines," p. 138).

natural environment, inhabited by Greeks or by citizens of Roman
Africa or by medieval Persia or by eighteenth-century Scots, who
stubbornly refuse to be or become vehicles of the self-realization of
Geist (p. 361).

It would be a mistake to read this as "foundationalism," for
MacIntyre, unlike the traditions he recuperates, does not make
any flat-footed claim for universality. His attack on relativism is
much like Rorty's – i.e., relativism is made possible by the idea of a
God's eye view, and once we give up the latter the former makes
no sense either. What MacIntyre's characterization of this position,
in terms of the problematic of tradition, does that Rorty's,
poststructuralism's, and Habermas's do not is make available
linguistic and ethical resources that the other problematics cannot.
For example, MacIntyre's idea of tradition complicates the so-called
Great Books debate not by challenging it from the outside but from
the inside: "Proponents of this type of Great Books curriculum
often defend it as a way of restoring to us and to our students what
they speak of as our cultural tradition; but we are the inheritors, if
that is the right word, of a number of rival and incompatible
traditions, and there is no way of either selecting a list of books to
be read or advancing a determinate account of how they are to be
read, interpreted and elucidated which does not involve taking a
partisan stand in the conflict of traditions" (*Three Rival Versions of
Moral Enquiry*, p. 228). Hence, Graff's proposal "to locate a
principle of coherence in the conversation itself" ("Teach the
Conflicts," pp. 59–60) is hopeless, not because of the undecidability
of signifiers and not because of oppression but because of two
intertwined hermeneutical difficulties: (1) how to sort out the
conflicts in the histories of traditions – for example, "Homeric
versus Platonic, Judaic versus Christian ... the Enlightenment
versus the Christian" (*Three Rival Versions of Moral Enquiry*, p. 229)
– and (2) how to clarify the interpreter's framework through which
he/she understands the conflicts of the past. The three frameworks
MacIntyre discusses in his *Three Rival Versions of Moral Enquiry* are
the encyclopedic, the genealogical, and the traditional. In his view,
the liberal university provides no way for the challenges of
genealogy and tradition-based inquiry to be addressed. This
failure also prevents the liberal university "from vindicating itself
against its external critics" (p. 230). He calls for his own version of
"teach the conflicts," in which "teaching and enquiry would each

have to play a double role" (p. 231): (1) the role of the partisan of a particular point of view; (2) the role "of someone concerned to uphold and to order the ongoing conflicts, to provide and sustain institutionalized means for their expression" (p. 231). Even though MacIntyre opposes the "arena of neutral objectivity, as in the liberal university" (p. 231), the second part of this proposal relies on liberal ideas – that dogmatic views of the good should not be imposed, that the public sphere can ask one to suspend one's commitment to tradition(s) for the sake of democratic discussion.

MacIntyre ties his presentation of tradition to a distinctive view of language, a view that he contrasts with the Davidsonian position advanced by Rorty. In MacIntyre's view, Davidson underwrites the impoverished, deracinated internationalized language spoken by most moderns, a language that helps us "be at home anywhere" and makes us "citizens of nowhere" (*Whose Justice?*, p. 388). Speakers of a cosmopolitan language reject the idea "that there may be traditional modes of social, cultural, and intellectual life which are inaccessible to it and its translators" (p. 387). This rejection of inaccessibility is a corollary of Davidson's attack on the intelligibility of radically alternative conceptual schemes: You can know something is inaccessible only if you can understand it. For MacIntyre, this follows only if one supposes "that the acquisition of the understanding of the inaccessible is a matter of translating it into our own language-in-use" (p. 387). In MacIntyre's view, the discovery of the inaccessible in another language requires two steps: (1) learning the second language from zero, just as a child would, not by matching phrases; (2) examining the first language from the perspective of the second, so that one can say what cannot be translated. MacIntyre gives the example of naming, where names are tied to a system of beliefs from which "no translation into the language of a different community with different beliefs can be achieved by simply reproducing the name or some version of it" (p. 377) – "Doire Columcille" in Irish and "Londonderry" in English, to use MacIntyre's example. Hence, "the conception of pure reference, of reference as such, emerges as the artefact of a particular type of social and cultural order, one in which a minimum of shared beliefs and allegiances can be presupposed" (p. 379). These incommensurabilities among languages emerge not only with names but with the language of virtues and action as well (p. 381).

In chapter 4, we will see how in *The Ambassadors*, "Paris" in the language of Woollett Massachusetts contrasts with "Paris" in the language of the Parisian community. In each case, the name locates a different semantic space and arrangement of virtues. As Cora Diamond says, "Grasping a concept . . . is not a matter just of knowing how to group things under the concept [the notion current in analytic philosophy]; it is being able to participate in life-with-the concept. What kinds of descriptive content there are is a matter of the different shapes life-with-a-concept can have" ("Losing Your Concepts," p. 266). In chapter 5, we will see the protagonist in *Invisible Man* struggle to escape from a "cosmopolitan language" that makes him invisible so that he can recover and rework the language and virtues of his cultural tradition. Ellison shows how a tradition-based problematic is especially important for those excluded from the dominant vocabularies.

MacIntyre's view of tradition thus puts on the table ways of understanding culture that ontologies of power and Habermas's philosophy of language cannot. Moreover, it challenges the link between language and ethics proposed by Rorty – that is, that radical difference has to be put in our terms, that "we" has an epistemological and hence ethical authenticity. If poststructuralism challenges Rorty because of his instrumental subject who emphasizes mastery rather than listening for difference, MacIntyre takes a different tack. Because Rorty/Davidson is insensitive to his tradition(s) and to the ways that tradition shapes language and ethics, he (Rorty/Davidson) cannot attend to the otherness in "our" conflicting traditions that requires one to speak alternative languages from the inside and make available what cannot be assimilated into "our" language.

MacIntyre's idea of tradition offers an enriched ethical vocabulary while it resists easy categorization as conservative in the political sphere, even though MacIntyre himself takes conservative positions. His concept of tradition provides a way of talking about critique and utopia in a richer way than Marxism or Critical Theory, because it does not offer an abstract, totalized truth that unmasks past achievements with only a vague vision of future possibility. By thinking of critique through traditions instead of against traditions, MacIntyre can focus on the linguistic and ethical specifics by which traditions perform their own internal revisions or react to external contacts. Hence, tradition-based reason provides a way of vindicating ethically thick stances, not the thin appeals to justice and negative liberty that we have seen. It is precisely this argumentative character of traditions that is lost in literary studies, since claims by texts or critics for the epistemic and ethical superiority of certain textual practices are usually labeled "foundationalist" or "hegemonic." This ethical/political vacuum can itself contribute to oppression. As Ralph Ellison says, "All novels of a given historical moment form an argument over the nature of reality and are, to a certain extent criticisms of each other" (*Shadow and Act*, p. 117). By backing away from this dimension of texts, critics live in the ethical vacuum outlined by MacIntyre, in which an Enlightenment understanding of "tradition" as naive dogmatism continues even as its own idea of reason has disappeared. All that is left for ethical reflection in the present is a withering reflexivity, otherness, and abstract justice, but no way of thinking about our current forms of life or their histories.

Despite the merits of MacIntyre's proposal, it leaves a number of unanswered questions. How does tradition-based inquiry insert itself into dialogue with alternative modes of inquiry and with competing first-order claims? At the end of *Whose Justice? Which Rationality?*, MacIntyre moves to defend his meta-theoretical position on tradition-based inquiry, to close the hermeneutic circle, to bring his argument into the present, and to clarify the site of his own speech: "The point in the overall argument has been reached ... at which it is no longer possible to speak except out of one particular tradition in a way that will involve conflict with rival traditions" (p. 401). That is, the book closes when he must leave his site of meta-philosopher and become first-order philosopher. The book ends by telling us "where and how to begin" (p. 401) to do this. Where is that? "We, whoever we are, can only begin enquiry from the vantage point afforded by our relationship to some specific social and intellectual past through which we have affiliated ourselves to some particular tradition of enquiry, extending the history of that enquiry into the present" (p. 401). However, we never get such an extension. Aspects of modernity leak through in unacknowledged ways – e.g., his acceptance of the Enlightenment idea of equality absent from the traditions he valorizes, the mobility of his narrator, who moves among the four traditions without establishing firmly the site of his own narration. How has MacIntyre, a product of modern culture who insists that no one can step outside his/her historical moment, avoided fragmentation like everybody else? MacIntyre's answer has two parts, neither one of which is adequately characterized. In the first, he says: "Even when marginalized by the dominant modern social, cultural, and political order, such traditions have retained the allegiance of the members of a variety of types of community and enterprise, not all of whom are aware of whence their conceptions of justice and practical rationality derive. The past of such traditions is encapsulated in the present and not always only in fragmented or disguised form" (p. 391). His second point is that the modern self can sort out the fragments of contemporary life and create its own substance through historical recuperation: "It is only insofar as these features of the polis which provide an essential context for the exercise of Aristotelian justice and for the action-guiding interpretive uses of the Aristotelian schema of practical reasoning can be reembodied in one's own life and one's own time and place that one can be an Aristotelian" (p. 391). This very modern formulation of how to overcome modernity's deracinating effects leaves too many unanswered questions. What does such a subject look like when it is living and arguing with modern culture? MacIntyre's entire discussion of modernity (one chapter in *Whose Justice?*) is so shallow and dismissive that we never see his problematic in a dialogue with any theory of democratic culture. The problem is not relativism but pluralism guided by democratic norms, and this problem requires first-order and not simply second-order arguments. By concentrating on the meta-theoretical level for tradition-based inquiry rather than spelling out what the Thomist tradition, which he prefers, offers to modernity, he simply sidesteps the problem that communitarians face in their argument with liberals. Stephen Salkever says this well when he claims that without "some concept of substantial historical progress in the manner of Hegel or Marx, the communitarian ignores or conceals the problem of distinguishing among better or worse communities, thus exhibiting a quandary that mirrors the perplexity inherent in liberal theory's neutrality" ("Lopp'd and Bound," p. 188).

MacIntyre, like Foucault whom he criticizes, writes from an Olympian distance, since he assumes that this entire book is a preliminary for addressing today's conflicts: "For it is here that contemporary substantive argument between, and for, and against traditions of enquiry and indeed for antitraditionalism in respect of both justice and rationality has to begin" (*Whose Justice?* p. 401). In making the case for tradition-based inquiry, he relies too heavily on a transcendental argument against other problematics rather than creating some common ground and engaging in first-order arguments with contemporary political theories. MacIntyre thus shares a transcendental focus with the figures we have examined in chapter 1 and with Rorty. In opting for this focus, MacIntyre misses an opportunity to make his tradition-based problematic for history work through what Hegel (and Habermas) tried but failed to do: to offer an historical account that can reconcile Aristotle and Kant, ancient and modern liberty, the good life and justice.

Moreover, his treatment of tradition does not address conflicts that are not thematized in his idealistic characterization of argument – for example, when power is at work or when there are heterogeneous speech communities that have contact with each other. How would tradition-based inquiry deal with the problem of W.E.B. Dubois's "double consciousness" – "this sense of always looking at oneself through the eyes of others, of measuring one's soul by the tape of a world that looks on in amused contempt and pity" (*The Souls of Black Folk*, p. 45), in which the individual is defined by a dominant and subordinate culture? He never asks how a woman or African American might situate herself/himself in regard to the traditions he discusses.[23] Can the political questions involved in the recognition of different cultural traditions in a society be addressed without the resources of modern political theory? In addition, he caricatures "postmodernist doctrines of the text" (*Whose Justice?*, p. 386), which emphasize the "indefinite multiplicity of interpretations" or "translations." Postmodern theories of the text, like the genealogies (Nietzsche, Foucault), are implicitly and explicitly criticized by MacIntyre, but he pulls up short of putting them in a productive dialogue with tradition-based inquiry by claiming that the massive incommensurability between such positions and his own prevents it. However, if MacIntyre were to characterize the modernity of his own position, this incommensurability would not simply diminish but could in fact be a resource. If contemporary theories do not formulate the resources and operations of traditions with MacIntyre's finesse,

---

[23] See Susan Moller Okin's critique of MacIntyre, "Whose Traditions? Which Understandings?".

preferring to collapse them into global characterizations (e.g., logocentrism, networks of power) that cut across humanistic categories, MacIntyre cannot bring his understanding of tradition into a modern world. Because MacIntyre totally neglects the political ideals of modernity in poststructuralism, Marxism, and liberalism, he does not characterize the deliberative space in which a member of postmodern culture recuperates tradition-based inquiry.

A good way of making MacIntyre's proposal a postliberal hermeneutic is to reformulate the liberal/communitarian debate. I have been laying the groundwork for this by pointing out how liberalism needs communitarian vocabularies and how communitarians assume modern positions – for instance, the recognition that a dogmatic view of the good cannot be imposed, that the vocabulary of equality, freedom, and rights needs a place. What this means is that we need to recuperate, and not just critique, modern notions of freedom and autonomy so that they can be part of a new political culture.[24] In order to do this, we can rethink these liberal ideals in terms of cultural practices and traditions rather than in terms of metaphysical imperatives or ahistorical doctrines of neutrality and procedural correctness. Rorty's meta-philosophical gestures in this direction simply drop the foundational language of liberalism without proposing a language for characterizing cultural practices. That is, liberal practices and values can be retrieved by wresting them from liberal theories and giving them a new articulation. As Salkever says, liberal theory "not only fails to defend liberal institutions properly, but in fact tends to undermine the work of these institutions" ("Lopp'd and Bound," pp. 177–78).

The route to mediating and transcending the liberal/communitarian debate is to treat liberalism as a tradition with practices and goods rather than as a neutral procedure for mediating conflicts.[25] Citizens participate in this tradition, not by abstracting themselves from their other traditions and their visions of the good through a Rawlsian thought experiment. Instead, liberalism can function as both a first-and second-order tradition. It is a first-order

---

[24] See Salkever's "Lopp'd and Bound" and *Finding the Mean* and William Galston's *Liberal Purposes*.

[25] Francis Fukuyama's *The End of History and the Last Man* is perhaps the best to look for a theory of liberal triumphalism, while Bhikhu Parekh's "The Cultural Particularity of Liberal Democracy" offers a warning to such claims.

tradition insofar as it fosters certain virtues – e.g., mutual recognition, tolerance, autonomy – and an ongoing historical argument about its development. These principles modify the understandings of particular traditions from the inside, as we see in Martin Luther King's or Cornel West's reading of Christianity. However, the influence goes in the other direction as well. Feminist and neo-Aristotelian critiques of liberal theory, for example, have exposed the poverty and cultural specificity of the self-understanding of democratic institutions in a way that makes liberal triumphalism a flight from history. Liberalism takes on a second-order dimension when it becomes the meta-language by which individuals and groups phrase their claims in the public sphere. Thus, instead of blocking out complex identities upfront in the Rawlsian or Rortyean ways, I understand a democratic tradition of justice as opening up to rich stories of difference. Here we have to leave behind liberal democracy for deliberative democracy, for liberalism omits the relationship between recognition, equality, and justice, as Ellison will show us in chapter 5. Deliberative democracy has an "ideal of politics where people routinely relate to one another not merely by asserting their wills or fighting for their predetermined interests, but by influencing each other through the publicly valued use of reasoned argument, evidence, evaluation and persuasion that enlists reasons in its cause" (Amy Gutmann, "Democracy," p. 417). To be sure, deliberative democracy discourages pre-modern attachments to tradition but this mobility of the self does not need to be underwritten spatially as a self separate from the contents it chooses. The practice of democratic autonomy does not require abandonment of the self-understandings provided by traditions but an ability to recognize and dialogue with different traditions, an ability that is fostered by democratic institutions, such as education. Democratic practices and values are thus woven into other traditions at the same time that they serve as a meta-language for negotiating conflict. Autonomy and freedom are achievements that democracy nourishes in its political culture (a communitarian point), at the same time that the vocabulary of rights protects individuals from tying autonomy and freedom to an oppressive view of the good (a liberal point). (I will say more about these issues – e.g., identity politics, public sphere – in chapters 3 and 5.) Democracy cannot be neutral toward all ideas of the good nor does it need to be.

Moreover, we need to abandon MacIntyre's global characterizations of the diversity of cultural practices with such labels as "liberal." The vocabulary of virtues has not disappeared; rather, it coexists and competes with instrumental, utilitarian values. The incommensurabilities in contemporary debates are not all signs of incoherence, as several reviewers of *After Virtue* were quick to point out.[26] By thinking culture in terms of practices, we can not only mediate the liberal/communitarian debate but bring it into a productive dialogue with the thinkers discussed in chapter 1. What conception of practice to use and how to connect this conception to language is the subject of chapter 3.

Summing up and looking forward

We now need to bring together the insights of the first two chapters to focus on what chapter 3 needs to resolve. The first chapter showed how the poststructuralists, Jameson, and Smith offered a new vocabulary of difference and power but no satisfactory way to situate the speaker of the present in such a way that he/she could not only critique the past but recuperate enough of its resources to project a future. Habermas argues against this totalizing view of power, but he does so by staking everything on a narrow philosophy of language that seeks only to defeat grand schemes of instrumentalism (with communicative action) and relativism (with procedural universalism), but that shows no interest in or capacity for exploring the ethical resources. The second chapter examined two different problematics that affirm agency and value but that also have serious problems. Whereas Rorty recuperates democratic values, his instrumental pragmatism gives us few resources for understanding the ethical and political dimensions of the subject. MacIntyre offers an important defense of the tradition-based understanding of the subject, yet he ignores the democratic practices of modernity. Both Rorty and MacIntyre,

---

[26] Taylor says in his review of *After Virtue*, "we are far more Aristotelian than we allow and hence our practice is less based on purely disengaged freedom and atomism than we realize ... Our way of life never sinks to the full horror that would attend it (I believe) if we could be truly consistent Benthamites, for instance" ("Justice after Virtue," p. 29). Taylor also makes bridges the other way by attacking liberal criticisms of Sandel. For Taylor, much of the criticism confuses ontological with advocacy issues. The former "concerns what you recognize as factors you will invoke to account for social life." Advocacy issues "concern the moral stand or policy one adopts" ("Cross-Purposes," p. 159).

like the philosophers in chapter 1, insist on totalizing their problematics for language. Each one either makes or depends on a transcendental argument against the opponents. Each one is guilty of the charge that Taylor makes against Rorty, which I cited earlier in the chapter – that is, each arrives "ex ante at some view of what knowledge has to be, and then dictat[es] to reality from that standpoint" ("Rorty in the Epistemological Tradition," p. 264). What binds them all together is the assumption that the function of meta-theoretical deliberation is to articulate "the validity criteria for every first-order discourse" (Nancy Fraser, "False Antithesis," p. 169). The effect of this assumption is to shift the focus away from the particular cultural resources of each situation and toward all-embracing truths that determine deliberation rather than inform it. In presenting and criticizing these positions, I have been opening a meta-theoretical space that lets third-person and dialogical problematics talk to each other so that we can sort out their contradictions, expose their weaknesses, and map their incommensurabilities. Of course, this is not a neutral space that can be separated from theoretical or political commitments, but this does not diminish the importance of a genre of argument that seeks to thematize theoretical conflict. What emerges from the last two chapters is the priority of dialogical hermeneutics to third-person problematics of critique. This priority is both logical – our understanding makes possible the distanciating operations of third-person critique – as well as ethical/political – the impetus for taking apart our self-interpretations with an anti-hermeneutics must come from a reworking of the traditions of value that are under critique. Kant's two realms are reconceived in terms of hermeneutics so that agency is not a necessary assumption that floats independently of history and embodiment. Rather, agency is embedded in complex historical languages, which can both oppress and enable. The next step in my argument might be to give my reading of the history of the West, as MacIntyre, Habermas, and others do. Instead, chapter 3 will work with existing accounts to develop and dramatize how my argument produces a new model of critical dialogue.

3

‡❖

Theorizing narratives of agency and subjection

❖‡

"We need a moral philosophy that can speak significantly about Freud and Marx, and out of which aesthetic and political views can be generated."   Iris Murdoch[1]

"I loved history as a child, until some clear-eyed young Negro pointed out, quite rightly, that there was no place in the American past I could go and be free. I now know that slavery neither eliminated heroism nor love; it provided occasions for their expression."   Sherley Anne Williams[2]

In her introduction to *Revaluing French Feminism*, Nancy Fraser brings into focus the central dilemma that emerges from the first two chapters: "Either we limn the structural constraints of gender so well that we deny women any agency or we portray women's agency so glowingly that the power of subordination evaporates" (p. 17). None of the theories traced in the first two chapters has offered a satisfactory account of the interplay between the two kinds of stories we need for critical theory: those that speak of the subject's determination and those that speak of the subject's ethical/political agency. Jameson and the poststructuralists tell different, but one-sided, stories of subjection. Habermas offers a narrative of agency to balance the one of determination, but his theory provides no way to characterize the richness of these narratives. Rorty's view offers agency without ethical depth or an account of oppression. MacIntyre gives new resources to narratives of agency, but he leaves them in a political vacuum.

This chapter falls into two parts. In the first, I will clarify the conceptions of the subject that have emerged over the first two chapters in order to show how stories of agency can work with stories of determination. My goal will be the creation of a meta-critical space of deliberation that can assess competing

---

[1] "On 'God' and 'Good,'" p. 68.   [2] *Dessa Rose*, p. x.

theories and their appropriateness for reading a given text(s). In the second half of the chapter, I develop my ideas through an analysis of the controversy surrounding an ethics of care versus an ethics of justice in the theory of Carol Gilligan and then through a discussion of the ethical practices of other texts by women.

Language, ethics, and the subject in critical dialogue

To characterize the dynamics of first-/second and third-person accounts of subjectivity in a schematic fashion, I will start with a dialogue between critical friends who are able to run the full register of discourse – that is, they can draw on the third-person accounts of psychoanalysis, social theory, or poststructuralism that can alter the assumptions at work in dialogue. During the course of the book, I will show how conflicting stories can work in a dialogue not just between two friends but between various kinds of interlocutors including text and reader. This starting point will bring out important issues that have been lost in contemporary theory:

1. *The need to recognize self-interpretations and to unmask self-interpretations.* The delicate and complex interplay between these theoretical needs brings to the surface two processes: first, the violence to the integrity of self that is involved in understanding how one's self-interpretations are crippling; and second, the complexities that are entailed in transforming these interpretations. Few things are as painful as being told that you do not know who you are, that your deepest loves and fiercest hates are not what you thought, that your achievements are part of a psychic or social survival mechanism. (This challenge may be made to entire schools of thought, of course, and not just to individuals.) Responding to such a story requires not simply changing one's mind but changing who one is. That is why this kind of exchange is not appropriate in most face-to-face encounters; however, it is also why this form of dialogue is important for our private and public lives, especially for our reading. Moreover, this kind of dialogue is going on in less direct and personal ways in the classroom and in meetings in the public sphere, because our stories always carry the potential to unmask interlocutors whether we intend to or not.

2. *The need to close the hermeneutic circle.* Dialogue between

friends – like psychoanalytic dialogue – forces out the need to respond to critique and to specify the utopian moment of deliberation in a way that none of the theorists we have examined so far does. Third-person accounts are always made by someone (first-person) to someone (second-person). The negative goal of critical friendship, like that of psychoanalysis, is to unmask our ideals, but this unmasking depends on new ideals and on the historical specification of the site from which they are constructed. Clarifying the relationship between third-person critiques and the dialogical traditions that are the object of critique provides a way of avoiding the performative contradiction that haunts genealogical maneuvers.

3. *The need to have narratives of recuperation interact with narratives of critique within the same interpretive space.* This dialogue will dramatize the importance of not collapsing the tension between the narrative of achievement (the utopian moment) and the deflating narrative of determination by psychic or social forces. The transcendental arguments against radical difference by Gadamer, Habermas, and Davidson and the transcendental arguments for radical difference by poststructuralists seek to drive out the possibility of such an interpretive space. The two persons in a dialogue must maintain a first-/second-person language infused with ideals that sustain their efforts at the same time that these ideals remain vulnerable to third-person redescriptions that characterize them as repetitions of patterns of the past.

But how does such a dialogue relate to reading literary texts? First, I assume that texts are always in implicit or explicit dialogue with other texts, both literary and nonliterary. Texts can rely on explicit general accounts (e.g., Freud's) about what a person is or what causes actions, etc., but literary texts usually dramatize their assumptions. For example, Flaubert's *Madame Bovary* does not tell us what its positions on language, subjectivity, and desire are, but the narrative shows its very definite stands on these issues. The novelistic practices in Kate Chopin's *The Awakening* "argue" against these assumptions as do the texts of Henry James, though none offers a direct theoretical challenge. A text participates in this dialogue through explicit commentary or through intertextual allusions of various kinds, as many theorists from Bakhtin to Barthes have discussed. What interests me here is not a new theory of reading but the enrichment of the characterization of the reader's deliberation about textual practices, so that the question of whether we are embedded in nourishing traditions or crippling disciplinary practices is not decided in advance by theory.

As a point of departure, I will use Ricoeur's three-part division of the hermeneutic circle of reading, what he calls "triple mimesis," in *Time and Narrative*. The first is the "prefigured" – that is, the reader's precomprehension of action that is necessary for the production and reception of narrative. I would expand this sense of "prefigured" from this phenomenological understanding to mean the historical argument in which the reader situates himself/herself. The second is the "configured" – the text itself, which Ricoeur rightly calls an action, an "emplotment" in the existing textual field. The third is the intersection between the world of the text and the world of the reader, whose world is articulated in language and narrative. Ricoeur's hermeneutic model gives a place to both structural and causal explanations (Mimesis 1, the "prefigured"), as well as to structural literary analysis such as narratology and intertextuality. If this model addresses the problem of understanding, it does not say much about the specifics of the dialogue between text and reader, in which texts are not only understood and classified but "applied" (to use Gadamer's term); that is, the way the text speaks to the reader's concerns.[3] The reader does not simply understand a text, but he/she comes to it with particular feelings and positions about the relationships among narrative, language, ethics, and politics – e.g., "Sartre is right and MacIntyre is wrong about narrative," "Proust's account of love is one-sided," "Hemingway's works are sexist." The text addresses these positions with its own explicit or implicit positions on these matters. Ricoeur's phenomenological emphasis in his monumental study leaves out this dimension; moreover, when he addresses poststructuralist thought – as he rarely does – he views it as an account that must be defeated rather

---

[3] Gadamer revises the three parts of traditional hermeneutics (explanation, understanding, and application) so that application is not an afterthought but part of understanding itself: "Application is neither a subsequent nor merely occasional part of the phenomenon of understanding, but codetermines it as a whole from the beginning . . . [The interpreter] must not try to disregard himself and his particular situation. He must relate the text to this situation, if he wants to understand at all" (*Truth and Method*, p. 324).

than incorporated into his own.[4] In brief, a text is in a dialogue of many kinds – e.g., sympathetic or reverential evocation, withering parody, trenchant argument – with other texts, particularly with the texts the reader uses to organize his/her identity. In doing so, the reader situates himself/herself in an historical tradition(s) and in future stories – e.g., in poststructuralist stories of oppression and negative liberty and/or MacIntyrean stories about the transformation of traditions. The reader's activity can thus be thought of in terms of the three dimensions of hermeneutics – explanation, understanding, and application – though now these dimensions have been extended to include the anti-hermeneutic challenges of chapter 1 and the refinements of chapter 2.

I will proceed by giving a narratological account of the conflicting stories produced in such dialogue among liberals, communitarians, and radicals. By focusing on the meta-theoretical dimension of this dialogue, I will minimize discussion of the controversies about the true account of human development or of the history of the West. Nonetheless, there is one theoretical issue that must be addressed immediately, and that is the ethical/political character of the meta-critical self that emerges from the dialogue established in chapters 1 and 2. This self draws on the communitarian accounts developed by MacIntyre and Charles Taylor because they offer the richest ethical language for characterizing the self historically and textually. The communitarian problematic for language is crucial not simply for the retrieval of the resources of the European traditions, which concern these two philosophers, but also for those excluded by dominant traditions. All citizens need a vocabulary of self-articulation that goes beyond Rorty's liberal holism and poststructuralism's vocabulary of difference. The key assumption of the communitarian view is that the self is not simply self-awareness but a self that is constituted by its understanding of the good. As Taylor says, "To know who you are is to be oriented in moral space, a space in which questions arise about what is good and bad, what is worth doing and what not, what has meaning and importance for you and what is trivial and secondary"

---

[4] The modernist texts (Proust's *A la recherche du temps perdu*, Woolf's *Mrs. Dalloway*, and Mann's *Magic Mountain*) Ricoeur selects are preoccupied like he is with mapping general philosophical or phenomenological issues – memory, subjectivity, and identity. Other writers, such as Ellison and Chopin, are concerned with the way such questions turn not on necessity or the nature of experience but on particular social constructions.

(*Sources of the Self*, p. 28). Thus, "our identity allows us to define what is important to us and what is not" (p. 30). There is a background against and through which the self finds its orientation, and this background can be interrogated but not invented.[5] The principal means by which the self achieves coherence in internal and external dialogues is through narratives of the past and the future, a point we have already found in MacIntyre and in Ricoeur.

The second strand of this self/subject comes from a revised liberalism. The guiding ideals that inform this self are drawn from liberal and radical democratic theory – autonomy, equality, liberty, and justice. Autonomy, however, is not the caricature of the isolated liberal self who joins society only to pursue self-interests. If we have transcended the stark opposition between liberal and communitarian views, we still have not addressed how autonomy needs to be rethought.[6]

The key figure in the theory of autonomy is Kant, who established his notion by separating theoretical accounts of determination from the practical realm of moral action. In order for us to be autonomous, our reason must be untouched by internal constraints, such as desire, or external constraints. In our contemporary perspective, the question of autonomy moves into areas ruled out by Kant. Not only does desire now play a key role but the issue of determination has been expanded. Kant saw determination in the form of the causality of Newtonian science, a causality that is equitably distributed and sealed off from the practical realm. Contemporary reflection brings social scientific and cultural theory into this "practical" realm in order to examine the cultural enablement or oppression of subjects. When we put the conditions for autonomy on the table the question concerns the ethical, historical, and social conditions that empower or oppress for particular projects rather than the universal problems of agency and determination. Although I maintain a double perspective that parallels Kant's division, I historicize these perspectives as tradition (agency) and genealogy (oppression) and bring these incommensurate accounts into a space of mutual interrogation so that the third-person perspectives can dialogue with first-/second-person

[5] Taylor gives a Heideggerian phenomenological cast to the notion of practice that is an important supplement to MacIntyre's reconstructed Aristotelian idea.

[6] See Gerald Dworkin, *The Theory and Practice of Autonomy*, chapter 1, for a variety of definitions of autonomy that currently circulate.

accounts and historicize both perspectives. However, I keep the two perspectives in tension rather than resolving them in Hegelian fashion. (There is no vision of reconciled subjectivity and the progressive advance of freedom driving my argument.) The tension is not a standoff, however, for the priority of the dialogical perspective and its vocabularies over the third-person perspective is established through the argument that I have made over the first two chapters – that is, the narrator of the genealogy employs the resources of traditions, quite often of the traditions that he/she is attacking. The finitude of the subject and the multiplicity and contingency of history are the conditions within which these perspectives operate.[7]

For my purposes the most helpful place to open the question of autonomy is with Gerald Dworkin's formal definition because it touches on points dear to liberals and communitarians: "Autonomy is conceived of as a second-order capacity of persons to reflect critically on their first-order preferences and desires, wishes, and so forth and the capacity to accept or attempt to change these in light of higher-order preferences and values. By exercising such a capacity, persons define their nature, give meaning and coherence to their lives, and take responsibility for the kind of person they are" (*The Theory and Practice of Autonomy*, p. 20). Such a view may not seem to have much bite – what isn't a second-order desire? However, its importance emerges when we connect this idea of second-order desires with an understanding of democratic self-interpretation developed by Taylor, which combines the Kantian theme of self-determination with the Hegelian idea of the subject's reappropriation and shaping of the content of consciousness.[8] Taylor develops this distinction into an account of human agency that connects autonomy to self-interpretation: "The human agent

---

[7] This historical justification of the ideals is precisely what Habermas avoids. As Robert Pippin says, "Habermas needs something like a *Phenomenology of Spirit*, or some sort of way of accounting for the modern affirmation of the values of reciprocity and self-consciousness that does not rely so heavily on the meager philosophic resources of developmental psychology ... Without invoking something like a Hegelian or narrative assessment of modernity and its implications, Habermas cannot defend a critical theory of modernity" ("Hegel, Modernity, and Habermas," p. 347). Although I have discussed the necessity for an historical argument for democracy in terms of MacIntyre's tradition, Pippin makes a similar argument through his reading of Hegel.
[8] The key essay on second-order desires is Harry Frankfurt's "Freedom of the Will and the Concept of a Person," in *The Importance of What We Care About*.

not only has some understanding (which may be also more or less misunderstanding) of himself but is partly constituted by this understanding" (*Human Agency and Language*, p. 3). This constitution is inevitably axiological as well, and Taylor calls such self-interpretations "strong evaluations." Such evaluations are often second-order desires that evaluate desires: "They involve discriminations of right or wrong, better or worse, higher or lower, which are not rendered valid by our own desires, inclinations, or choices, but rather stand independent of these and offer standards by which they can be judged" (*Sources of the Self*, p. 4). This view of the subject is opposed to utilitarian efforts to maintain a subject who is outside any context and who weighs alternatives: "Whereas for the simple weigher what is at stake is the desirability of different consummations ... for the strong evaluator reflection also examines the possibility of different modes of being of the agent" (*Human Agency and Language*, p. 25).[9] The idea of the agent as strong evaluator, like the idea of the intersubjective creation of identity, has both an empirical and normative dimension. That is, an atomistic, utilitarian conception of the self misses something important about the nature of self-interpretation and what this conception misses is of ethical/political significance. I would not deny that there are exceptions to Taylor's characterization, exceptions that can come not only from utilitarians but also from unreflective beings such as Tolstoy's peasants, as Owen Flanagan points out ("Identity and Strong and Weak Evaluations," pp. 46–47) in his critique of Taylor's notion as excessively intellectualist. For my purposes here, what is most important is the normative dimension of this claim. Democratic subjects need to esteem this kind of self-understanding because such a view permits us to thematize the richness of our lives at the same time that it urges us to deliberate democratically on our interconnections. This is the perfectionist dimension of the conception of the democratic subject that I advocate. Moreover, I would add an historical aspect to Taylor's phenomenological account, an aspect that places strong evaluations in historical arguments that recuperate them.

What we need to see (and what the other theorists, except for

---

[9] Sandel likens this "simple weigher" in Taylor's definition to Rawls: "Since for Rawls the faculty of self-reflection is limited to weighing the relative intensity of existing wants and desires, the deliberation it entails cannot inquire into the identity of the agent" (*Liberalism and the Limits of Justice*, p. 159).

MacIntyre and Taylor, never show) is what it looks like to live through these vocabularies. Even Rorty, who affirms agency and modern traditions, acknowledges his embeddedness and then speaks of vocabularies as matters of word choice and not as alternative complex practices.[10] The only values that he discusses are the meta-values of liberalism – justice and negative freedom – which ask for a meta-philosophical subject who admits to being caught in the particularities of social history but who seeks to avoid characterizing such a subject as if it were unimportant.

Moreover, my model of the democratic subject draws on the radical, genealogical model to understand the ways subject positions in a society are created. These third-person stories include unflattering accounts of the traditions that make them possible, and these accounts enact a kind of radical third-person critique that liberal and communitarian theories block. These stories are precisely the ones that MacIntyre and Rorty leave out, for the critiques they offer never cut deeply into the presuppositions of the subject. This is also true of Taylor's own work, which suffers from his refusal to include a dimension of critique that takes either Marxism or poststructuralist analyses seriously. The result is that he remains caught in a nostalgia for Romantic expressivism, which he plays off against the Cartesian strain of modernity, while ignoring postmodern cultural interpretations.[11] Unlike poststructuralist genealogists, my conception of genealogy puts on the table the resources on which its critiques depend; the narrator of the story does not just gesture toward a negative liberty but tells the story of the positive liberty embodied in his/her texts. That is, the

[10] Rorty's commentary on Taylor's essay illuminates the importance of the notion of "strong evaluations" for my purposes. Rorty wants to drop any such distinction: "The interesting line is not between the human and the nonhuman, nor between material objects and emotions, but between behavioral patterns which you and the natives share and the patterns which you do not" (*Essays on Heidegger and Others*, p. 104). Rorty ignores Taylor's claim about the subject and dissolves the question of things into behavior. But the problem here is not just the second-order claim about problematics but a first-order claim about the subject, a debate about what Rorty would call "final vocabularies" – that is, "a set of words which [humans] employ to justify their actions, their beliefs, and their lives" (*Contingency, Irony, and Solidarity*, p. 73). In short, these vocabularies include much of what Taylor calls "strong evaluations"; however, Rorty, unlike Taylor, does not give "final vocabularies" the status of second-order desires, which order and shape first-order desires.

[11] See Quentin Skinner's "Modernity and Disenchantment," for a critique of Taylor's sometimes uncritical appeal to traditions – e.g., Judaeo-Christian, and institutions – e.g, the family, and community.

narrator needs to discuss his/her understanding of the traditions that underwrite the critique as well as the relationship of this narrative self(ves) to these traditions. (The second part of the chapter as well as chapters four and five will give examples of why these perspectives are necessary and how they work together.)

An individual's autonomy is not just a matter of his/her right to be recognized as a responsible agent worthy of respect, for the question of identity is closely connected to the issue of autonomy. Autonomy includes the capacity to articulate an identity and having access to the discursive means necessary to do so. As Nancy Fraser says, "To be autonomous here would mean to be a member of a group or groups which achieved a degree of collective control over the means of interpretation and communication sufficient to enable one to participate on a par with members of other groups in moral and political deliberation" ("Toward a Discourse Ethic of Solidarity," p. 428).[12] Autonomy, justice, equality, and liberty depend on having access to sources of ethical nourishment, such as stories and traditions, and having these stories recognized in the public and private spheres.

This new understanding of liberal ideals requires a revision of the moral/political psychology that subtends the ontology of the liberal self, a self who acquires independence through a process of separation from others who threaten to smother (the mother) or destroy (the father). We find this view of the self in Freud, Kohlberg, and others, and it has been challenged by thinkers using relational models of development. These models provide a basis for thinking of autonomy as an intersubjective process of mutual recognition among equals, as Jessica Benjamin's *The Bonds of Love*, Seyla Benhabib's *Situating the Self*, and other works have shown.[13] I do not mean to conflate the ontological and psychological issues with political ones but to connect these issues, which liberal theory

---

12 See Fraser's "Rethinking the Public Sphere," in which she shows how the public sphere provides "arenas for the formation and enactment of social identities" (p. 122).
13 The psychological research that lies behind these two books includes the work of D. W. Winnicott, Heinz Kohut, Nancy Chodorow, and Carol Gilligan. For the debate between Lacanian and object-relations theorists such as Chodorow, see Teresa Brennan's Introduction to *Between Psychoanalysis and Feminism* and Claire Kahane's "Object-relations Theory." Benjamin's account recognizes one of the principal reproaches of Lacanians against object-relations theorists: that the psychic is not reducible to the social (Brennan, Introduction, *Between Psychoanalysis and Feminism*, p. 8).

urges us to keep separate. Thus, Rorty says to communitarian critiques of Rawls, "Rawls is not interested in the conditions for the identity of the self, but only in the conditions for citizenship in a liberal society" (*Objectivity, Relativism, and Truth*, p. 189). Certainly, Rawls has a point here. If we tie autonomy to a narrow normative and/or psychological theory such that people who do not conform are denied autonomy, then we have missed the mark. On the other hand, if we make autonomy a purely formal notion, we block out the social and psychological histories that make autonomy not just a matter of private but public concern. Rawls wants to abstract his conception of the person from philosophies of history and human nature, claiming his view "is not a psychology originating in the science of human nature but rather a scheme of concepts and principles expressing a certain conception of the person and an ideal of citizenship" (*Political Liberalism*, pp. 86–87). Even a formal political self cannot be completely abstracted from psychological presuppositions. As Owen Flanagan says, "Kant is the most famous autonomy theorist of all ["autonomy" here concerns the separation of ethics and psychology]. But even he is best read as assuming that psychology matters to ethics. His conception of the kingdom of ends, a community in which each accords every other noninstrumental respect, is best understood ... as based on the belief that such a kingdom is realizable of what is psychologically and sociologically possible for us" (*Varieties of Moral Personality*, p. 27). The point is not to prevent theories of history from becoming part of deliberation for fear that these theories will become oppressive "meta-narratives" of Hegel or Marx but to work through them in terms of democratic ideals. The unacknowledged theories that lie behind the narrow liberal view of autonomy are reinforced by ideologies that perpetuate domination through cultural scripts that make agency male and passivity female and whose content feeds the nightmarish side of the liberal ideals – isolated competitive monads who seek community only for self-interest. Liberalism prevents us from thematizing these scripts through such deliberative strategies as the original position.

Instead, I follow Benjamin in imagining the emergence of an autonomous self through a process of recognition in which the abstract right to be treated as an autonomous agent is supplemented by the ethical and cultural support necessary to participate in democratic institutions. This support will include attention to an individual's differences and to creating the dialogical capacities needed to articulate and rework these differences in encounters with others. In this view of the subject, agency does not depend on domination, and integrity does not depend on separation. Such a self can have the porous boundaries needed to negotiate the problems involved in meeting the needs for critique and community that are inherent to the lifeworld of liberal democracies. In short, the theory of the self that I have sketched gives some minimal presuppositions for underwriting the kind of critique and recuperation I have done in chapters 1 and 2 and will do in the rest of the book.

But how does this dialogue between constructing and constructed views of the subject take place? For the moment, let us assume that the challenge to the self is made through the notion of an unconscious, by which I mean any force operating behind the agent's back. The challenge presented by this idea is nicely formulated by Rorty when he says that "it looks like somebody is stepping into our shoes . . . like a person is using us rather than a thing we can use" (*Essays on Heidegger and Others*, p. 146).[14] In this manner of thinking, the unconscious is not a collection of seething drives but an alternative package of beliefs – that is, an alternative self whose sets of beliefs are incommensurate with the familiar set that is available to introspection. In this way, the question of the force of the unconscious – or any other third-person agent – is separated from the logical problem posed by its mere existence. In addition, this view of the unconscious does not tie it to a particular story of development. Our relationship to the unconscious is articulated in holistic language games in the same way that our disputes with other critics are. The effects of psychic forces cut across the intentionalities and beliefs of the conscious self – e.g., in patterns of repetition, slips of the tongue, symbols, etc. In the narrative of critique, these fissures in belief appear in stories with nonhuman agents such as "drives," "compulsions," etc. The forces that cut across the first-person statements can be called another agent or self who is "outside" the conscious self. The disjunction between the conscious and unconscious selves means that they have only a causal relationship with each other rather

---

[14] Rorty relies on Donald Davidson's "Paradoxes of Irrationality" for his view of the person. A person is "a coherent and plausible set of beliefs and desires" (Rorty, *Essays on Heidegger and Others*, p. 147).

than a rational justificatory relationship. That is, they have a relationship of force rather than argument. As Ricoeur says, "Man's alienation from himself is such that mental functioning does actually resemble the functioning of a thing" ("The Question of Proof," p. 261). The story told by the unconscious is not only different but incommensurate with the one told by the conscious self – e.g., a story of the father as aggressive tyrant versus the one that makes him a fellow sufferer.

How does the idea of competing stories help us think through the tension between explanation and understanding? Let us say that Ernest Jones were to ask a real-life Hamlet why he is waiting to kill Claudius, and Hamlet replies, "Conscience doth make cowards of us all." Jones may interpret this generalization as a defense against certain unconscious motives rather than accepting Hamlet's maxim at face value. Jones's causal explanation points toward a second, unconscious self that has a different cluster of beliefs and that tells a different story. The conscious and unconscious selves are "part of a single unified causal network, but not of a single person" (Rorty, *Essays on Heidegger and Others*, p. 147). (There can, of course, be more than two selves at work.) Predicting an individual's behavior requires knowledge of all of these selves, "but only one of these persons is available (at any given time) to introspection" (p. 148). This view replaces Freud's hierarchical conception of the relationship of consciousness and the unconscious – e.g., the famous archaeological metaphor that speaks in terms of the unassimilated fragments of the past that press against the conscious activity of the present – with a "lateral" metaphor in which two or more languages, two or more selves, are trying to speak at the same time. (The hierarchical vocabulary of Marxist explanations, such as base and superstructure, can be made lateral in the same way.) The critical friend ferrets out the story of the unconscious self, perhaps linking the two selves through a third narrative – what Habermas calls a "general interpretation" of the story of development, a story that may use causal language about "drives," "cathexes," etc. The respondent, however, cannot use such causal language in his/her story but only compares the two stories. Of course, it is important to remember that these third-person accounts emerge within a dialogical (I–you) relationship, in which the speakers, and not just the words, are crucial. Moreover, the account given above simplifies the dialogical interactions that blur the boundary between one person's speech and another's. As Bakhtin reminds us, "the speaker strives to get a reading on his own word, and on his own conceptual system that determines this word, within the alien system of the understanding receiver" (*The Dialogic Imagination*, p. 282). That is, the critical dimension is never a view from nowhere and is itself tied to ideals and background assumptions of some community.

After the speaker has grasped the stories of his/her subjection, the question is not "new stories" *per se* but what new stories to inhabit, what new stories will help constitute the new self the person is seeking to forge. "Inhabit" and "constitute" do not fit with Rorty's instrumental liberalism but with Taylor's view that certain kinds of linguistic usage are constitutive, strong evaluations. For example, let us say someone is battling with a problem about weight,[15] and a dialogue with a friend has established the presence of a crippling inner voice that connects with the troubled person's parents and oppressive cultural norms about beauty and self-esteem. In the course of the dialogue, both first-/second-person and third-person accounts emerge, so that the troubled person's self-understandings are made part of the stories of which he/she was not aware but which were imprisoning him/her. These third-person stories can be drawn from theories of psychological development, the history of gender relations, the history of ethics (e.g., Nietzsche's *Genealogy of Morals*), and the history of confessional practices, such as psychoanalysis (Foucault), or personal history. We should remember that a "third-person" account here may emerge implicitly from listening to another person's first-person story if this story makes one aware of agents operating behind his/her back. For example, hearing a woman recount the story of abuse by her husband may force other women to examine their own complicity with the practices that informed the abusive marriage. (I will look at an example like this in the second part of the chapter.) Indeed, this is usually the case for readers of literary

[15] I am expanding Taylor's example in *Philosophical Papers*. By speaking of a therapeutic dialogue with a communitarian view of language, I am contesting MacIntyre's point that the therapist – one of modernity's main character types – is concerned only with the manipulation of the self to achieve health, with the functionalist goal of "making people workable" (Iris Murdoch, "On 'God' and 'Good,'" p. 72). The functioning of the person is always part of a larger context about ethical constitution and the narrative understanding of the self offered by MacIntyre. The work of therapeutic dialogue, like the critical dialogue I am proposing, is not directed simply toward understanding but to emotional renewal.

texts, texts that do not usually offer extensive social explanations but that dramatize social or emotional forces that challenge the reader's self-understanding. The dialogue between text and reader is not always a Socratic dialogue but often an emotional exchange filled with accusations, anger, joy, despair, love, etc., in which no holds are barred.

The work of critical dialogue not only requires the emotional resources and the mutual recognition developed through the relationship but the articulation of a new identity, "a place to land" – that is, an ethical vocabulary that the person can inhabit individually and communally. In the narrative terms for this dialogue worked out so far, this means that we have not only the narrative of the conscious self, the narrative of the unconscious self, and the third-person stories that problematize these selves; we also need a fourth narrative. This fourth narrative is what the two interlocutors construct in order to reconcile the language game of the conscious self with that of the unconscious. An evaluative language of constitution must be negotiated so that one not only accepts the unwelcome story of his/her unconscious self but invents a self/language game that offers a meaningful existence. The person exposed to a third-person account of his/her actions does not simply "understand" what the unconscious self is saying and become liberated (Habermas). He/she does not only delight in the diversity of possible alternatives (Rorty's ironic liberal) or in the appeal to negative freedom we find in various poststructuralist projects. Rather, he/she finds a site and an ethical language for integrating this story into a new one. The "hidden story" that the process of working through unfolds becomes available only through the utopian projection of a new self (fourth narrative). The narrative dynamics of this account expands MacIntyre's idea of the self and the tradition as forms of narrative quests to include explanatory challenges. Explanatory accounts, or genealogies, must ultimately be redeemed in terms of the ethical/political ideals of the person(s) and tradition(s) in question, even as these ideals themselves undergo critical assessment and transformation. Moreover, the dialogue sketched above could take place in any number of deliberative contexts about public, as well as private matters.

It is worth noting here that Taylor ignores the role of third-person accounts in his discussion of identity crises. His examples come from competing strong evaluations. Like MacIntyre (*After Virtue*, pp. 30–31) and other communitarians, he seems to hold the therapeutic perspective in low esteem because it deracinates us from the moral "sources of the self" and redescribes these languages so as to strip them of their ethical character. In my view, this is precisely the value of third-person accounts, for they open the possibility of otherness inside and outside our self-interpretations. The goal of third-person accounts is to make these denied possibilities available so that they can be democratically "cured," as Ralph Ellison will show us. Instead of seeking otherness in this world, Taylor pursues a theistic solution in "epiphanic" works of art, in which we are brought "into the presence of something which is otherwise inaccessible, and which is of the highest moral order or spiritual significance; a manifestation, moreover, which also defines or completes something, even as it reveals" (*Sources of the Self*, pp. 419, 518).

But what about the well-known objections to third-person accounts, like psychoanalysis, for democratic dialogue, such as Gadamer's reply to Habermas: "the generalization of the physician-patient model to the political practice of large groups . . . runs the risk of encouraging an uncontrolled exercise of force on the part of self-appointed elites who dogmatically claim a privileged insight into truth" (cited in McCarthy, *The Critical Theory of Jürgen Habermas*, p. 206)? In my view, this is not a problem with third-person accounts *per se*, for such accounts are part of our everyday conversations. When we listen to a friend talk about her lover or her mother, we do not limit ourselves to the self-interpretations of our interlocutor but draw on explanations from many sources. Moreover, our discussions with others are often about the nature of self-interpretation and not about local issues. The problem comes when the third-person accounts are in the hands of institutions of power and there is no reciprocity between the speakers so that third-person accounts can be used to dismiss the self-understandings of citizens as mere ideology. The institutional power of theoretical discourse haunts all theories, not just third-person ones. This threat is one reason why autonomy has to be a normative rather than just an empirical claim. During our lives, we go through countless redescriptions of ourselves that we often understand as more autonomous than our former selves. Our conception of political autonomy needs to be kept distinct from such reincarnations. However, autonomy cannot be divorced from our identities because it is tied to recognition. (I develop this connection in chapter 5.) Autonomy is a democratic, intersubjective ideal that needs to be nourished. Thus, I am tying autonomy to a conception of radical, deliberative democracy, as Habermas does, in which democratic participation produces individuals with democratic virtues and dispositions. This perfectionist dimension of democracy is opposed to liberalism's emphasis on neutrality toward the good and on checking power.[16] Liberals like Rawls set up a wall not just against third-person accounts but also against the limited perfectionism of a democratic society.[17] In my view, the attempt to block out our particularities and our theories is not the way to interpret democratically. Instead, citizens can bring all they want to the table, but what they bring must be couched in the language of democratic interpretation, as we will see in chapter 5.

My proposal does not mean that first-person constructs are unassailable; indeed, a person's (or a community's) wish to remake his/her personality by using a new vocabulary can often be redescribed as a new version of an old pattern of repetition. Thus, the tension between first-/second- and third-person accounts cannot, and should not, be resolved, whether the tension comes from the third-person accounts of social science or from the competing linguistic theories of Rorty, Derrida, and Lyotard. This means that subjectivity is mobile and not reducible to discursive positions; the subject can respond to challenges that are thematized in argument as well as to challenges that address the forms of life the subject inhabits. It is the latter form of challenge that the notion of "otherness" designates, and we have seen how otherness emerges within, as well as outside, the self in critical dialogue. Because the subject in the West has had a pernicious mobility that either colonizes or banishes beings that fall outside its categories, theorists have been suspicious of

[16] See Amy Gutmann's entry "Democracy" in *A Companion to Contemporary Political Philosophy* and Jayne Mansbridge, *Beyond Adversarial Democracy*, for a discussion of deliberative democracy.

[17] See Rawls's arguments against "comprehensive doctrines" throughout *Political Liberalism*. Pursuing third-person accounts and democratic citizenship as a form of life does not mean that I want to abandon the self-understanding of freedom Rawls presents but to enrich his notion: "Citizens think of themselves as free in three respects: first, to pursue a conception of the good; second, as being self-authenticating sources of valid claims; and third, as capable of taking responsibility for their ends" (p. 72).

dialogic views of the relations among subjects as simply another way of disguising hegemony. In my view, we should not let this danger block a dialogical, intersubjective account of language in favor of a totalizing critique that situates itself beyond dialogue with the present. Third-person accounts challenge dialogical relations, because they threaten the integrity of the speakers; however, they cannot totally incapacitate response without becoming a dogmatic positivism.

By maintaining such a dialogical tension, we can pursue the richness of communitarian ontologies while thematizing what these ontologies cover over. What this dialogue does is foreground the paradox of politics, a paradox that William Connolly phrases as follows, "The human animal is essentially incomplete without social form; and a common language, institutional setting, set of traditions, and political forum for enunciating public purposes that are indispensable for the acquisition of an identity and the commonalities essential to life [the communitarian position]. But every form of social completion and enablement also contains subjugations and cruelties within it [the poststructuralist point]" (*Identity and Difference*, p. 94). In Connolly's view and mine, democracy needs a political space in which these different perspectives can be discussed, and the commitment to such a space is a liberal commitment: "Politics is the means through which these ambiguities can be engaged and confronted, shifted and stretched ... A society that enables politics as this medium is a good society because it enables the paradox of difference to find expression in public life ... This perspective is, of course, a liberalism" (p. 94). A political/ethical commitment to this space, where claims about liberty, equality, and the good life can be debated forces all participants out of the bunkers that define their ethical, political, and linguistic horizons. Communitarians – both in the dominant culture and in marginal ones – must connect their traditions to the democratic principles that inform society; radicals must connect their critiques to democratic institutions and virtues; liberals must give up their mask of neutrality and hear claims that draw on stories of oppression and stories of difference that their social ontology blocks.

Commitment to democratic political values does not leave participants unaltered, for it means giving these values a trump value over substantive views of the good life. Defenses of liberal democracy and the self-understandings of the subjects of democracy need to draw on communitarian vocabularies of tradition and virtue in order to articulate their positions and forms of life. This will not be a semantic concession to nonfoundationalism, as it is in Rawls, or a holistic background for "us," as it is in Rorty; instead, defenses will be specific about virtues and principles of this political form, as the work of Salkever, Nussbaum, Mouffe, and Galston shows. Thus, the insistence that we thematize the ways social ontologies enable and oppress is not based simply on a commitment to truth but on a liberal virtue. As Salkever says, "the commitment to and even joy in self-consciousness and self-scrutiny is a different sense of the good life either from zealous sectarian dogmatism or essentially passive toleration or neutral neutrality. The liberal virtue here is the ability to maintain a balanced tension between moments of commitment and moments of doubt" ("Lopp'd and Bound," p. 188). Democratic subjects must play multiple roles, in which they are partisans of particular traditions but also partisans of democratic culture. Mary Louise Pratt describes this kind of politics in her classroom, "The classroom functioned not like a homogenous community or a horizontal alliance but like a contact zone. Every single text we read stood in specific historical relationships to the students in the class . . . Everybody had a stake in nearly everything we read, but the range and the kind of stakes varied widely" ("Arts of the Contact Zone," p. 39).

But isn't this dialogical model just a Bakhtinian dialogue? The value of thinking of critical dialogue in the terms I propose needs to distinguish itself from Bakhtin in order to clarify its theoretical contribution. First, I am in substantial agreement with his meta-linguistic position about the dialogical character of language, and I applaud the way he complicates MacIntyre's picture of the dialogue within and between traditions by showing complex interconnections among utterances that operate in subtler ways than MacIntyre's philosophical argument allows; however, Bakhtin never addresses what is the key for MacIntyre and for me – how we need to deliberate about the ethical shape and direction of the self or of its traditions. Furthermore, Bakhtin simply banishes third-person accounts from his dialogism rather than broadening his meta-critical space to include them.

The easiest way to see the difference between Bakhtin and the MacIntyrean point I emphasize is to put out of play the point on which we agree – that language and identity are dialogical. Bakhtin devotes most of his argument to precisely such meta-theoretical battles – e.g., the dialogical account of the self versus a monological account. In a conversation with MacIntyre (or with the other theorists discussed earlier), meta-linguistic claims against monologism are not pertinent since no one believes it. Ethical/political defenses of monologism are out because they are incompatible with the democratic assumptions that inform the dialogue. Hence, the focus of discussion – which can take place in conferences, political meetings, classrooms, bedrooms, etc., – shifts to alternative views of ethics, politics, and aesthetics and how they are to be sifted, rejected, and revised. Ethical vocabularies get status not because of their unexamined hegemonic position but because they are self-consciously privileged and debated. What particular linguistic/ethical practices enable and shape agency in a positive sense? What does it look like to live in them as opposed to others? How do we compare them? It is not that Bakhtin's meta-linguistic views are incompatible with my own; it is rather that he is not interested in assessing the ethical/political forms of rationality provided by particular practices.[18]

Bakhtin never tells the ethical/political stories that would put his critique in a democratic project. He gives a merely formalistic definition of his idea of critique without inserting this idea into an historical argument. We can see this in the famous example of the emergence of critical consciousness in the illiterate peasant who "prayed to God in one language (Church Slavonic), sang songs in another, spoke to his family in a third" (*The Dialogic Imagination*, p. 295). But "as soon as a critical interanimation of languages began to occur in the consciousness of our peasant . . . then the inviolability and predetermined quality of these languages came to an end, and the necessity of choosing one's orientation among them began" (p. 296). This Rousseauesque example of the linguistic state of nature is detached from history. What are the historical debates that inform this critical moment and how do these debates connect to the historical account in which Bakhtin locates his own project? Of

---

[18] Bakhtin does give a place to higher order forms than dialogue, such as his conception of genre: "Genres (of literature and speech) throughout the centuries of their life accumulate forms of seeing and interpreting particular aspects of the world" (*Speech Genres*, p. 5). I discuss Bakhtin's work at greater length in "Ontologie linguistique et dialogue politique chez Bakhtine."

course, Bakhtin tells the story of the development of dialogism, but this is just a literary history that turns on the opposition between monologism and dialogism, between the evil of authoritarian discourse and the good of polyphony. These histories permit us to follow the triumph of dialogism, but they do not explore the complex conditions that harm or nourish democratic subjects. What are the positive forms that a society should seek to reproduce? To respond to this question requires a discussion of positive and not just the negative liberty that Bakhtin celebrates.

Another difference between Bakhtin and the dialogue sketched above is that Bakhtin conflates his ontological claim with a normative, ethical claim – e.g., dialogism is not only true but requires a particular ethical stance toward this truth. Ontologies and norms are connected, but they need to be connected in a thematized way so that we do not let the necessary truths about language structure debate, as the first two chapters have shown. We can see this problem in Bakhtin's discussion of *Notes from Underground*. After saying that the Underground Man's "consciousness of self lives by its unfinalizability, by its unclosedness and its indeterminacy," he goes further: "And this is not merely a character trait of the Underground Man's self-consciousness, it is also the dominant governing the author's construction of his image" (*Problems in Dostoevsky's Poetics*, p. 53). The Underground Man's experience of, and engagement with, the meta-linguistic truth of unfinalizability is not the only possible one and indeed a highly undesirable one. We have seen other stances toward "unfinalizability" – Derrida's writing under erasure, Rorty's ironic redescription, MacIntyre's vulnerable traditions, etc. (I am assuming here that Bakhtin's theory of language is not so different from those discussed so far as to be radically incommensurate with them and to *entail* an alternative political/ethical stance.) Bakhtin runs together the meta-linguistic claim of the observer with the first-/second-person claim of the participant. (In chapter 2, we saw Rorty make a similar move when he uses the meta-linguistic claim that the self is a web of beliefs to justify an instrumental view of the self rather than creating a two-tiered theory in which meta-philosophical notions of "webs of belief" and "unfinalizability" play the role of critical background to the first-order theories of the agent.) Bakhtin affirms the emergence of the self through dialogue: "One's own discourse and one's own voice, although born of another, will sooner or later begin to liberate themselves from the authority of the other's discourse" (*The Dialogic Imagination*, p. 348). But this meta-linguistic account finds first-/second-person embodiment only in ethical selves who are absorbed in questions of the unfinalizability of dialogue or the authority of the discourse.[19] Thus, we can agree with Bakhtin's ontological claims about the dialogical self and unfinalizability but also ask for richer characterizations of the ethical stances that accompany this recognition – that is, which ethical goods, virtues, ideas of the good life. His effort to achieve not merely self-consciousness but de-positioned self-consciousness is precisely the error of modernity that MacIntyre so pointedly exposes.

If MacIntyre were to discuss the speech of the Underground Man in Dostoevsky's *Notes from Underground*, he would not just talk about Dostoevsky's dialogical view of reality or the way he resists imposing an authorial voice on his characters; MacIntyre would talk about the Underground Man's maniacal dialogism as a symptom of the breakdown of tradition-based reason that isolates and fragments selves. MacIntyre would not just insist on a dialogical truth instead of the Enlightenment's monological truth; he would insert the argument(s) of the text into an historical argument, in which Dostoevsky is arguing not simply for the meta-theoretical case for dialogism but for first-order ethical, aesthetic, and political claims. (Bakhtin's silence about the democratic legacy of the Enlightenment when reading a text that is so preoccupied with its failures is particularly significant.) MacIntyre would not, of course, explicitly recuperate this breakdown of authoritarian traditions in the way Bakhtin and I do.

In addition, Bakhtin fails to address the shape that emotions (pain or love) or goodness give to linguistic personhood. If we think of the Underground Man's spiraling speech "with a loophole" only from the perspective of its dialogical relations to intertextual voices, as Bakhtin does, we leave untouched the psychological wound that makes his speech revolve around destructive patterns of domination and submission. This wound is created by damaging dialogical patterns that require normative assessment. A sociolinguistics that merely situates the subject in intertextual dialogues does not

---

[19] It is a simplification to speak of *a* Bakhtinian position, since his work changed considerably over the course of his life. There are heated debates over how to read these changes.

examine the ethical/political value of different dialogical forms. When Bakhtin says that Dostoevsky's artistic form "liberates and de-reifies the human being" (*Problems in Dostoevsky's Poetics*, p. 63), he refers to the way Dostoevsky refuses to shape monologically the voices of his characters but says nothing about the crippled beings in the texts; he shows how much his argument for dialogue is aimed at the meta-linguistic issue of its opposition to monologue.[20] Bakhtin gives too much emphasis to the liberatory force of the dialogical problematic, as if merely recognizing this truth were enough to liberate us. The Underground Man's de-centered speech dramatizes not an ethical ideal but the psychic nightmare of a peculiarly modern narcissistic quest to be a meta-person.

Another difference between the critical dialogue that I have characterized and Bakhtin's account is that he is hostile to the third-person accounts of Freud and Marx, since both use a grand monological theory of truth to redescribe the self-interpretations of individuals and groups in terms of external "forces that lie outside consciousness, externally (mechanically) defining it: from environment and violence to miracle, mystery, and authority. Consciousness under the influence of these forces loses its authentic freedom, and personality is destroyed" (*Problems in Dostoevsky's Poetics*, p. 297). Bakhtin wants to make psychological complexity only an affair of consciousness: "The depths of consciousness are simultaneously its peaks . . . Consciousness is much more terrifying than any unconscious complexes" (p. 288). For Bakhtin, Freud and Marx pose two problems that also concern my dialogical model: reductive falsification and political repression. The first issue concerns the positivistic assumption that often emerges in both Freud and Marx, in which an explanatory truth flattens dialogical self-interpretations into data and ethics into utilitarianism (Freud) or mystification (Marx).[21] Bakhtin's claim for the priority of

---

[20] In "The Poetics of *Ressentiment*," Michael André Bernstein examines precisely this point when he speaks of "the immediate, intractable, and existence-embittering suffering, from which Bakhtin's theories (although certainly not his life) are so remarkably free" (p. 202). *Notes from Underground*, one of the centerpieces for the analysis of dialogism, shows how "the dialogic status of their words, ideas, and sentiments is expressed as pure entrapment" (p. 208).

[21] As Ricoeur says, Freud made "no separation between the utilitarian enterprise of dominating the forces of nature (civilization) and the disinterested, idealist task of realizing values (culture)" ("Psychoanalysis and the Movement of Contemporary Culture," p. 304). I discuss these points in more detail in "Explanation, Understanding, and Incommensurability in Psychoanalysis."

dialogical understanding of human reality exposes the positivism that haunts both thinkers and the ways that monological views diminish ethical reality. Bakhtin is also making the hermeneutic point consistent with my view that Freudian and Marxist modes of interpretation have inadequate ways of recuperating cultural achievements. Of Lunacharsky's study of Dostoevsky, which explains his (Dostoevsky's) novels in terms of psychological and capitalist forces, he says: "The exceptionally acute contradictions of early Russian capitalism and the duality of Dostoevsky as a social personality, his personal inability to take a definite ideological stand, are, if taken by themselves, something negative and historically transitory, but they proved to be the optimal conditions for creating the polyphonic novel ... and this was without question a great step forward in the development of the Russian and European novel" (p. 35). Bakhtin's second criticism is that these theories had menacing political consequences, because they could be used to ignore the dignity of first-/second-person constructions made by individuals and groups and to justify treating these self-interpretations only as ideological mystifications or psychic processes (e.g., defense mechanisms). This danger was, and is, very real, but it is no reason to ignore how third-person accounts can reveal fissures within voices or forces that control them.

Bakhtin's ontology places the self in social voices – inside and outside the self – but offers no account of internalized oppression, of the way that "domination is anchored in the hearts of the oppressed" (Jessica Benjamin, *The Bonds of Love*, p. 5). This kind of domination requires a more complicated examination of the role of authority/power – e.g., seductions and rewards. (For example, Bakhtin examines only the linguistic relations among adults, not between parents and children, in which the dynamics of dialogism do not capture the shaping power in these relationships.) Bakhtin is reluctant to integrate stories about the particular socioeconomic or psychological forces that cripple human agency into the dialogical stories of achievement, preferring to acknowledge and seal off the existence of these forces, as the above remark on Lunacharsky shows. Third-person accounts need to heed what Bakhtin says in his ethical/political discussion of the relationship between authors/narrators and characters: "Only a dialogic and participatory orientation takes another person's discourse seriously"

(*Problems in Dostoevsky's Poetics*, p. 64), but they need not limit themselves to Bakhtin's dialogic ontology in which self-under-standings are inaccessible to explanation. As Charles Taylor says: "One has to understand people's self-interpretations and their visions of the good if one is to explain how they arise; but the second task can't be collapsed into the first even as the first can't be elided in favor of the second" (*Sources of the Self*, 204). If my meta-theoretical model of critical dialogue has shown how Bakhtin can be appropriated, it still has not shown how it can assess theories that address the issue posed by Nancy Fraser at the beginning of the chapter – women's achievement under oppression. I will conclude this section by comparing the way Sandra Gilbert and Susan Gubar theorize language, agency, and oppression in "Sexual Linguistics," the last chapter of *No Man's Land*, with Jessica Benjamin's approach in *The Bonds of Love*.

Gilbert and Gubar begin by rejecting Lacan's theory that makes the father's position crucial in the acquisition of language, and they assert – with a couple of footnotes to psychoanalytic works – the primacy of the mother. They say this new truth is in fact an old tradition of masculine and feminine linguistic fantasy that "implies the intuition of the primacy of the mother rather than the father in the process of language acquisition that assimilates the child into what Kristeva calls the 'symbolic contract'" (*No Man's Land*, pp. 228–29). To "support" this speculative thesis, they gather quotations from what male and female writers say about gender and language. Deprecating remarks by male writers about women's language, like patriarchal hierarchies in general, "have been historically erected as a massive defense against the deep throat of the mother and the astonishing priority that the mother tongue is common to both men and women" (p. 266). The effects of domination on women, particularly the internalization of patriarchal language, are ignored; the cause of patriarchal culture is simply a male defense. Gilbert and Gubar do not describe male and female linguistic practices and relate them to any present or future possibility for what gender might mean. That is, their utopia seems to require only the recognition of this truth that has already been realized. They offer no account of how these views of language relate to historical forces or linguistic theory. This kind of gender point scoring falls exactly into the trap Fraser describes, in which "we portray women's agency so glowingly that the power of subordination evaporates" (*Revaluing French Feminism*, p. 17). Benjamin puts Fraser's problem of radical politics on the table at the beginning. The "weakness of radical politics [is] to idealize the oppressed, as if their politics and culture were untouched by the system of domination, as if people did not participate in their own submission" (*The Bonds of Love*, p. 9). Benjamin challenges Freud not simply by condemning his bias; instead, she sets up an alternative model of development to replace his monadic model: "The idea of intersubjectivity reorients the conception of the psychic world from the subject's relation to its object toward a subject meeting another subject" (p. 20). Intersubjective space becomes the site for explaining oppression: "Domination and submission result from a breakdown in the relationship between self-assertion and mutual recognition that allows self and other to meet as sovereign equals" (p. 12). At the same time, it serves as the utopian site, for Benjamin uses it to locate not only neglected psychological evidence about gender and development but resources as well (e.g., the potential for intersubjective and equal recognition). Here, we see the importance of the investigator's ideals – in this case, intersubjectivity, agency, etc., – in reconstructive research. In order to explain oppression and project a transformation, Benjamin problematizes and mobilizes gender itself, so that what we are explaining and what we are seeking to bring about are not held hostage to existing gender categories. She does not avoid the complicity between oppressor and oppressed, so that women's work is not idealized on the grounds of gender alone. Moreover, she does not try to leap outside the forces she is describing. Her model touches all the theoretical bases necessary for critical theory. We are now ready to deal with specific texts and with Gilligan's ethical theory.

Ethics and gender: achievement, oppression, difference

The debates surrounding the work of Carol Gilligan show why we need to bring third-person narratives of critique into dialogue with first-/second-person narratives of reconstitution in the way that the first section of the chapter outlines.[22] Gilligan asks us to reexamine ethical theory so that we esteem rather than ignore the contribution of women's practices. Her work has created a controversy because the practices that she valorizes are ones that other feminists regard as the products of internalized oppression. How do we assess her claim to achievement against the claims made by theories of oppression? What clearly will not work is dogmatic theoretical commitment either to a third-person account of women's oppressive construction by the patriarchy or to first-/second-person narratives that account for and valorize women's agency. Diana Meyers phrases the problem for psychoanalytic theory pointedly, "In short, can psychoanalytic feminism explain the inbred handicaps limiting women's life prospects while generating a vision of human agency that would eliminate those handicaps?" ("The Subversion of Women's Agency," p. 138). I am not going to offer a new psychoanalytic narrative of development. My goal is to show how different levels of meta-theory, theory, and first-order criticism that I have outlined work together in a reading of textual subjects. I will assess Gilligan's claims about the importance of women's practices and then play my reading of Susan Glaspell's short story "A Jury of Her Peers" against hers. I close by extending my model to texts by Kate Chopin and Hélène Cixous.

Since Glaspell's story may be unfamiliar, I will summarize it briefly. The story begins when Mrs. Hale is called from her work in the kitchen to join her husband, Mr. Peters (the sheriff), and his wife. Mrs. Hale, the center of focalization for the third-person narrative, learns that Mr. Wright, the husband of an old friend, has been killed. The sheriff suspects that Mrs. Hale's friend Minnie has killed her husband. The group proceeds to the Wrights' home, where it splits up. The men go to the barn to look for evidence that can establish a motive for Minnie, while the women go to the kitchen to wait. In the kitchen, which is their separate physical and

---

[22] I cannot enter into all of the controversy surrounding Gilligan's work – see *Signs* 11 (1986). From my point of view, the most compelling critique, such as Linda Kerber's "Some Cautionary Words for Historians," is the one Gilligan herself acknowledges – i.e., she does not explain gender difference or dominance. See Joan Tronto for a political critique of the ideals Gilligan esteems: "In suggesting that care is gender related, Gilligan precludes the possibility that care is an ethic created by modern society by the condition of subordination" ("Beyond Gender Difference," pp. 646–47).

semantic space, the women find not only the text of Minnie's life but their own, a text that forces them to see themselves and their husbands in a new way and that requires a new language. What they discover through Minnie's text of madness is the psychological torture that her husband has put her through, a torture that culminates in his strangulation of Minnie's double, her pet bird. However, this is not simply detective work but a progressive hermeneutical self-interrogation, in which they must become "mad." They would not know before this moment how to read the bird at the beginning of the story. Mrs. Peters, who does not know Minnie and who is "married to the law" ("A Jury of Her Peers," p. 280) fights the revolutionary demands that Minnie's text makes on her. Mrs. Hale, who feels guilty for never having visited Minnie since her [Minnie's] marriage, leaps at the clues. That their husbands share Mr. Wright's ideology is brought home to them during the visit, since every time the men pass the kitchen, they make a condescending remark about the triviality of women's preoccupations when the issue is murder. The women recognize that the values and textures of their own lives are neither read nor appreciated by their husbands and that the forces that drove Minnie mad operate around and within them as well. They begin to understand how they have internalized their own domination as part of the "bonds of love," to recall Jessica Benjamin's evocative title. Unlike Minnie, they are able to create a way of speaking and being that unites them and separates them from the men. Here, we see how narratives of the self must include radical changes in the understanding of identity, practices, and traditions, which MacIntyre never considers. At the same time, we see the importance of recovering from a de-centering third-person story with a new first- and second-person narrative that is sustained by an account of practices and traditions. Moreover, the agency of the protagonists is not simply hermeneutical; they must choose whether to conceal evidence from the men and protect Minnie or to remain true to "the law" and turn the bird over to them. The story ends when they choose to conceal the bird and become the jury that Minnie needs.

In "Moral Orientation and Moral Development," Gilligan develops the ideas she advanced in *In a Different Voice* and applies them to Glaspell's story. Gilligan claims that traditional theories of moral development emphasize justice and autonomy (Freud and Kohlberg) and that these theories apply to men rather than women. According to Gilligan, these theories are not simply biased but impoverished; they leave out ethical resources that come about through women's social practices; these resources emphasize contextualized caring about relationships rather than disinterested rule-governed judgment. Moreover, Gilligan urges us to critique Freud/Kohlberg's conception of autonomy as separation and to rethink the processes of individuation in relational terms. She lays out complementary optics for ethical understanding: an ethics of care, which is associated with women, and an ethics of justice and autonomy, which is associated with men.[23] Gilligan describes the different ethical shapes of the self as follows: "These perspectives denote different ways of organizing the basic elements of moral judgment: self, others, and the relationship between them . . . [E]ach organizing framework leads to a different way of imagining the self as moral agent" (pp. 22–23).

Gilligan has certainly uncovered neglected ethical resources that challenge the dominance of the liberal subject of justice and its moral psychology as *the* moral subject. However, her analysis does not adequately theorize the women's ethical practices or the conditions under which they develop them. Gilligan emphasizes how the women think holistically about the pressures on Minnie, but, as we will see, she ignores the causes of these pressures, the changes in their self-understanding during the course of the story and the complexity of their ethical dilemma. In addition, she does not mention the women's relationships with their husbands but focuses only on the differences between the men's and the women's understanding of Minnie's plight. In doing so, Gilligan not only overlooks the political forces involved but ignores the critical understanding that Mrs. Hale and Mrs. Peters achieve and their power to act on this understanding. The "different voice" is the one that emerges during the course of the story and not the one they bring to Minnie's house. Gilligan also leaves the justice/care opposition intact rather than rethinking both ethical resources from the perspective of utopia, where the damage of historical oppression can be sorted out from the achievement under oppression. Her utopia is a balance between the two orientations.

---

[23] Gilligan qualifies her claim about gender as follows: "The contrasts between male and female voices are presented here to highlight a distinction between two modes of thought rather than to represent a generalization about either sex" (*In a Different Voice*, p. 2).

At the beginning of the story, the women's voices are dominated by their husbands' perspectives, but in very different ways. Mrs. Peters defends the men and cites moral authority: " ' It's no more than their duty' ... and 'The law is the law' " ("A Jury of her Peers," pp. 266, 270). Every time Mrs. Peters speaks with her husband's voice, Mrs. Hale responds not with a competing moral argument but with a qualification and resistance. After the first comment, we read, " 'Duty's all right,' replied Mrs. Hale bluffly; 'but I guess that deputy sheriff that come out to make the fire might have got a little of this on' " (p. 266). To the remark about the law, she says, " 'The law is the law – and a bad stove is a bad stove' " (p. 270). This is not so much about the conflict between "justice" and "care" as it is about broader differences in the textures of the men's and women's lives, textures that explode the rigidity of the care/justice opposition: " 'I'd hate to have men comin' into my kitchen,' she [Mrs. Hale] said testily – 'snoopin' round and criticizin' " (p. 266). Mrs. Hale is not objecting to the law or opposing care to justice; she is objecting to having an alien, condescending ethical understanding invade her cultural space, the kitchen.' She and Mrs. Peters are coming to a new understanding of the distinctiveness and importance of this space. A better way of characterizing what is at stake is to say that there is a conflict between competing conceptions of the good life and identity, for the men's judgment is not just of Minnie but of them.[24]

As the women decipher Minnie's text of madness, and as their alienation from their husbands grows, they start to question their ethical understanding. The men call their preoccupations "trifles" – the title of the dramatic version of the story. When Mrs. Peters says of Mr. Wright, " 'They say he was a good man' " (p. 267), she is repeating the received opinion of what a good man is. He was economically self-sufficient, and he did not drink or break any laws. He was autonomous. Mrs. Hale challenges this definition of goodness to include recognition of and attentiveness to others, kindness, and generosity, a mixture of liberal and communitarian virtues. Until now, they have accepted their differences from men as insignificant. Henceforth, however, they must face the fact that they do not get to partition off social space or to determine the virtues and norms that give identity and worth in the public and

[24] Annette Kolodny and Judith Fetterley show how the story's exile from the canon replays the men's judgment of the women in the text.

private spheres. Indeed, the story points out the need for a "politics which extends the terrain of political contestation to the everyday enactment of social practices and the routine reiteration of cultural representations" (Kirstie McClure, "On the Subject of Rights," p. 123).

The violence in the Wrights' marriage thematizes the conflict – the differences and the inequality – that the two women do not want to see. They begin as analysts trying to understand the "causes" of Minnie's madness, the forces that could make her do the unthinkable; however, they shift from explanation to understanding when they start to identify with Minnie. The "causes" of her actions become motives when these causes are tied to similar forces in their own lives – their own experiences of loneliness caused by their husbands – that is, they see these causes speaking for them; they understand them from the inside. Suddenly, they are the analysands and not the analysts. The particulars of Minnie's story function like a third-person critical social scientific account because they make available a new way of telling their own stories, in which they were unknowing victims and not agents; however, just as in analysis, the effects of the story are more powerful because they are spoken in a particularized first-person account to them and then suddenly for them. When Mrs. Peters discovers the strangled bird, she recalls the anger she felt as a young girl when a boy took a hatchet to her cat: "'If they hadn't held me back I would have' – she caught herself, looked upstairs where footsteps could be heard, and finished weakly – 'hurt him'" ("A Jury of Her Peers," p. 277). The anger here is not just about care and sympathy for Minnie nor about the anger she had to suppress at the time but about the anger she has discovered in and about the present. In the same way, Minnie's bird is not only a symbol of her lost, or never realized, happiness but of their own.

The friendship that develops between Mrs. Hale and Mrs. Peters gives them a context for mutual recognition and support that was not available to Minnie. Here is where they draw the strength to betray their husbands, to stop "caring" for them in order to realize themselves. The women establish a critical understanding, and in order to do so, they have to change the strong evaluations they use to make sense of their identities in, and outside of, their marriages. They are not so embedded in relationships they care about that they cannot assess the character of these relationships. (Of course, the story ends before we see any of these changes fully realized or thematized.) The text shows the need for an ethics and politics that goes beyond justice and care to explore the richness of practices and for a critical assessment of the nourishing and imprisoning aspects of social communities.

What I have been doing here is trying to sort out ethical issues without ignoring or essentializing gender categories. This kind of critique is important because so much of recent feminist criticism has been concerned with the opposition between those who want to deconstruct gender distinctions and those who want to have a separate space for women. Since I cannot summarize the debates over essentialism in feminist theory here,[25] I will cite the provocative critique of essentialism recently made by Chantal Mouffe and then comment on it: "The whole false dilemma of equality versus difference is exploded since we no longer have a homogeneous entity 'woman' facing another homogeneous entity 'man,' but a multiplicity of social relations in which sexual difference is always constructed in very diverse ways ... To ask if women should become identical to men in order to be recognized as equal or if they should assert their difference at the cost of equality appears meaningless once essential identities are put out of the question" (*The Return of the Political*, p. 78). First, I agree that one part of our understanding of "woman" and "man" needs to be made in terms of multiple subject positions so that the question of essentialism drops out. However, this poststructuralist mapping operation, which Mouffe calls "articulation," is simply a third-person positivism unless it is accompanied by an assessment of these subject positions through critique and recuperation. The "politics of difference" leaves unanswered the question of how this difference is characterized – in particular, whether it is characterized through a third-person or dialogical problematic. Discovering diversity in what were taken to be unities is simply not enough, for it does not point in any ethical or political direction. The whole opposition between essentialism and de-centered multiplicity is produced by the poststructuralist insistence that *any* first-/second-person account of the subject is an essentialism that reinstates a discredited humanism. Constructs concerning gender or any other identities do not have to be written on the skids of the signifier in order to be

---

[25] In "Feminist Theories: Beyond Essentialism and Constructivism," in *Contemporary Critical Theory: From Hermeneutics to Cultural Studies*, I discuss this debate at length.

provisional, partial, and vulnerable constructs. Since I pursue this critique of poststructuralism in chapter 1, I will just insist here that the dialogical dimension of the articulation of subject positions be made explicit. "Articulation" is addressed by someone to someone in the name of something.[26] Because this dimension is omitted, the political conclusion Mouffe makes is not argued for but asserted. What practices should be valorized and recuperated? Do practices associated with women make a contribution to ethical/political life? What forms of agency are important for public and private life? How does gender figure in utopian constructions?

The failure to think through the relationship between agency and oppression produces disputes such as the one between Joan Scott and Linda Gordon. In her review of Gordon's *The Heroes of Their Own Lives: The Politics and History of Family Violence*, Scott accuses Gordon of idealizing the agency of the women she studies. Scott thinks Gordon could have avoided this problem through the adoption of a "conceptualization [that] would see agency not as an attribute or trait inhering in the autonomous will of autonomous individual subjects, but as a discursive effect" ("Review of Linda Gordon," p. 851). For Gordon, such a way of understanding agency "drains that notion of any meaning" ("Response to Scott," p. 853). What concerns me is not the empirical question about these particular historical subjects; rather, my point is that neither model of agency has the whole story. To Scott, I would say that she must recuperate the agency of some of her predecessors in order to make her analysis possible and that this account of her story needs to intersect with the women whose stories she analyzes. To Gordon, I would say that her agents have internalized oppression and not just fought against an external force.

Thus, in my reading, I prefer to keep the third-person vocabularies of critique in a dialogical connection with the first-/second-person vocabularies of constitution. The women's ethical identities at the beginning of the story are shaped by confining social and

---

[26] The notion of "articulation" that Mouffe employs here, which she develops with Ernesto Laclau in *Hegemony and Socialist Strategy*, is for the most part a third-person account. The third-person character of this theory emerges in her definition of discourse: "The type of coherence we attribute to a discursive formation is ... close to that which characterizes the concept of 'discursive formation' formulated by Foucault: regularity in dispersion" (*Hegemony and Socialist Strategy*, p. 105). In my view, a narrative identity is an articulation by a subject, not about a subject.

psychological forces of which they are unaware. Their own marginalized practices can be recuperated only in a utopian space where gender and power are reconfigured, and they make steps toward such a reconfiguration in the story. By maintaining the tensions between critique and utopia, we can avoid the oscillation between essentializing and deconstructing gender, which is like the foundationalist/relativism debate that we examined earlier. Both positions in the debates are generated by the attempt to assume an unsituated view that will establish the truth of the matter beyond dialogue: gender categories are pure versus gender categories are heterogeneous. What we need are better ways to understand the patchwork of languages and practices that constitute existing identities and how we want to change them.

Moreover, working out the complexities of critique and utopia in each particular case cannot be done with a single theoretical stroke. Such deliberation will require the tough Nietzschean questions about power and ethics that Claudia Card puts to Gilligan's ideas: "The claim that a people has been oppressed implies that its members have been damaged – perhaps not all, not always irreversibly, and usually not thoroughly, but enough to require careful appreciation in appraising their perspectives" ("Women's Voices and Ethical Ideals," p. 130). It will also mean not totalizing Nietzsche's genealogy of power in the poststructuralist manner so that all goods that have ever produced some suffering are illusions. The nostalgia for a God's-eye view outside the ambiguity of culture appears in ethical reflection in the following form: If ethical goods have any complicity with power or do not live up to what they say they are, then they are worthless or dangerous mystifications that need to be discarded, not reworked.

Thus, the "different" voice does not repudiate the language of rights, autonomy, and justice, either. Rather, the language of rights can be appropriated by those who were excluded – for example, women and slaves – as the women's, abolitionist, and civil rights movements show.[27] This appropriation into different practices brings these liberal vocabularies into new discursive worlds, whose challenge to the white male tradition is not simply that this

---

[27] See Barbara Bardes and Suzanne Gossett's *Declarations of Independence* for an account of how women used Jefferson's language for their own purposes. I am indebted to Greg Jay's unpublished paper "Not Born on the Fourth of July: Cultural Differences and American Literary Studies.'

tradition contradicts itself when it excludes them. Instead, the new voices, such as those Glaspell depicts, challenge the norms and values that dominate the lifeworld and the public sphere. The distinctiveness of women's voices emerges in their capacity to transform the existing parameters of cultural debate, and these voices are not limited by existing gender distinctions, which have all too often worked against their interests.

However, it is not just the genealogies of power that block reflection on issues of cultural difference and domination but the way the issue of inequality is conflated with the issue of the recognition of cultural specificity/difference (Taylor, *Multiculturalism and the Politics of Recognition*, p. 37). The former appeals to the universal dignity of all persons, while the latter demands "that one accord equal respect to all actually evolved cultures" (p. 42). The two are intimately related but not identical, and the context of their application is crucial. If we were to employ the second principle, the men's judgment of the women's practices would not be a "particular mistake in evaluation but a denial of a fundamental principle" (p. 42). This is not an effective route to take in attacking the men's judgment, since it implies that all practices (texts) are of equal worth. This move leads to relativism and to the uncritical celebration of the marginal. Instead, critique should be focused on the particular failings of the dominant practices and on the particular strengths of the women's practices when reconstructed from specific utopian sites. As far as principles go, we can invoke the right of all members of a community to be recognized in their own terms, a phrasing that captures the way difference and equality connect but that does not lead to relativism. The "worth" of the women's practices emerges then through critical reflection and dialogue, not by an appeal to equality that ironically levels as it celebrates difference. A democratically biased hermeneutics – which I will discuss further in chapter 5 – is not just about recognizing otherness and letting voices speak but about creating ethical/political selves. In such a theory of value, the field of ethical understanding is transformed; care is not simply added to justice.

The dynamics of first-/second- and third-person accounts are not limited to showing unsuspected oppression, however; they can also expose unsuspected resources, as Kate Chopin's *The Awakening*, another work of the same period that examines women's oppression, will illustrate. Unlike "A Jury of Her Peers," *The Awakening* does not thematize the way women come to transform their self-understandings through dialogue. Instead, the text aims directly at the reader's intertexts in its dense reworking of various traditions in women's and men's writing in terms of plot, symbols, and narrative style. In this text, the protagonist, Edna Pontellier, recognizes the unsatisfactory confines of her marriage and the entire institution, moves into her own house, and takes a lover. Unable to find, or even to foresee, happiness in this society, she walks into the sea.

Edna grasps early in the novel the deep social story (third-person account) operating within and without her that the women in Glaspell's tale sense only at the end; however, what is at stake for Chopin is also a different third-person account about psychological and symbolic processes that she is not sure the reader will grasp. Edna does not simply walk away from society into the sea; Chopin walks away from the realistic novel, especially *Madame Bovary*, and the implicit sociopsychological models that subtend it.[28] Instead of "undoing" the linguistic assumptions of realism as Flaubert does, Chopin seeks to revise her readers' existing assumptions so they will not read it in the way they would "A Jury of Her Peers." However, the narrator does not give us a Balzacian lecture about how to read; instead she coaxes us toward a new view of the psyche and of the novel. Some of the critique of realism comes through discussion of Edna's relationship to the other arts: her nonrepresentational paintings (*The Awakening*, p. 13), her Schopenhauerian response to music (chapter 9), which goes behind representation to the will itself (p. 27).[29] What is more important for us here is how the narratological dimensions of the changes operate, and chapter 6 of the text provides a good example.

The chapter contains only seven very short paragraphs and appears to be offering an explanation for Edna's actions in the preceding chapter. We find first a report of Edna's confusion: "Edna Pontellier could not have told why, wishing to go to the beach with Robert, she should in the first place have declined, and

---

[28] See Elaine Showalter's "Tradition and the Female Talent," in which she locates the text's originality against the backdrop of other women writers of the time who work in local colorist or sentimentalist modes.

[29] Chopin alludes to Schopenhauer's theory, in which music is elevated over the other arts because of its nonrepresentational character.

in the second place have followed in obedience to one of the two contradictory impulses which impelled her" (p. 14). Then we find a one-sentence paragraph that offers a tentative metaphor for the process: "A certain light was beginning to dawn dimly within her, – the light which, showing the way, forbids it." This "it," then, is the cause of her feelings: "it served to bewilder, it moved her" (p. 14). In the next sentence, the narrator asks us to clarify this for ourselves by bringing to the passage what we already know about novels of development. "In short, Mrs. Pontellier was beginning to realize her position in the universe as a human being and to recognize her relations as an individual to the world within and about her" (pp. 14–15). However, the narrator problematizes these intertexts with irony, since the traditional *Bildungsroman* concerns male protagonists and different problems: "This may seem like a ponderous weight of wisdom to descend upon the soul of a young woman of twenty-eight" (p. 15). The realistic novel usually maps its universe by invoking and expanding the reader's assumptions about the literary and extraliterary world.[30] The protagonist of a novel of development discovers this world through a combination of action and dialogue. In *The Awakening*, much of the important action is internal and beneath the level of consciousness and dialogue, for the style and sociological *idées reçues* of the *Bildungsroman* cannot be brought to a woman's identity crisis.

Edna's relationship with Adele, who is cast in the familiar role of the older advisor, is important not because of what they say – there is an ideological gulf between them – but because her love for Adele permits her to discover repressed psychic resources (p. 15). The narrator confesses that her narrative dilemma parallels Edna's confusion: "But the beginning of things, of a world especially, is necessarily vague, tangled, chaotic, and exceedingly disturbing. How few of *us* ever emerge from such a beginning! How many souls perish in tumult!" (p. 15, my emphasis). The world here is one that the narrator is trying to evoke. She is urging us toward a novelistic world that she, like Edna, has difficulty articulating. The text asks us to loosen our background assumptions about what a person is but does not come out with an alternative third-person account. Instead, the narrator breaks down the existing conventions about building a textual world and reworks symbols through

---

[30] See Philippe Hamon, "Un discours contraint" and my *Realism and the Drama of Reference* for a discussion of the conventions of realistic discourse.

direct commentary: "The voice of the sea is seductive; never ceasing, whispering, clamoring, murmuring ... The voice of the sea speaks to the soul. The touch of the sea is sensuous, enfolding the body in its soft, close embrace" (p. 15). Edna's relationship to the sea is crucial to her renewal, and the narrator is not content to let the reader interpret it.[31] This relationship, like her bond with Adele, is not transmittable in dialogue. In fact, we do not find the reality-testing dialogue of the realistic novel, in which the protagonist seeks to understand and adapt; rather, the heroine knows all too well what narratives await her and seeks inward resources – ways of feeling that are not available in existing culture. The novel thus mixes realism and romance. These resources will help in the telling of new stories like *The Awakening*, a story that Edna could live but not recount.

Because of Edna's rejection of all the existing social and narrative structures and her recovery of a pre-Oedipal world, her story has been ripe for precisely the kind of oscillation that Fraser frames so nicely – the airtight oppression of patriarchal society and the jubilant liberty of the marginalized subject. These two elements are certainly important. What keeps them from being contradictory is the agency of the implied author of the text, whose intertextual revision of the way we map subjectivity is more important than Edna's self-understandings. Indeed, Edna's regressive narcissism, which helps her escape from some aspects of the patriarchy, is itself one of the results of assigning agency to men. Edna cannot stand the give-and-take of intersubjective relations, of mutual recognition with anyone.[32] The text's insistence on *both* intersubjectivity and on the restorative resources of regression is our guide here, not a reading that idealizes Edna's solipsism and demonizes all of nineteenth-century culture. This makes the particularities of Edna's case, and not global patriarchal discourse, take on importance – e.g., the absence of a mother, the ways Leonce actually facilitates Edna's regression by giving her space – the achievements of the other women in the novel and their accommodations with society – e.g., Mlle Reisz. The point here is

---

[31] In "The Second Coming of Aphrodite," Sandra Gilbert emphasizes the mythic, utopian dimension of Edna's journey (Aphrodite being reborn from the sea).

[32] See Cynthia Griffin Wolff's psychoanalytic study "Thanatos and Eros" and Patricia Yaeger's poststructuralist reading of the gaps in the text, "'A Language Which Nobody Understood.'" Yaeger emphasizes the opening of social possibilities, but she gives no account of an agent who can realize them.

that the third-person account can be a story of rejuvenation and not just one of critique. What is going on behind one's back may not just be bad news but unforeseen opportunity. The point of redescribing our self-understandings is not limited to unmasking; redescription can also unfold potential for renewal.

My model of critique and recuperation can also help improve the critical dialogue about postmodern texts, for it is in this dialogue that the conflicts between claims about women's oppression and women's agency appear most dramatically and confusingly. Indeed, a text's value and its feminist character are often defined only negatively against the patriarchy, as we see in the reading of Hélène Cixous. The first line of Cixous's "La Venue à l'écriture," we read, "Au commencement, j'ai adoré." The standard reading of Cixous and of *l'écriture feminine*, in general, is at the level of the sign, and this reading talks of the reversal of binary oppositions. Toril Moi, who makes Kristeva's work her model, cites the oppositions that appear in Cixous's work and comments, "Her whole theoretical project can in one sense be summed up as an effort to undo this logocentric ideology: to proclaim woman as the source of life, power and energy and to hail the advent of a new, feminine language that ceaselessly subverts these patriarchal binary schemes where logocentrism colludes with phallocentrism in an effort to oppress and silence women" (*Sexual/Textual Politics*, p. 105).[33] In the pages that follow, Moi pursues this point with a discussion of Derrida's notion of *différance* and *ecriture*. Here, we see the directionless poststructuralist critical vocabulary of "undoing" and "subverting" tied to "woman." By defining "woman" against the monolithic evil of the patriarchy and not characterizing the productive new subject positions developed by the text, Moi leaves no critical space to assess the achievements of, or the problems with, Cixous's textual strategies.

The deconstructive dimension is only part of the text's complex reworkings of the relationship among language, subjectivity, and value, reworkings that become available through my model. First, we have the intertextual link with the Bible, "Au commencement était la Parole"; this is not simply an undoing of the logos but a challenge to the patriarchal pragmatics that articulates values and

---

[33] Verene Conley makes a similar point to Moi: "Cixous reads and writes at the interstices of Lacan's theory of language – that of the chain of signifiers – and not that of the phallus – and Derrida's différance" (*Hélène Cixous*, p. 9).

subject positions, that uses the "neutral" constative utterance as the paradigm so that other illocutionary forces are simply "propositional attitudes."[34] Instead of the de-positioned report of the installation of the word and its truthful correspondence to things, we see a positioned site of writing – the "je" of the enunciation – and the agency of the subject – the "je" of the utterance – who performs the value of adoration. The absence of a complement frees this value from a developed intention and thus tries to capture the inaugural power of adoration, the privileging of love over truth. The text does not simply "undo" or announce the differends suppressed by existing discourses; it offers a normative challenge and offers its own utopian dimension. By distinguishing linguistic practices in this way, we get a vocabulary for describing a particular moment of subjectivity and the distinctive disclosure of the world associated with that moment. Instead of saying that Cixous offers tales of critique and joy told from an unmappable site, we can say that Cixous offers new ethical practices for subjects to inhabit, put into dialogue, and assess. Such an interpretation requires that we give up understanding "phallocentrism" only through Derrida's ontology of sign or Kristeva's notion of the symbolic order. Neither of these offers an understanding of conceptual revision, intersubjective relations, or innovative linguistic practices. In my model, Kristeva's opposition between the semiotic and the symbolic can be recuperated provided this relationship is not reduced to a nonnegotiable conflict, in which the semiotic either ruptures the symbolic or is repressed by it, but thought of in expressive terms as well.[35] By thinking of writing in these terms, we can contextualize and assess textual practices for the strengths or weaknesses in given situations rather than being forced into the position of opting for or against massive metaphysical categories. Thus, in the example above, we can say

[34] I am using "illocutionary force" to distinguish linguistic practices, thus giving it a power that speech-act theory does not when it reduces illocutionary force to a modality that does not affect content. I develop this idea in chapter 4.

[35] Kristeva keeps ethics locked into Freudian and Lacanian formulations that renounce all connection with the semiotic, the body, and the other. Hence, she calls for a "heretical ethics separated from morality . . . , which makes bonds, thoughts, and therefore the thought of death, bearable: heretic is undeath, love" (*Tales of Love*, p. 247). See Eleanor H. Kuykendall's "Questions for Julia Kristeva's Ethics of Linguistics" in which she concludes that Kristeva "endorses an ethics resolutely located in an irrational, pre-Oedipal preconscious, her conception of 'feminine subjectivity' is, in the end, a contradiction in terms" (p. 191).

that while the linguistic practice evoked by Cixous's text can offer access to pre-Oedipal dimensions of subjectivity and to affective resources blocked by the norm of the disengaged subject, it is not a very desirable position for political debate, in which attention to the boundaries and ethical particulars of one's own self and those of others are crucial.

Conclusion

Critical theory needs to distinguish between meta-theory, theory, and first-order criticism, and the level of theory is the appropriate place to begin, for it is here that we find the most important conflict in contemporary debate emerges. First, we need a theory of the constructing subject that includes language and practices so as to give a rich characterization of ethical/axiological shapes of identity. Second, we need theories that identify conflicts not just between but within linguistic practices. These stories are of three types: (1) causal theories, such as psychoanalysis or sociohistorical explanations; (2) reconstructive (Habermas) accounts of pre-theoretical know-how; (3) stories that are as skeptical of the presuppositions of explanatory stories as they are of self-interpretations (poststructuralist accounts). These stories unmask the self-interpretations of a culture by redescribing them but do not connect these redescriptions to causes since hasty explanations risk reproducing what they are trying to expose. Instead, these stories work with nebulous relational forces, such as power.

The contradictions among these frameworks brought out the need to adopt a meta-theoretical perspective. Meta-theory is a genre of discourse that tries to thematize the conflicts and commonalities among these accounts so as to realize theoretical and first-order needs. Of course, this meta-theoretical space is not neutral terrain divorced from theoretical and first-order commitments, but it is a distinct genre of dialogue that focuses on tensions between competing problematics. My meta-theoretical work has sought to overcome the theoretical rifts among competing problematics by thematizing the sources of the rifts, by bringing out common areas, by arguing against the totalizing claims of power or philosophical idealism, and by distinguishing their incommensurability from incompatibility (chapters 1 and 2). In some cases, my meta-theoretical work resorted to transcendental argument in order to crack a theory's self-presentation so as to open a space for contact with another view – e.g., my argument against poststructuralism's failure to account for its own agency or for ethical/political resources to which it appeals. At other times, the meta-theoretical discussion was directed to the theoretical need for a rich understanding of the constructing subject's complex ethical and axiological shapes. Lastly, I affirmed the importance of the meta-theoretical dimension for democratic hermeneutics, since it is here that many of the contemporary disputes about identities, traditions and problematics need to be situated. Meta-theoretical talk is not a permanent, fixed genre that grounds criteria for theory; rather, it arises in an *ad hoc* fashion when people start to talk past rather than to each other. I brought home the significance of my arguments by looking at conflicts in feminist theories and by offering first-order readings of texts by women that show why we need a rich account of the constructing subject that is open to stories of its own oppression.

My examples so far have concentrated on how theories of dialogical agency need to work together with theories of oppression, but I have not developed an inside view of the dialogical subject's movement among values. I will now turn to Henry James's *The Ambassadors* in order to explore new ways of discussing how the question of value animates the dynamics of language and subjectivity. Instead of concentrating on the meta-theory/theory level, as this chapter did, I will be thickening my theoretical conception of the dialogical subject and then doing first-order criticism to show how it works. My goal will be to recuperate James for current debates so that we avoid reading his work either as a fold in the discourse of power or as a fossil of modern humanism.

4

✛✛

Truth, beauty, and goodness in James's
The Ambassadors

✛✛

In chapter 3, I showed how my model of dialogue helps inform deliberation about women's achievement and oppression; now I will show how extending this model can revivify a canonical modernist text for postmodern ethical dialogue. If my model is to provide a meta-theoretical clarification of the current disputes, it must be able to address the hermeneutic issues posed by these different kinds of texts. I selected *The Ambassadors*, because it presents a subject with the ethical density of the communitarian subject combined with the diversity and mobility of the liberal subject. Indeed, the central drama of the text is the reconfiguration of the subject around shifting ethical and linguistic practices. This drama of "textuality and ethics," to recall Martha Nussbaum's phrase,[1] is absent from most contemporary ethical/political discussions in literary theory and philosophy, as we have seen. Nussbaum's work, which bridges the gap between communitarians and liberals and between philosophy and literature, is the most important ethical reading of James's work in recent theory, but it never seeks to rectify the disjunction of textuality and ethics. Instead, she uses James with Aristotle to show the failure of Anglo-American ethical philosophy, especially liberal theory, to characterize ethical deliberation in a richly satisfying way, in a

---

[1] *Love's Knowledge*, p. 170. While Nussbaum thinks that contemporary theories of "textuality" preclude ethics, she, nonetheless, makes style central to ethics: "Only the style of a certain sort of narrative artist (and not, for example, the style associated with the abstract theoretical treatise) can adequately state certain important truths about the world, embodying them in its shape and setting up in the reader the activities that are appropriate for grasping them" (p. 6). Thus, "Henry James's belief that fine attention and good deliberation require a highly complex, nuanced perception of, an emotional response to, the concrete features of one's own context" could be stated abstractly, but then the text's "formal choices seem to be making a different and incompatible set of claims" (p. 7).

way that can help it address the starting point for ethical reflection: "How should one live?" (*Love's Knowledge*, p. 23). Nussbaum recuperates James's texts, because they highlight the kind of ethical deliberation she thinks is an important corrective to Rawls's liberal depictions of this process – disengaged, rule-governed, action-oriented reflection; however, unlike Sandel and MacIntyre, she tries to supplement and revise Rawls, not reject him.[2] This critique of the Rawlsian subject is important, but she avoids talking about language, communities, and traditions. Indeed, Nussbaum never discusses the communitarian critique of liberalism. Instead, she focuses on the meta-ethical claim for immersion and emotion against detachment and rules, not on first-order considerations of the kinds of practices one is immersed in. Thus, while I agree with her meta-ethical premise, I will direct my attention to giving a textual/linguistic characterization of the ethical dimension of the work and will show how language and ethics are compatible.[3]

To carry out my development, I will draw on the pragmatics of Lyotard, Bakhtin, and John Searle, as well as the neo-Aristotelian vocabulary offered by MacIntyre. Lyotard's *Le Différend* is the most promising poststructuralist theory for reading James, because it develops a philosophical pragmatics that permits us to break with holistic vocabularies at strategic moments. Working with Wittgenstein's notion that language is not a homogeneous system of signification but a miscellany of heterogeneous language games, Lyotard distinguishes among various types of sentences – e.g., cognitive, ethical, aesthetic, etc. – and discusses the dangers of subordinating one type to another or of mediating the *différend* between types. Thus, for Lyotard, analyzing the ways that sentences are linked is a means of unmasking a politics: "Politics consists in the fact that language is not language but sentences" (*Le Différend*, p. 200). Unlike the speech-act theories of Habermas or John Searle, Lyotard's pragmatics makes the sentence, not the person, the agent and thus attacks "the reader's prejudice, anchored in him by centuries of humanism and 'human sciences,' that there is 'man,'

---

[2] Nussbaum connects the critique of Rawls to *The Ambassadors* by using the character of Mrs. Newsome as a caricature of Rawlsian principles and opposing her to Strether's and James's styles of being.

[3] This chapter will not refer to much recent James criticism until after my reading, since this criticism employs approaches I have already examined and since its critique of the Jamesian project serves as a point of departure for my discussion.

that there is 'language,' and that man uses language for his ends" (p. 11). For Lyotard, speaker and listener "are situated in the universe that the sentence presents in the same way as the referent and meaning" (p. 27). While such a view helps us analyze the ways that we are structured by linguistic forms, it does not address satisfactorily the relationship of sentences to various kinds of subjectivity, the history of cultural practices, or the space from which the theorist performs such analyses.[4] For this, we need to complement Lyotard's theory of the constructed subject with MacIntyre's idea of practice and with a pragmatics that gives a place to agency. These complementary philosophical positions will make available the dynamics of value and subjectivity in James's text. The novel does not weave its values into a modernist humanism, as other readings propose; rather, the Jamesian text articulates the tensions among these values and the consequences of these tensions for the subject. The three principal values at work in James's text are the referential (assertive), the ethical, and the aesthetic, which correspond to Kant's three critiques. Kant's works provide common intertexts for James and Lyotard (the centerpiece of *Le Différend* is a reinterpretation of Kant) as well as for major figures in Anglo-Saxon (especially Rawls) and Continental philosophy.

But how do we make pragmatics consistent with the complex narrative of *The Ambassadors*, in which the protagonist's subjectivity is presented not only by his own speech-acts but by a third-person narrator? For my purposes, I shall divide subjectivity into pre-intentional states – those feelings, sensations, etc., that exceed our awareness (unconscious or preconscious) – and intentional states, which are directed acts by which we represent an object of consciousness. This distinction fits the philosophical and nar-

---

[4] Lyotard defines a *différend* as follows: "A *différend* takes place between two parties when the 'settlement' of the conflict that opposes them is made in the idiom of one while the injury from which the other suffers does not signify in that idiom" (*Le Différend*, pp. 24–25). I translate "phrase" as "sentence," not "phrase." As Geoff Bennington points out, "sentence" shows the relationship of the text to the Anglo-Saxon philosophical tradition (*Lyotard: Writing the Event*, pp. 123–24). Lyotard rejects politics as an autonomous genre of discourse and makes it hinge on the question of linkage among sentences (*Le Différend*, p. 200). See his discussion of Marx in "Le signe d'histoire," in *Le Différend* for the potential of the study of the sentence in the critique of ideology. I discuss the strengths and weaknesses of Lyotard's view of language in "Lyotard's Politics of the Sentence."

ratological terms of the preceding chapter and is consistent with Dorrit Cohn's excellent typology of mental representation in *Transparent Minds*. To bring mental acts and speech acts into a common frame, I will use Searle's analogy between speech acts and intentional states:

Intentional states represent objects and states of affairs in exactly the same sense that speech acts represent objects and states of affairs ... In the ... speech act cases there is an obvious distinction between the propositional content "that you will leave the room" and the illocutionary force with which that propositional content is presented in the speech act ... Equally in ... intentional states, there is a distinction between the representative content "that you will leave the room," and the psychological mode, whether belief or fear or hope or whatever, in which one has that content.[5]

For Searle, the content is "the conditions of satisfaction," yet he is not concerned with how this content is realized, a crucial question for the Jamesian text and one that Strether takes up: "It was the proportions that were changed, and the proportions were at all times, he philosophized, the very conditions of perception, the terms of thought" (*The Ambassadors*, p. 196). That is, for James, our concepts are not simply resting in our language waiting to be actualized; rather, they can be modified or recast, though neither characters nor readers can ever make all of their presuppositions explicit. As Searle says, "The understanding of the literal meaning of sentences, from the simplest sentences, such as 'The cat is on the mat,' to the most complex sentences of the physical sciences, requires a pre-intentional Background" (*Intentionality*, p. 145). Hence, Searle agrees with Heidegger and Taylor that intentionality is not transparent but embedded in the cultural practices we live in. Moreover, the text does not simply represent Strether's consciousness, his intentional states, but also, through the narrator's voice, the hero's pre-intentional states. As Paul Ricoeur says, "temporality cannot be spoken about in the direct discourse of a phenomenology; it requires the mediation of the indirect discourse of narration" (*Temps et récit*, p. 349). Thus, the drama of subjectivity in James is not just the drama of consciousness but a movement between two kinds of states and among different kinds of

---

[5] "What is an Intentional State?," p. 260. I use Searle's theory for reasons of economy and accessibility despite my differences with him. Also see Paul Armstrong's fine book *The Phenomenology of Henry James*, which relates concepts from Husserl, Sartre, Ingarden, Heidegger, and others to the work of James.

sentences.[6] The narrator represents states and objects that exceed Strether's intentional acts, and we watch his tenuous subjectivity as it is struck, solicited, and transformed by the welter of impressions that swim in and out of his power to name them.

These intentional states are informed by three principal illocutionary values that appear in the narrator's presentation of Strether's subjectivity. Because the sentences in question are the narrator's rather than Strether's own speech acts, the illocutionary value for the protagonist is reported in the sentence.[7] In the assertive mode, the sentence seeks to locate truth and particular reference, as in the following passage: "The intimation had the next thing, in a flash, taken on a name – a name on which our friend seized as he asked himself if he weren't perhaps really dealing with an irreducible young Pagan. This description – he quite jumped at it – had a sound that gratified his mental ear, so that of a sudden he had adopted it" (*The Ambassadors*, p. 99). In the ethical mode, which has much in common with what Searle calls "commissives," (e.g. promises), "whose point is to commit the speaker to some future course of action," the subject looks for consistency in moral norms, for virtues as well as rules, and the language is frequently argumentative.[8] In the following passage, we see Strether involved in the determination of his principles as well as in the determination of "what" the situation is: "He *must* approach Chad, he must wait for him, deal with him, master him, but he *mustn't* dispossess himself of the faculty of seeing things as they were" (p. 79, my

---

[6] Lyotard prefers the term "presentation" to "intentionality": "A sentence presents a universe . . . There is what is signified, that about which it is signified, to whom and by whom it is signified: a universe" (*Le Différend*, p. 108). Lyotard avoids the concept of intentionality since it is too closely associated with a psychological subject: "Our 'intentions' are tensions to link [sentences] in a certain way that genres of discourse exercise on senders, referents and receivers, meanings. We think that we want to persuade, seduce, convince . . . but this is because a certain genre of discourse – dialectic, erotic, didactic – imposes itself on 'our' sentence and on 'us' its mode of linkage" (p. 197).

[7] As Searle says of reported intentional acts, "The reporter repeats the propositional content but *reports* the illocutionary force" (*Intentionality*, p. 191). In his example, Searle asks us to suppose that a sheriff asks, "Is Howard an honest man?" In the indirect statement the interrogative illocutionary force is reported: "The sheriff asked whether Howard was an honest man."

[8] Searle, *Expression and Meaning*, p. 14. Lyotard distinguishes between normative sentences and sentences of obligation (or prescriptives): "The norm makes a law of the prescription. 'You must perform such an action' says the prescription. The normative sentence adds: 'It's a norm decreed by X or Y'" (*Le Différend*, p. 206). The importance of Lyotard's distinction for my reading emerges later in this chapter.

emphasis). In the aesthetic mode, the subject spins out and plays with possibilities, and this play is informed by a search for harmony or teleology of meaning rather than truth. After returning from Gloriani's party, Strether gets a glimpse of his host, an impression that solicits his imagination: "He was in fact quite able to cherish his vision of it, *play* with it in idle hours, only speaking of it to no one and quite aware he couldn't have spoken of it without appearing to talk nonsense" (pp. 120–21, my emphasis).[9]

The dynamics of these three types of sentences comes from the tensions produced by their incommensurability – that is, there are no necessary links between any two – and by the inevitability of their linkages by genres of discourse (persuasion, laughter, etc.) and other social practices of Woollett and Paris. As Lyotard says, "Linking is necessary but the mode of linkage never is" (*Le Différend*, p. 52). Thus, the incommensurabilities come from two sources: the tensions among the three values at any synchronic moment; and the tensions between the configuration of practices that informs these values for Strether at the beginning and the different configuration that informs them at the end. Incommensurability does not mean each set of practices is unintelligible to the other, for they can be compared with a meta-language. Thus, on one hand, illocutionary force becomes a site where conflicting social practices seek mediation. At the same time, the analysis of the sentence reveals the cost of mediating different values, of suppressing the *différends* among them.

This list of values is not exhaustive, and James's text cannot be easily partitioned. Nonetheless, such an elementary taxonomy will highlight the compatibilities and conflicts among Jamesian values and illustrate the consequences for the subject of living "in" one of these modes (cultural practices) to the exclusion of the others.

In the following example, we see the dynamic interaction of these forces. After going to the theater with Maria Gostrey,

---

[9] The use of the word "play" is informed by Kant's notion of aesthetic judgment, which is founded on "the feeling (of internal sense) of that harmony in the play of mental powers, so far as it can be felt in sensation" (*Critique of Judgment*, p. 65). Other examples of this use of "play" are: "The historic sense in him might have been freely at play – the play under which in Paris indeed it so often winces like a touched nerve" (James, *The Ambassadors*, p. 59); "such were the liberties with which his fancy played after he had turned off to the hillside" (p. 303). There are at least thirteen such usages in *The Golden Bowl*: "This backward speculation had it begun to play, however, would have been easily arrested" (James, *The Golden Bowl*, vol. I, p. 323).

Strether must deal with a new impression for which he has no language:

> It would have been absurd of him to trace the ramifications of the effect of the ribbon from which Miss Gostrey's trinket depended, had he not for the hour, at the best, been so given over to uncontrolled perceptions. What was it but an uncontrolled perception that his friend's velvet band somehow added, in her appearance, to the value of every other item – to that of her smile and of the way she carried her head . . . He had in addition taken it as a starting point for fresh backward, fresh forward, fresh lateral flights. The manner in which Mrs. Newsome's throat was encircled suddenly represented for him, in an alien order, almost as many things as the manner in which Miss Gostrey's was. (*The Ambassadors* p. 42)

In this passage, an impression explodes Strether's system of signification. The simplicity of the object and the language of designation that names it make its effect on Strether a source of embarrassment: "What, certainly, had a man conscious of a man's work in the world to do with red velvet bands?" (p. 42). (Compared to the "somethings" and other invisible referents of the Major Phase, the phrase [red velvet band] is unusually concrete.) In order to develop an adequate language for this referent, Strether takes "flights." We are in James's favorite space – that is, semantic space that is opened and marked by the appearance of a difference. The significance of this object (group of words), "velvet band" is not transparent but part of a system designated by a proper name ("Maria"), not a conceptual language that is adequate to the impression. When language is no longer the instrument by which the subject names familiar objects, both subject and object tremble. Strether is forced to take "flights" for new significations that will make reference possible, and he moves through a space that is not mapped by common nouns but by proper names. (Later Strether uses "Maria" to try to fathom Mme de Vionnet: "Confronted with Mme de Vionnet, he felt the simplicity of his original impression of Miss Gostrey" [p. 150].)[10]

---

[10] This idea of semantic space often comes up in dialogue in which characters talk about "where they are," such as the following exchange between Maria and Strether:

"She's [Mme de Vionnet] coming round to see me – that's for *you* . . . but I don't require it to know where I am."
The waste of wonder might be proscribed; but Strether, characteristically, was even by this time in the immensity of space.
"By which you mean that you know where *she* is?" (*The Ambassadors*, p. 136)

William Veeder notes forty-one different appearances of this expression and its variants ("Strether and the Transcendence of Language," p. 132).

The band is part of an entire belief system, a competing moral tradition that surrounds Maria and that challenges the vocabulary of Woollett. Thus, when he locates the same "image" or "impression" – that is, the complex of language and perception – he finds that "it" no longer has the same meaning or referential resonance. His first stop in his flight is, of course, the way in which Mrs. Newsome's throat is encircled; however, when he gets "there," he finds that the known on which "he" wants to ground his understanding has become "alien": "The manner in which Mrs. Newsome's throat was encircled suddenly represented . . . almost as many things as the manner in which Miss Gostrey's was" (p. 42). Then he extends Mrs. Newsome's resonance by recalling that he once compared her to Queen Elizabeth. This simile unleashes a swarm of "things": "All sorts of things in fact now seemed to come over him, comparatively few of which his chronicler can hope for space to mention. It came over him for instance that Miss Gostrey perhaps looked like Mary Stuart: Lambert Strether had a candour of fancy that could rest gratified for an instant in such an antithesis" (p. 43). By metaphorically extending Mrs. Newsome's meaning, Strether arrives at an opposition that momentarily contains for him the difference generated by the sight of Maria's band. Strether's emotions and sensibility have also moved – that is, the illocutionary force or value of the sentences has changed. Initially, he is confused by the meaning of the band and by his fascination with it. Conceptual knowledge – the language of Woollett that he is presently using – fails, and the mysterious power of the band (which is obviously sexual) plunges him into a frenzied search for a new idiom. When the search stops, the sexual desire and its ethical consequences, as well as the desire for a unifying referential language, have been displaced by an aesthetic satisfaction and a delight in the play of semantic richness. The paradox of aesthetic play is that even though it generates new meanings and referents, the possibilities that it creates do not carry the same referential weight (illocutionary force) as assertive sentences. That is, Strether is able to entertain meanings without considering the world disclosed by these meanings or the consequences of such a disclosure for his subjectivity. Thus, the aesthetic mode does not subsume or embrace possibilities available in other sentences but has its own positionality. Strether is attracted to the play of semantic resemblance and difference that becomes possible only when the forces of assertion and of ethics are diminished. By containing desire within the aesthetic, the subject diminishes the demands of reference and ethics: Who is this person? How am I going to act with her? This is one sentential possibility for the famous Jamesian observer who represses his own positionality.[11]

However, Strether is not so receptive to the contemplation of infinite semantic expansion when he is ready to meet Mme de Vionnet. At this point in the novel, he and Miss Barrace are trying to name Mme de Vionnet's "magnificence." She starts by naming Mme de Vionnet's shoulders: "'No,' said Strether, 'one was *sure* of her shoulders'" (p. 157, my emphasis). When Miss Barrace tries "charm," he replies, "'Of course it's her charm, but we're speaking of the difference.'" Miss Barrace tries to contain the difference by standing above the question and enclosing it within a facile pluralism: "'Well,' Miss Barrace explained, 'she's brilliant, as we used to say. That's all. She's various. She's fifty women.'" But he is waiting with the referential question, albeit a rather clumsy one: "'Ah but only one' – Strether kept it clear – 'at a time'" (p. 157). Contemplation of an indeterminate being without invoking ethical or referential interests is not the same as having to act on the basis of what this person is. This is not to say that Mme de Vionnet "is" a unified person or that she is a succession of unified persons. (For the moment, the idea of narrative identity proposed by Ricoeur and MacIntyre is enough to keep this issue off the table.) My point is that the referential force that truth, ethics, and action require is in conflict with the infinite extension of meaning that we frequently see in the aesthetic mode. The question in James is not whether the aesthetic is an illusion or an isolated value; the aesthetic gives an important space to play, in which we get access to new kinds of truth but lose connection to others; the aesthetic is distinct but not isolated from other values. The question is whether it is appropriate and how it is connected to referential and ethical values. Thus, we see how the connection of value and subjectivity can provide insight that anti-humanistic views of meaning have no way of discussing.[12]

---

[11] See Kaja Silverman's psychoanalytic reading of the Jamesian observer in *Male Subjectivity at the Margins*, pp. 166–81.

[12] Nussbaum discusses how in James's *The Golden Bowl*, Maggie Verver comes to connect the aesthetic and the ethical in the second half of the novel, after holding them apart during the first half (*Love's Knowledge*, pp. 146–47). In *Henry James and the Art of Power*, Mark Seltzer's Foucauldian reading of James explores the

The interaction of these values and referents plunges Strether into a discontinuous ontological drama that can be seen in the text's grammar and diction. That is, the novel dramatizes the continual reconstitution of the hero's subjectivity and world. The most obvious examples appear in sentences in which Strether is an object and an idea or an impression is an actor: "What carried him [Strether] hither and yon was an admirable theory" (p. 57); "the thing indeed really unmistakeable was its rolling over him as a wave that he had been, in conditions incalculable and unimaginable, a subject of discussion" (p. 129). These grammatical constructions, which many have noted,[13] must not be reduced to Strether's psychological nature (e.g., his passivity), but taken as part of the text's innovative evocation of subjectivity and reference. However, the most interesting feature of James's style is his use of nontransitive verbs (copulas, intransitives, passives) in conjunction with abstract nouns and deictics. For example, early in the novel we read, "Nothing could have been odder than Strether's sense of himself as at that moment launched into something of which the sense would be quite disconnected from the sense of his past and which was literally beginning there and then" (p. 20). In this passage, not only is Strether an object rather than an actor, but the cause is unnamed. The world appears in abrupt movements whose relationship to what has come before is differential, not causal. Neither the character nor the narrator is interested in causal explanation; rather, we see an ontological rupture that explodes subject and object. The "something" is not an entity that is outside of him but a force that envelops his subjectivity, and the narrator does not offer a master vocabulary that tells the reader what is "really" going on. Unlike aesthetic sentences in which the subject plays with meanings, these sentences have "bewilderment" as their illocutionary value for Strether. (I allude to James's well-known line from the Preface to *The Princess Casamassima*: "if we were never bewildered there would never be a story to tell about us.")[14] If the aesthetic sentence is like Kant's discussion of the beautiful where the faculties are in harmony, "bewilderment" is James's ontological rewriting of the sublime, in which the subject's

complicity between his understanding of art and the material conditions from which he wished to keep it separate.
[13] See, for example, Seymour Chatman, *The Later Style of Henry James*.
[14] James, *The Art of the Novel*, p. 63.

categories and practices are overthrown. The differences that produce bewilderment are not simply "ambiguities," "gaps," or polysemic possibilities that we find in the epistemological workings of the phenomenological subject; rather, they are ontological ruptures that fracture the very site of comparison between this "something" and all that came before.[15] As Maria says to Strether early in the novel, "'Nothing for you will ever come to the same thing as anything else'" (p. 53). This is not to say that all referents are unique but that the power of these "somethings" cannot be contained within the existing ontological horizon.

The ontological drama of the text anticipates the concerns of postmodernism, as Brian McHale says: "The dominant of postmodern fiction is *ontological*. That is, postmodern fiction deploys strategies which engage and foreground questions" such as these: "'Which world is this? What is to be done in it? Which of my selves is to do it?'" (*Postmodern Fiction*, p. 10).[16] This linguistic and ontological drama is obscured by James's own critical vocabulary and plot structures – that is, the perceptual and epistemological vocabulary that he employs in his *Prefaces* (e.g. point of view, reflector, "house of fiction") – and his use of secrets and centers of focalization to structure plots.[17] These features have led critics to categorize James's work as "modernist," which McHale defines as follows, "the dominant of modernist fiction is *epistemological*. That is, modernist fiction deploys strategies which engage and foreground questions such as ... 'How can I interpret this world of which I am a part? And what am I in it'" (p. 9). But such a reading of *The Ambassadors* misses the whole point. Everyone knows "what" the secret is (the sexual nature of Chad's affair with Mme de Vionnet) except for Strether. The drama of the story is not hide and seek with the secret but the ethical/axiological reconstitution of self

[15] I develop the idea of ontological discontinuity in "The Drama of Reference in James' The Golden Bowl," and "Maggie Verver's Ontological Voyage," chapter 8 in *Realism and the Drama of Reference*.

[16] McHale claims that if we examine "the various catalogues of features [of postmodernism] proposed by Lodge, Hassan, Wollen, and Fokkema ... we would find ... that most (if not all) of these features could easily be seen as strategies for foregrounding ontological issues. In other words, it is the ontological dominant which explains the selection in clustering of these particular features; the ontological dominant is the principle of systematicity underlying these otherwise heterogeneous catalogues" (*Postmodern Fiction*, p. 10).

[17] See chapter 5, *Realism and the Drama of Reference*, in which I discuss Todorov's and Jameson's reading of James.

and world around such mysteries. The novel anticipates the postmodern preoccupation with ontology at the same time that it participates in the modern preoccupation with epistemology.

Of course, *The Ambassadors* does not speak to many aspects of postmodern experience, as more recent fiction does – e.g., the way the subject is imploded and flattened by social and economic forces, to use Jameson's well-known point.[18] However, the novel contributes to postmodern dialogue in three important ways. First, it shows how language and ethics can work to enrich our ontological dramas so that those dimensions of our lives that are not dominated by overpowering and often unnameable forces are given a place; postmodern fiction, like postmodern theory, tends to foreground the constructed subject and the bankruptcy of ethical practices. Second, it shows how reflexivity and fragmentation are simply moments of postmodern experience and not such deep or totalized "truths" about the postmodern world that any claims for reference or coherence are simply old-fashioned and misguided. Such a view flirts with the performative contradiction of taking a position that does not account for its own utterance; that is, this postmodern position takes on a kind of nostalgia for a God's-eye narrative, since it presumes to stand outside narrative in order to judge its failure. I read the postmodern features in James as prospective appeals to postmodernism to think in terms of the fallibility and incompleteness of narrative that points to the need for perpetual reworking rather than to the failure.[19] Third, the postmodern reading of James includes a meta-critique of his fictional norms and of his ethical/political limits.

One way to grasp James's contribution to postmodern dialogue in theory and literature is to look at what separates Henry's text from the pragmatism of his brother or Rorty.[20] What separates Henry from the pragmatists is that pragmatists believe that the collapse of foundationalist philosophy based either on the subject or the external world can simply be recognized and appropriated

[18] See Jameson's discussion of the subject of postmodernism in chapter 1 and the conclusion of *Postmodernism*.

[19] See the last two chapters of Gerald Prince's *Narrative as Theme*, in which he shows how the works of Claude Simon and Patrick Modiano emphasize the need to rework narrative in the face of its fallibility and incompleteness rather than the failure of narrative as judged against some nostalgic hope for final truth.

[20] In *The Trial of Curiosity*, Ross Posnock develops the connections between Henry and William and the importance of the work for contemporary thought.

by the subject – i.e., since we know there are no foundations for epistemology, we need to proceed instrumentally according to what is useful. William James, who precedes Rorty in rewriting truth into what it is efficacious to believe, shows an impatience with language in his famous complaint about the style of the Major Phase:

The method seems perverse: "Say it out for God's sake," they cry, "and have done with it." And so I say now, give us one thing in your older directer manner ... For gleams and innuendoes and felicitous verbal insinuations you are unapproachable, but the core of literature is solid.[21]

In William's formulation, Henry's novels are about "something" that could be stated clearly in another language. William's pluralistic view of the universe does not consider the irreducible dimension of language in generating these worlds. Even though we find common metaphors in both of their writings (e.g., water and organicism) the fluid relations that William finds among different spheres (e.g., ethics, truth, etc.) contrast with Henry's concern for the textuality of conflicting values in the construction of subjectivity. In Henry's text, water charts the flow of subjectivity beneath the intentionality of speech and perception, but it is not a privileged ontological metaphor. Rorty shows a similar impatience with, and disinterest in, the dynamics of language, subjectivity, and value, as if the end of foundationalist metaphysics rendered such issues moot. Strether's movement in the novel is not from Woollett's absolutes to a pragmatic pluralism; rather, we see an ethico-ontological drama, in which the subject undergoes experiences that fracture the integrity of the self and then seeks to establish a self-understanding and a narrative about this self-understanding that tells how he got there.

If the sight of Maria's band starts to alienate Strether from the language of Woollett, the sight of Chad carries this process even further and makes him change his way of approaching the world, so that aesthetic value dominates truth and ethics. Chad is the point of reference that Strether has with Woollett. If they can agree on a description, then they will work together. When he sees Chad and recognizes the "sharp rupture of an identity," most of the categories that bind him to Mrs. Newsome evaporate: "A personal relation was relation so long as people perfectly understood or

---

[21] *Letters of William James*, vol. II, p. 278.

better still didn't care if they didn't. From the moment they cared if they didn't it was living by the sweat of one's brow" (pp. 90, 92). The tension between the referring and describing functions of proper names explodes. Names, Searle says, "enable us to refer publicly to objects without being forced to raise issues and come to agreement as to which descriptive characteristics exactly constitute the object" (*Speech Acts*, p. 172). However, the space of Jamesian reference is not physical but moral. No one in the novel disagrees about Chad's physical location, but Strether is confused by the beauty of Chad's presence and looks for ethical, aesthetic, and referential practices that can embrace him. Strether's dilemma dramatizes MacIntyre's point about how the issue of reference is deeply embedded in moral tradition. The descriptive and referring functions cannot be separated out if rival traditions (Woollett and Paris) are at issue. MacIntyre says, "Names are used *as* identification *for* those who share the same beliefs, the same justifications of legitimate authority, and so on. The institutions of naming embody and express the shared standpoint of the community and characteristically its shared traditions of belief and enquiry" (*Whose Justice?*, p. 378). James shows what is involved when one loses a sense of embeddedness in a tradition, becomes aware of the virtues of another, and seeks to invent and inhabit a new ethical space.

In order to gain access to such a framework, Strether recognizes that he must abandon "his odious suspicion of any form of beauty . . . He periodically assured himself – for his reactions were sharp – that he shouldn't reach the truth of anything till he had at least got rid of that" (*The Ambassadors*, p. 118). One of Strether's ethical principles is not simply the fulfillment of his duty and the condemnation of Chad's behavior but a commitment to truth, to find out what the situation is, as we saw earlier: "He mustn't dispossess himself of the faculty of seeing things as they were" (p. 79). When he sees Chad, Strether revises the practices that enable him to describe and refer to "things" that are not in his present world. Such a revision has consequences for the way he phrases his experience. Strether does not simply acquire more "knowledge" or "expand" the horizon of his existence. The Jamesian text does not work like a *Bildungsroman*, in which the protagonist moves from ignorance to mastery, from the provincial to MacIntyre's liberal cosmopolitan self who is at home everywhere and nowhere, even though Strether tries to give such a reading of his life near the end of the novel. Instead, we see Strether's positionality change.[22] Indeed, a new practice may take away or transfigure all that someone takes for knowledge. When two rival traditions confront each other, what counts as an adequate translation in one may not count as adequate in the other (MacIntyre, *Whose Justice?*, p. 381). Moreover, such incompatibilities occur not only in names but in lists of virtues. As MacIntyre says, "By ascribing a particular virtue to someone a speaker precludes that person's having a certain range of vices" (p. 381). We can see such incompatibilities in the different understandings of "Chad" and "Paris" offered by Paris, Woollett, and Strether.

The principal effect of these new practices appears in Strether's elision of referential and aesthetic sentences and his repression of ethical ones. One of the verbs that enacts the linkage of the assertive and aesthetic values is "appreciate." When Strether speaks of Sarah's obtuseness, he says, "'She doesn't appreciate him [Chad]'" (*The Ambassadors*, p. 245).[23] There are countless examples of aesthetic vocabulary applied to actions. "The mother's eagerness with which Mme de Vionnet jumped at this was to come to him later as beautiful in its grace" (p. 151). (This is a feature of Parisian vocabulary – Bilham says that the relationship of Chad and Mme de Vionnet is "quite beautiful" [p. 123].) Strether begins to confuse the aesthetic and referential, so that the artistic analogies he uses to read people and places become fetishized objects of contemplation. During his reflections on Mme de Vionnet, we read, "Her head, extremely fair and exquisitely festal, was like a happy fancy, a notion of the antique, on an old precious medal, some silver coin of the Renaissance" (p. 160). Proper names lose their reference in aesthetic sentences and become a hook for the play of analogy. James's texts give many examples of the way sentences that first appear in the aesthetic mode are appropriated by referential sentences. The slippage then goes from referential to ethical sentences. The most obvious examples of characters who

---

[22] James was aware that his material was hackneyed and could be read without appreciation – e.g., Jim Pocock's reading of Strether in the novel.

[23] For other examples of "appreciation" or "appreciate," see pp. 45, 61, 68, 92, 322, and 327, where it appears as a rationalization by Strether of the unscrupulous business practices of the Newsomes. There, of course, are changes at the level of the word as well. For example, "virtuous" in the phrase "virtuous attachment" has a different meaning in the first part (p. 112) than it does at the end (p. 330).

use artistic analogies to control others are Gilbert Osmond in *The Portrait of a Lady* and Adam Verver in *The Golden Bowl*, as many critics have noted. That is, the presence of an artistic analogy does not mean that an aesthetic illocutionary value is present.

Strether quickly becomes attached to the aesthetic mode, and one of the means by which he achieves this is Chad; the young man becomes the link between Strether's past and his present. At Gloriani's, Strether is hit by "an assault of images" (p. 120), the most powerful of which is the vision of Gloriani himself.

Was what it had told him or what it asked him the greater of the mysteries? Was it the most special flare, unequalled, supreme, of the aesthetic torch, lighting that wondrous world for ever, or was it above all the long straight shaft sunk by a personal acuteness that life had seasoned to steel? . . . [I]t was for all the world to Strether just then as if in the matter of his accepted duty he had been positively on trial. (p. 121)

Gloriani's face wrenches Strether from the comfortable seat of speaker in his consciousness. In these sentences, Gloriani not only appears as an admirable figure for contemplation but as a challenge to Strether's values and his self. Gloriani is not only a fully realized alternative to Woollett; he is a man who has achieved this difference without the psychic wound that leaves Strether so afraid and subject to domination. The hero's response to this challenge is complex. Strether starts to revise his ethical practice, so that goodness is comprised not only of a narrow conception of duty but also of a notion of self-development. Ethics is no longer merely the avoidance of wrong (a morality of laws) but a morality of virtues, an active practice that brings the concepts of beauty and excellence into his idea of what one ought to do and be. He sees this kind of ethics in Chad as well as Gloriani, and it is a practice that is not possible in Woollett. However, in making this revision, he tries to write himself out of the sentences of obligation; he wants to be the all-knowing spectator who makes the "right" judgments – beyond moral or referential reproach. It is just such obfuscatory fusion that the text shows to be unethical. Strether's rewriting is driven by his fear, by his sense of being on "trial," but this story of repetition does not negate his achievement; rather, it helps us understand how first- and third-person perspectives can work together without canceling each other out.

Thus, even though Strether feels drawn toward the figure of

Gloriani, he also retreats from this vision with declarations that make action impossible. He says that for him "it is too late" but that Bilham should follow the moral injunction derived from his vision: "'live all you can'" (p. 132). Strether continues to seal off the challenge by moving to universal propositions about the forces that determine all actions: "It's ["the affair of life"] at best a tin mould ... into which, a helpless jelly, one's consciousness is poured – so that one 'takes' the form" (p. 132). Thus, he tries to step away from the challenge and to explain it in a way that makes his choice to remain a spectator a scientific conclusion, not an ethical decision. Having lost his language of ethics and truth, Strether decides to adopt the aesthetic mode, to give himself up to "appreciation." That is, as we noted earlier, Strether starts to repress the incommensurability that separates assertive and ethical statements from aesthetic ones. Moreover, he does not simply make statements to this effect but comes to live "in" this choice.

At this point, we need to address how gender informs the dynamics of Strether's psychic economy and ethical development. At the beginning of the novel, Strether judges himself to be a failure because he is not, like Waymarsh, a successful businessman. Thus, he pursues that of social and aesthetic practices – ways of speaking, thinking, and being – that do not exist as "things" of value in Woollett, for they are not material products that one gets in exchange for the performance of certain behavior – what MacIntyre calls "external goods" – but rewards that result from this behavior, such as insight and pleasure.[24] Moreover, the pursuit of such goods is blocked, because they are "acquired" through an ethic of self-cultivation. Strether recognizes that "there was a whole side of life on which the perfectly usual was for leading Woollett business-men to be out of the question" and that Woollett society "was essentially a society of women" (p. 213). Thus, his own participation "was an odd situation for a man." In this society, the "sins" of business are, in Maria's words, "expiated" (pp. 50, 52) through such projects as Mrs. Newsome's review. Aesthetic sentences thus play an important role in the economy of

---

[24] See chapter 2 for a full discussion of MacIntyre. For this distinction between internal and external goods, see *After Virtue*, pp. 181–203. He gives the example of getting a child to play chess by offering him candy – an external good – and then watching the child start to play for the internal goods he gets – "in the achievement of a particular kind of analytic skill, strategic imagination, and competitive intensity" (p. 187).

Woollett's cultural practices. Strether's refusal to name the product that is responsible for the Newsome fortune parodies the way the aesthetic tries to disown its material connections.[25] This gender split is not just about different ideas of the good life; rather, it is informed by the structure of domination described by Benjamin (see chapter 3), a structure that gives agency only to men and undermines intersubjectivity among all people. Strether has slipped off the male socialization track. For our purposes, we can simply say that Strether, like many Jamesian heroes, has not fully identified with the father and emerges from the Oedipal drama as a wounded narcissist who cannot take up the male subject positions of domination. Although he is critical of men produced by Woollett, he is still haunted by this "failure." His failure is not just a product of chance but of his inability/unwillingness (third- or first-person account) to fit into the roles available to him without the internalized authority to carve out an alternative. Instead, he submits to a phallic mother who controls his financial and moral life while offering him an acceptable, though menaced, position outside the agony of male competition. In Paris, he finds a society with a different axiology, an axiology that esteems the aesthetic uniqueness of social beings. This permits him to redescribe himself in fantasies that do not have to submit to intersubjective judgment and to revenge himself against Woollett (the men and Mrs. Newsome).

The Jamesian subject's deviation from male socialization opens new possibilities, as my reading has emphasized, but it also has weaknesses. I will mention the most important weakness for the intersection of the psychological and the ethical – the problem of autonomy. Strether does not simply reject Woollett's idea of autonomy; he is still controlled by a fear that makes any identity a painful and fragile reaction to the demands of others. Even though he is extremely sensitive to the possibilities of fine-tuned intersubjective relations, as well as to the incommensurabilities in dialogue, he is unable to place himself inside a dialogue exchange as an ideal ethical being – that is, as a being with defined, yet porous, boundaries. Strether's boundaries are porous, but he is incapable of articulating his shape in intersubjective space, of becoming a

[25] For James's relationship to feminism, see Carren Kaston's *Imagination and Desire in the Novels of Henry James* and Priscilla Walton, *The Disruption of the Feminine in Henry James*.

realized agent equipped for give and take with others. He still occupies a distinctly male position. Strether's extraordinary vulnerability helps keep him from what everyone else knows and enables him to develop important and productive linguistic fantasies; however, the achievement is built on a structural problem. By attending carefully to others' words, by reinterpreting them with blindness and insight, and by keeping back his self-descriptions, he can escape embodiment, always have the last word, the final rewrite of the text of his life. This quest to be sublimely unreadable maintains his self-esteem and his fragile sense of autonomy, but this is achieved at the cost of relationships with others. My reading of the rest of the story will show how this process works.

Before pursuing Strether's uses of the aesthetic, we need to consider not only the sentences but the narratives in which Strether locates himself. When he arrives in Europe, his principal narrative is that of the ambassador who goes to bring Chad back. The narrative depends on a stable ontology that offers criteria for knowledge and value. The text dramatizes the disintegration of this story around the proper names – "Chad," "Mme de Vionnet," "Paris," and "Strether" – whose referential, ethical, and aesthetic value cannot be phrased in his linguistic practices. At crucial moments, the text's narrative movement is suspended – usually through past perfect retrospection – so that we find the sentential drama of value and subjectivity that we saw with Maria's band, not a temporal sequence. (For other examples of this movement around a name, see "Paris," pp. 64–65, "Chad," 89–94.) Another narrative – the story of Strether's life independent of his relationship with Mrs. Newsome, a story that does not use the same lexicon or narrative structure – begins to dominate his thinking. The conflict between these two narratives emerges in the first sentence of the novel. ("Strether's first question, when he reached the hotel, was about his friend; yet on learning that Waymarsh was apparently not to arrive till evening he was not wholly disconcerted" [p. 17].) However, when Strether starts to phrase his life in the aesthetic mode, he tries to suspend this conflict by giving himself over to a *Bildungsroman* that will serve as a preliminary to choosing between the alternatives.

Perhaps the most important step in his adoption of this mode is the substitution of Chad for the threatening and unfathomable figure of Gloriani. Instead of confronting an alien presence whose maturity forces Strether to question his present self, Strether places Chad at the center of his reveries. Chad has the familiarity of New England and the youth that engages Strether's image of his own past. The switch occurs while Strether admires "the glossy male tiger" (Gloriani) (p. 133) – a menacing sexual image unlike any that Strether applies to Chad – and asks Bilham if he knows who he (Strether) should enjoy being like. Bilham follows Strether's eyes and guesses Gloriani. However, at this moment "another impression had been superimposed" (p. 133), as Strether sees Chad with Jeanne de Vionnet: "Chad was, oh yes, at this moment – for the glory of Woollett or whatever – better still than Gloriani" (p. 134). In Chad, Strether finds a surrogate, so that he can avoid the direct challenge of Gloriani – the sentence of obligation – and yet participate in the world he imagines.

Moreover, aesthetic value can conflict with ethical as well as referential value. An easy way to see this is through Strether's question to Bilham at Gloriani's party: "'You've all of you here so much visual sense that you've somehow all "run" to it. There are moments when it strikes one that you haven't any other.' 'Any moral,'' little Bilham explained" (p. 126). Strether's question is not just a defensive Puritanism but a question about ethics. Indeed, this lack that he sees may result not in tolerance but in a rigid, moral code. The ethical sense in James is not just a supple sensibility for an individual's values and language, for the ways in which the individual transcends the categories of society, but a crack in the fortress of the self. This absence of a moral sense should not be equated with any specific behavior (e.g., libertinism); rather, it means the absence of a moral dimension of experience. The brutality and inflexibility of the judgment of the apparently refined Parisian society is what Mme de Vionnet fears so and why she feels such refuge in talking to Strether. If the complexity of European civilization enriches the possibilities of social being, this tradition also threatens to ossify the moral imaginations of those who live in it.

Strether must endure the consequences of his attachment to the aesthetic mode, an attachment that culminates in the famous recognition scene. Here, Strether goes to the country in order to escape the pressure of the Americans, the Parisians, and his own desires. Strether's physical distance from the others becomes aesthetic distance when he begins to indulge in analogies between art and the landscape. By writing his situation in the aesthetic mode, Strether redirects these pressures into sentences that suspend issues of truth and goodness, as well as the question of narrative. At the beginning of the scene, we read, "It [this area] had been as yet but a land of fancy for him – the background of fiction, the medium of art, the nursery of letters" (p. 301). Strether has come to use the aesthetic mode as a means of repressing and displacing sexual desire as well as his ethical and referential values.

Strether's reverie culminates when he feels the unity of this semantic space, a unity that is called "the thing": "the thing, as he would have called it ... was the thing that implied the greatest number of the things of the sort that he had to tackle" (p. 306). This thing is then called a "text," which "was simply, when condensed, that in *these* places such things were" (p. 306, my emphasis). Strether's aesthetic play produces a new word but the force of this word is meta-linguistic. The function of "the thing," like the words "picture," and "text," is to name and give ontological force to the difference between Woollett and the world in which he finds himself, a force that is emphasized by the demonstrative. The "thing" is like a Kantian Idea that organizes the play of signification but that has no ostensive reference. If the aesthetic play permits such creation, it also insulates the subject from other modes of engagement with himself and the world.

Thus, Strether's drama becomes an allegory of the problematic of interpretation, in which Roland Barthes's textual play confronts E. D. Hirsch's intentionality. James's text rewrites the demands of both. If subject and object are both products of texts, so that neither intention nor reference has an extratextual ground, this does not obliterate referential value in favor of aesthetic value. Without the free play, the subject closes itself off from enrichment; without the value of reference, aesthetic sentences spin possibilities that lose the power to disclose the world, that lose their link to the referential and ethical values that seek particular individuals. Strether must move from contemplation in an aesthetic mode to the ethical mode of choice and action, where he must determine what things are and how to act. If we find Strether's subjectivity de-centered and pluralized, we also see the demand for agency. Strether is not just a text but an agent. If this cultivation of the aesthetic mode has helped to establish intersubjective relations with Marie and Chad, it has also blinded him to what they are. Mesmerized by beauty, he forgets the challenge of truth, the impossibility of containing flux in a "picture." The couple's appearance on the water draws the self and the world back from fantasies of containment.

This is not to say that Strether's misunderstanding vindicates the language of Paris or of Woollett, since both communities were "right" about the sexual nature of Chad's relationship. Such an empiricist reading, which uses a limited "error" to reduce Strether's new language to "illusion," does not account for the ontological drama of the text. Strether has worked out his own language and practice, and he does not retreat to the assumptions of either community. Instead, he moves to solidify his language through conversations with the three people who have participated in his development – Maria, Chad, and Mme de Vionnet – conversations in which Strether and his interlocutors articulate their differences.

Of course, Strether's language includes a dimension of fantasy and self-mystification, but here is where we need to clarify the relationship between philosophy of language and identity. On the one hand, we are embedded in holistic webs of language that make massive errors about our understanding of the world unthinkable. On the other hand, we are such profound mysteries to ourselves that we must struggle to get a grip on the reality of our selves and others through various therapeutic and analytic dialogues. In the former case, the reality of our world is a presupposition; in the latter, it is an achievement. We need to keep both of these in mind so that we neither dismiss Strether's language as a mere illusion nor elevate it to a sacred constitution. Strether's fantasies offer new possibilities for disclosure at the same time that they are fraught with weaknesses for him and others. Other people's fantasies can always be our truths. Nonetheless, I do not want to offer Strether as the Jamesian ethical ideal nor the ideal that I would propose. To show his limits, I will focus on Strether's final dialogues with Maria, in which linguistic sophistication works with the failed autonomy we saw earlier.

What dominates these scenes is the presence of Strether's new narrative for his life. This emerges when he explains his stay in Paris by Mme de Vionnet's beauty: "'A basis seemed to me just what her beauty supplied'" (p. 330). Strether has moved out of the present into retrospective teleological explanations. (Before the recognition scene, he could confess, "'What I want is a thing that I've ceased to measure or even to understand'" [p. 294].) Now, however, we see his narrative become prospective as well, and beauty, or "magnificence," as he says this time, once again becomes the thread of the plot: "'Well, that's what just once in all my dull days, I think I shall have been'" (p. 194). The future perfect tense shows how Strether leaps to the end of this part of his life in order to look back on it as a narrator. He starts to situate himself in a story that already decides the questions that Maria is posing. He speaks from the site of a future self who has already left.

This narrative of magnificence reemerges in the next scene when he says: "'That, you see, is my only logic. Not, out of the whole affair, to have got anything for myself'" (p. 344). His justification is that he wants "'to be right'" (p. 344). Here, we see the vocabulary of Woollett in this teleological narrative justification. The narrative genre is particularly adept at reconciling and obscuring *différends*, as Lyotard points out: "The multitude of types of genres and genres of discourse finds a way to neutralize *différends* in narratives" (*Le Différend*, p. 228). If we wish to ascribe an intention to this usage, we could say that Strether uses Woollettese in order to emphasize his differences from Maria, to show that he does not belong and thus make his departure easy. At the same time, this statement permits him to give himself some cover from Woollett's judgment, a judgment that still operates inside, as well as outside, him. (James's characters are never postconventional – that is, they never subject existing social norms to a full interrogation.) Maria instantly challenges this claim – and the presupposition that he is the master of his language – by saying that he has gotten a good deal, his "wonderful impressions" (*The Ambassadors*, p. 344). The "anything" that Strether refers to is what I, following MacIntyre, have called an "external good" – that is, a good that is "externally and contingently attached to" a given practice (MacIntyre, *After Virtue*, p. 188) – e.g., money to an athlete. This "anything" makes sense only in the vocabulary of Woollett. Maria checks his attempt to avoid her by pointing out that they now share a vocabulary in which "impressions" – that is, "internal goods" that are acquired through participation in a cultural practice – also count as things. However, it is more than Strether's "'being right'" that troubles Maria: "'It isn't your *being* "right" – it's your horrible sharp eye for what makes you so'" (*The

Ambassadors, p. 345). Strether is not simply a speaker who is situated within a narrative that tells him what values to pursue; he also stands outside of this first-order narrative. His "horrible sharp eye" is focused on a larger narrative he wants to bring about and not on the demand that Maria is making on him. The meta-self represented by this "eye" and situated in this superordinate narrative, is not in a dialogue with Maria but only with Strether's internal demands (including his reformulation of the demands of others). By refusing to step out of this evasive narrative, he does not permit the present to erupt. As Lyotard says, "One never knows what *Ereignis* is . . . The mistake is to anticipate it – that is, to forbid it" (*Le Différend*, p. 129). Using narratives to reposition oneself outside of a dialogical encounter with others appears most notably in "The Beast in the Jungle."[26] In this tale, the hero cloaks himself in the story of the beast as a way of escaping contact with others and himself. James's texts expose the ethical shortcomings of these fantasy narratives by his fearful heroes.

Strether's ethical failure is driven home when he makes explicit his consideration of Maria as a thing in the aesthetic economy of renunciation. He says that she is something that he cannot have: "'It's you who would make me wrong'" (*The Ambassadors*, p. 345). The decision is then held up and played with by both of them, as they feel all that lies behind this statement – e.g., Strether's love for Mme de Vionnet and his feelings for Maria, which are primarily feelings of understanding and concern but not desire. However, Strether does not desire to have Mme de Vionnet but to be like her, to be magnificent, and this kind of magnificence requires suffering that is incompatible with Maria's offer. Strether then outflanks Maria's accusation by saying that his "horrible sharp eye" is just what makes him desirable for her: "'You can't resist me when I point that out'" (p. 345). But Maria – no doubt weary with his agonistics – repeats only "'I can't resist you.'" In the last line of the novel, Strether takes Maria's retort, and, indeed, the entire text to this point and puts it in a "picture," a statement that gestures toward an all-embracing semantic space that objectifies them – he says "there," not "here" – and that forecloses any action: "'Then *there* we are'" (p. 345, my emphasis). By making "then" both a logical and temporal link to all that has preceded, Strether moves

---

[26] See my "Narration and the Face of Anxiety in James's 'The Beast in the Jungle'" for development of the role of narrative as means of escape.

out of the horizon of their conversation and lets himself off. This meta-textual gesture by which he seals his rhetorical victory does not close the text. (Indeed, Strether's line is a *mise en abyme* of the nineteenth-century narrator's gesture of closure.) Rather, the sentence exposes the ways that such speculative sentences mask the tensions that inform them – the tension between the "I" of the enunciation and the "I" of the utterance, between argument and narrative, between the two individuals of the "we," etc. Strether's closing statement foregrounds the way the heterogeneity of sentences can never be overcome but only provisionally bridged for certain purposes.

Because the Jamesian text shows the dynamic mobility of the subject in negotiating changes in ethical and linguistic practices, it has a meta-philosophical importance for us today that transcends many of its dated particulars.[27] Nonetheless, the Jamesian text does not represent an unassailable ethical/political ideal; it can figure in unflattering stories of various types as well. I would criticize Jamesian ethics for the way it ignores relationships among strangers, for its cultural conservatism, for its suffocating intellectualizing, and for the shallowness of its liberal understanding of culture.[28] Moreover, James's theory and practice of the novel have been used as doctrine to exclude other writers. James's texts do not have much to say about race or class relations, and these omissions are important, particularly in the formation of the American canon. However, it does not necessarily follow that his texts are politically useless. Indeed, part of my point is that the dynamics of language, ethics, and subjectivity in James can improve the way we talk about ethics and politics today. In contemporary theory, there is a tendency to react against the denial of the political by conservatives and aestheticists with the platitude "everything is political." Of course, there is a political dimension to everything, and all dimensions of culture need to be interrogated. The

---

[27] This is the claim MacIntyre, Nussbaum, and Gadamer make for Aristotle.

[28] Nussbaum makes an important defense of James against the charge of elitism. She distinguishes between an aristocratic ideal – "that only members of a certain class have, by nature, the refinement of mind that is essential to good governing, and that they therefore should govern for everyone" (*Love's Knowledge*, p. 201) – and "a perfectionist view that insists that not all human lives are equally complete, equally flourishing – even where moral development itself is concerned – and that it is so, in great part, because the central human capabilities have, for their development, material and educational necessary conditions that are not, as things are in most actual societies, available to all" (p. 201).

question is whether the text has to address all of the political matters on the current agenda in order to avoid blanket condemnation. In order to particularize my own critique of James, I will not just read him through the grid of contemporary theory; instead, I will give my reading of James a different interlocutor – Ralph Ellison. In Ellison's work, we see the need to excavate, critique and recuperate the ethical/political resources of American, African American, and European cultures in a way no Jamesian text ever does. As Ellison says, "The diversity of American life with its extreme fluidity and openness seemed too vital and alive to be caught for more than the briefest instant in the tight well-made Jamesian novel, which was for all its artistic perfection, too concerned with 'good taste' and stable areas . . . Understatement depends after all, upon commonly held assumptions and my minority status rendered all such assumptions questionable" (*Shadow and Act*, p. 103).

The subject of democracy in the work of Ralph Ellison

Ralph Ellison's work is the most complex ethical/political work discussed thus far, for it employs the ethical vocabularies of liberals, communitarians, and radicals. Ellison speaks the language of the liberal, who affirms individualism, justice, and liberty; he also speaks the language of the communitarian, who extols the virtues of different traditions and who is critical of liberal neutrality toward alternative views of the good; lastly, he plays the role of the radical, who excavates and unmasks the self-understandings of American culture across racial lines. In his work, the dynamics of language and subjectivity are ceaselessly called into question in a way they never are in James. For Ellison, the culture in which we are embedded is a deceptive one that must be relentlessly critiqued; unlike poststructuralists, however, Ellison does not set up the site of critique on an unspecifiable planet. He recognizes that cultural critique requires resources from the very ethical/political traditions that he is attacking. There is nowhere else to go. But how does he do this? What kind of site or subject position(s) enables Ellison to move with such flexibility among these vocabularies? Ellison himself takes up this issue in many of his works, particularly *Invisible Man*, which can be read as a meta-philosophical quest for a site for the telling of his story. This meta-philosophical dimension of his work will synthesize and dramatize the theoretical questions I have addressed throughout the book. Ellison's search for a site parallels my own meta-critical search for a more productive site for theoretical discussion.

I will divide the chapter into two sections. In the first, I will set the stage for my analysis by looking at some contemporary debate on the issue of race. I do this because it is impossible to get access to Ellison's work without sorting out this debate. In the second part, I use my critical model to dialogue with Ellison's understanding of tradition, democracy, oppression, and liberalism.

Agents and constructs in racial politics

"The major function of Afro-American critical thought is to reshape the contours of Afro-American history and provide a new self-understanding of the Afro-American experience which suggests guidelines for action in the present."   Cornel West[1]

The debate over race in contemporary literary theory is not a biological issue but a cultural one. Race has disappeared as a referent in the language game of science;[2] however, it continues to play an important role in the languages that oppress and nourish African Americans. What makes up the cultural traditions of African American identity? What kind of vocabulary should be used to talk about it? The focus of the debate that will orient my remarks is the adoption of poststructuralist and other theoretical vocabularies to read African American literature by Henry Louis Gates, Jr. and Houston Baker, Jr.[3] The charge is that these vocabularies are not only alien to African American literature but that they are not responsive to the ethical, political, and aesthetic needs of African Americans. Since there is no space to review all the contributions to this issue, I will outline my position briefly and then look at Gates's own efforts to connect poststructuralism and black vernacular theory.

As a point of departure, I will use Cornel West's definition of "blackness": "After centuries of racist degradation, exploitation, and oppression in America, blackness means being minimally subject to white supremacist abuse and being part of a rich culture and community that has struggled against such abuse." ("Black Leadership and the Pitfalls of Racial Reasoning," p. 393).[4] There

---

[1] *Prophesy Deliverance!*, p. 22.
[2] Anthony Appiah, "Illusions of Race," *In My Father's House.*
[3] Joyce A. Joyce, "The Black Canon"; Gates, "'What's Love Got to Do with It?'"; Baker, "In Dubious Battle." Joyce responds to these criticisms in "'Who the Cap Fit.'"
[4] West's work on the history of philosophy (*The American Evasion of Philosophy*) and the African American tradition (*Prophesy Deliverance!*) does not negotiate the meta-theoretical difficulties between tradition-based stories and genealogical accounts. For an incisive critique of West's history of pragmatism, see Robert Gooding-Williams's review essay, "Evading Narrative Myth." Gooding-Williams points out how West tacks on the word "genealogy" to his ungenealogical

are two parts to the definition – a story of oppression and a story of agency. That is, there are distinctive traditions (in MacIntyre's sense) that provide resources of various kinds – aesthetic, ethical, emotional, etc. Although stories of oppression can be told without poststructuralism, poststructuralism can deepen these stories by showing how African American culture has internalized oppressive linguistic and social structures. Poststructuralist vocabularies should not replace the vocabularies of resistance offered by the traditions, but poststructuralist analysis can supplement and critique traditional vocabularies. There are two reasons for this. First, poststructuralism aims at discursive practices that transcend race – e.g., processes of rationalization, capitalism, etc. – and that are important for all. Second, poststructuralism is particularly adept at providing a critique of the vocabularies of self-under-standing precisely because it works in anti-hermeneutical categories. The critique of self-understanding addresses such phenomena as internalization, which is crucial to the African American theoretical project. This strength of poststructuralism is also its greatest weakness; as we have seen, it is a weakness that must be supplemented by an account of agency and tradition that enables individuals and communities to close the hermeneutic circle and theorize meaningful spaces in which to live. In short, African American cultural theory needs a self-conscious meta-critical dimension that can make use of the first-/second- and third-person theoretical models available.

These needs require that we go beyond both poststructuralism and the other popular position in contemporary theory – identity politics. And West's discussion does just that by insisting on the democratic ethical/political norm, by which individuals contest these ethnic identities: "Hence, all black Americans have some interest in resisting racism . . . Yet how this 'interest' is defined and how individuals and communities are understood vary. So any claim to black authenticity – beyond being the potential object of racist abuse and heir to a grand tradition of black struggle – is contingent on one's political definition of black interest, and one's ethical understanding of how this interest relates to individuals and communities in and outside black America" (pp. 393– 94).

organic history of pragmatism. Gooding-Williams shows how West forces a pragmatic reading onto Dubois in order to give pragmatism a dimension of ethical/political critique that he (West) can appropriate.

This is not simply a right but a demand on the cultural critic to step out of a merely descriptive role, to close the hermeneutic circle and identify the ideals that inform his/her understanding of African American cultural history and its relationship to other histories. This demand challenges "appeals to black authenticity," for "such appeals hide and conceal the political and ethical dimension of blackness ... Every claim to racial authenticity presupposes elaborate conceptions of political and ethical relations of interests, individuals, and communities. Racial reasoning conceals these presuppositions behind a deceptive cloak of racial consensus" (pp. 393–94). Here, West avoids the oscillation between essentialism ("black" has an unchanging meaning and reference) and constructivism ("black" refers only to a network of signifiers and signifieds) that haunts much of the argument about race. For West, "black" is situated in a tradition that is open to discussion, a discussion informed by views of language that affirm the power of reference, that give place to the ethical richness of the traditions, and that connect the African American traditions to existing social and political institutions.

In *The Signifying Monkey*, Gates attempts to heal a split between the vocabularies of poststructuralism and the vernacular critical language of the African American tradition by defining terms from the African American tradition in the vocabulary of Derrida and Bakhtin. He gives a promising definition of the tradition as linguistic practices: "The blackness of black literature is not an absolute or a metaphysical condition ... Rather, the 'blackness' of black American literature can be discerned only through close readings. By 'blackness' here I mean specific uses of literary language that are shared, repeated, critiqued, and revised" (p. 121).[5] However, his historiographical goals and principles are not clear aside from the positivistic claim that there is an African American tradition with its own critical language. Does he want to reconstruct the self-understandings of the writers? Does he want to make them speak to current concerns? How does his reading of this tradition relate to other readings of the tradition?

---

[5] Gates cites Ellison on this point: "It is not skin color which makes a Negro American but cultural heritage shaped by the American experience, the social and political predicament; a sharing of that 'concord of sensibilities' which the group expressed through historical circumstance and through which it has come to constitute a subdivision of the larger American culture" (Ellison, *Shadow and Act*, p. 131).

What does he want to critique and recuperate from the African American tradition, from the canon, or from existing theory? Why does he select these authors? Why doesn't he critique any of the authors in his pantheon? Why are gender conflicts within the African American tradition ignored? (Alice Walker is discussed only in relation to Zora Neale Hurston.) By avoiding these issues and by using linguistic problematics that cannot give constitutive characterizations of the tradition, Gates constricts the argumentative space within which African American traditions operate and makes "black vernacular" function as a term of "racial authenticity."

He sets up his view of literary history by citing Ralph Ellison: "Protest is an element of all art, though it does not necessarily take the form of speaking for a political or social program. It might appear in a novel as a technical assault against the styles which have gone before" (Ellison, *Shadow and Act*, p. 137). Gates then interprets this remark as follows: "This form of formal revision is what I am calling critical signification or formal Signifyin(g) and is my metaphor for literary history" (*The Signifying Monkey*, p. 106). Gates defines formal Signifyin(g) through Bakhtin's idea of the double-voiced discourse, focusing on parodic narration and hidden polemic. The former uses another's words, but with different intention, while hidden polemic argues implicitly with other views on the same topic.[6] Gates comments, "Ellison's definition of the formal relationship between his works and Wright's is a salient example of the hidden polemic: his texts clash with Wright's 'on the ground of the referent itself'" (p. 111). However, instead of addressing the alternative referential and ethical languages offered by Wright and Ellison, of finding how Ellison's language transforms the self-understanding of the African American tradition, we read, "Ellison in his fiction Signifies upon Wright by parodying Wright's literary structures through repetition and difference" (p. 106). The multiple voices in Gates's use of Bakhtin usually serve to "parody,"

---

[6] Gates uses the following citation from Bakhtin: "In hidden polemic the author's discourse is oriented toward its referential object, as in any other discourse, but at the same time each assertion about that object is constructed in such a way that, besides its referential meaning, the author's discourse brings a polemical attack to bear against another speech act, another assertion, on the same topic. Here one utterance focused on its referential object clashes with another utterance on the grounds of the referent itself" ("Discourse Typology in Russian Poetics," cited in *The Signifying Monkey*, p. 111).

"subvert," or "undo."[7] This is an impoverished hermeneutic vocabulary that helps Bakhtin dovetail with poststructuralism, but it fails to address the hermeneutic needs of African American critical thought.[8] Gates makes some insightful readings, though they are often disconnected from his theoretical commitments: "Wright's *Native Son* and *Black Boy*, titles connoting race, self and presence, Ellison tropes with *Invisible Man*, with *invisibility* as an ironic response of absence to the would-be presence of blacks and natives, while man suggests a more mature and stronger status than either *son* or *boy*; Ellison Signifies upon Wright's distinctive version of naturalism with a complex rendering of modernism" (p. 106). All this is fine as far as it goes, but Ellison is not simply playing off Wright's text or making poststructuralist points about essence; he is offering an alternative form of life to inhabit. Another quotation from Ellison (one that I cited in chapter 1 with regard to poststructuralism) brings into focus the issues that formalism and poststructuralism do not address: "I would write my own books and they would be in themselves, implicitly, criticisms of Wright's just as all novels of a given historical moment form an argument over the nature of reality and are, to an extent, criticisms of each other" (*Shadow and Act*, p. 117). Ellison's understanding of the idea of tradition is closer to MacIntyre's than it is to Bakhtin's, although other texts of Bakhtin give a richer hermeneutic sense to the ideas of genre and tradition than the ones Gates cites.[9] In short, because Gates employs limited notions from Bakhtin and Derrida, he cannot articulate the rich dynamics of the argument formed by the African American traditions or the potential of the theorists he employs. Ellison's concept of tradition forces us to go beyond the presence of intertextual relations within a given set of works, to assess their diverse positions through

---

[7] There are exceptions to this rhetoric, such as Walker's signifyin(g) on Hurston, in which the parody is a form of homage. What is needed here are other generic categories, just as different kinds of signifying speech acts need to be distinguished.

[8] By trying to make Bakhtin consistent with Derrida, Gates misses the productive incommensurability between their problematics. Bakhtin resists all third-person accounts of language for political reasons, as his well-known polemics against Marx and Freud make clear. Hence, Derrida's ontology of the sign offers an avenue of critique unavailable to his dialogism.

[9] Other texts by Bakhtin – see *Speech Genres and Other Late Essays* – emphasize hermeneutics more than the ones Gates cites. For a reading of Bakhtin that develops this dimension, see Gary Morson and Caryl Emerson, *Mikhail Bakhtin: Creation of a Prosaics*.

critique and recuperation, and to establish our relationship to the multiple dimensions of this tradition.

Nonetheless, Gates does feel a need for an agent-based vocabulary. However, he does not get any help on this when he tries to yoke Derrida's ontology of the sign to the practice of Signifyin(g). I will give a couple of illustrative quotations that show not only Derridean but de Manian vocabulary. Sometimes he talks about Signifyin(g) only at the level of the sign as these two theorists do: "Signifyin(g) is a trope in which are subsumed several other rhetorical tropes, including metaphor, metonymy, synecdoche" (*The Signifying Monkey*, p. 52); "the importance of the Signifying Monkey poems is their repeated stress on the sheer materiality and willful play of the signifier itself" (p. 59). However, at other moments, Gates recognizes the need for an agent-centered vocabulary that is incompatible with the ontology of the sign: "The Monkey is called the Signifier because he foregrounds the signifier in his use of language. Signifying, in other words, turns on the sheer play of the signifier. It does not refer primarily to the signified; rather, it refers to the style of language, to that which transforms ordinary discourse into literature" (p. 78). If there is one thing Gates's analyses do not show, it is the "play of the signifier"; rather, he shows the appropriation of the signifier "signification" by African Americans to designate a variety of linguistic practices. As Gates says, "Black people vacated this signifier [*signification*] – then, incredibly substituted as its concept a signified that stands for the system of rhetorical strategies peculiar to their own vernacular tradition" (p. 47). What is called for here is not just analysis of changes at the level of the sign but at the level of the sentence – i.e., pragmatics, where the relationships of speaker, listener, referent, and practices to social conflicts can be examined.[10] The ontological liberty of the signifier may help underwrite change, but it does not articulate specific practices nor does it provide a space for assessing the ethical sustenance or

[10] In chapter 2 of *The Signifying Monkey*, Gates reduces the research of Claudia Mitchell-Kernan and Geneva Smitherman to a narrow notion of tropes as signs. He praises Mitchell-Kernan for showing that signifying is a "pervasive mode of language use rather than merely one specific verbal game" (p. 80). What the linguists offer is an analysis of signifying through pragmatics – study at the level of the sentence, where speakers, listeners, and referents are at issue. Gates never distinguishes between semiotics, analysis at the level of the sign (the focus of Saussurean linguistics), semantics, analysis at the level of the sentence, and pragmatics, analysis of the entire situation of enunciation.

political strength these practices gave to those who inhabited them. A more productive use of Derrida's problematic would be as a third-person strategy for unmasking racial vocabularies inside and outside the African American traditions rather than as part of a first-/second-person story of agency. Gates does break with Derridean strictures in his analysis, but he never makes a theoretical break; instead, he just adds on an agent-centered vocabulary: "He [the Signifying Monkey] is the principle of self-consciousness in the black vernacular, the meta-figure itself" (p. 53). At other times, he tries to heal the split between a vocabulary of consciousness and the antihumanist vocabulary of deconstruction: "The Monkey, in short, is not only a master of technique . . .; he is technique, or style, or the literariness of language" (p. 54). The most important formulation he gives to Signifyin(g) is the one that has no place in the Derridean or the Bakhtinian terms he employs: Signifyin(g) is "an adult ritual, which black people learn as adolescents, almost exactly like children learned the traditional figures of signification in classically structured Western primary and secondary school" (p. 75). Such a definition – like the vocabulary of consciousness or Bakhtin's notion of voice – is not compatible with Derrida's theory of language, which is designed precisely to cut across the intentional structures of historical practices. To appropriate deconstruction for the project of African American critical theory requires that it appear as one theoretical option within a broader horizon and not as the site of theory. The linguistic theories of Derrida, of Bakhtin, and of those who think in terms of practices require meta-theoretical sorting out in view of the ethical, political, and aesthetic needs of the African American critic. What is lost in such a conflation is the competing strengths and weaknesses of Derrida and Bakhtin. Bakhtin's pragmatics can bring forth aspects of discourse that are not available through Derrida's analysis; by the same token, the critique of the sign is a third-person account that cuts across Bakhtin's pragmatic categories.

Here, it is useful to recall Rorty's meta-philosophical reflections on the relationship between the theoretical problematic one uses to tell a story and the canon that one reads. In Rorty's terms, Gates's history can be called "doxography" – that is, "the attempt to impose a problematic on a canon drawn up without reference to that problematic, or, conversely, to impose a canon on a problematic constructed without reference to that canon" (Rorty, "The Historiography of Philosophy," p. 62). This concept of history is exactly the one Gates criticizes in his analysis of the exclusion of African American texts and the ways that they were forced to conform to existing standards. However, Gates replaces an old doxography with a Derridean/de Manian one based on tropes, in which the value of texts derives from the dynamics of their figures.[11] But Rorty's lesson here is not just the bias in a given set of criteria but the absence of self-consciousness about the relationship of the problematic to canon, and the call to thematize the relationship of theory to value. Since I will pursue these theoretical issues in the next section, I would like to close with an example of how Gates's idea of Signifyin(g) can be enriched by thinking of it in terms of constitutive vocabularies and practices.

My text is Ellison's short story "Flying Home," in which we see Jefferson, a poor, elderly farmer, "signify" on Todd, an "upwardly" mobile black pilot. The signifying does not operate through argument but through a challenging redescription of Todd's self-understanding. We could say that Jefferson "parodies" Todd. But the point of the parody is not retrospective unmasking but prospective reinvention. The point is not to "trope a dope" (Gates, *The Signifying Monkey*, p. 52) but to break down a self-understanding that internalizes debilitating white judgments, while it obscures his connection to African American culture and its resources. Jefferson's signifying has both referential and ethical dimensions; however, the "corrections" that Jefferson offers to Todd are so profound that the intersubjective space of argument is uprooted. To get Todd to see his point, Jefferson must go after the young pilot's entire self-understanding and urge him toward a new language for constituting himself and the world. Jefferson's first-person narrative pushes Todd toward a third-person understanding of himself. The identity of the speaker, an elderly, uneducated man who "fathers" him like an analyst – not the materiality of the signifier – is where the story turns. Jefferson renews what Todd "already knows" but cannot hear. Like *Invisible*

---

[11] Gates's desire to make African American texts available to tropological analysis is understandable within the context of the politics of English departments during the 1970s and 1980s, when deconstruction was gaining popularity. Texts that could not be read this way were ignored. In 1984, Gates argued against the "curious valorization of the social and polemical functions of black literature," because "the structure of the black text has been repressed and treated as if it were transparent" ("Criticism in the Jungle," pp. 5–6).

Man, this text takes the Freudian pattern of repeating, remembering, and working through – we see Todd remember his desire to fly and the force of the racism he has tried to deny – and politicizes the process by which a particular shape of identity is excavated and overcome. This change is linguistic as well, and it shows the need not simply to speak of "signifying" in terms of pragmatics but to understand the way pragmatics needs to be placed in the larger horizon of forms of life that offer practices and axiologies of existence. Signifying is not just subversive; it is constitutive of a positive style of being that is inaccessible to poststructuralism (and to Rorty's behaviorism, for that matter.) In this way, Ellison's dialogue is not just with the African American tradition but with the politics of subjectivity in canonical Modernism. If Modernism foregrounds the aesthetic exploration of the inner world of the subject – e.g., Proust's first-person narrator frames issues of identity, memory, language, etc., in terms of general philosophical problems – Ellison's first-person narrator makes these ideological questions, questions that do not turn on necessity or on the nature of experience but on the worth of particular social constructions. By placing the shape of different social constructions before us, by unmasking and reinventing the resources of the past, Ellison's texts urge us to take on the ethical, political, and aesthetic tasks of connecting stories of oppression with stories of recuperation. How his texts make these points will be the subject of the next section.

Traditions and genealogies in democratic interpretation

"Instead of proclaiming the ideological and illusory character of the so-called 'formal bourgeois democracy,' why not take its declared principles literally and force liberal democratic societies to be accountable for their professed ideals." Chantal Mouffe[12]

This section will develop a reading of Ellison that shows how his work speaks to the ethical/political needs of the present. The focus of my reading is Ellison's understanding of the subject in deliberations about identity in a liberal democracy, an understanding that shows how to work simultaneously in a tradition based problematic and a genealogical problematic. Unlike Baker and

---

[12] Mouffe, *Radical Democracy*, p. 2.

Gates, I will read Ellison against much of contemporary theory so as to highlight what is missing. This is not to say that in 1997 we can simply read off Ellison's text as if it could speak to the present without mediation. There are many aspects of Ellison's texts that date them and that limit their vision; however, these differences from the present can become resources once they undergo a critique and a recuperation that negotiates the gap between his vocabulary and ours (mine). By laying out the deliberations through which a text's unwelcome features are sorted out, I will be dramatizing a critical dimension lost in many contemporary anti-hermeneutical readings, in which a text is selected either as an oppressor text or a liberator text and then read from this perspective. Moreover, through a dialogue with Ellison, I will be sketching how we can improve our self-understandings as postmodern subjects.

Ellison's work offers a radical genealogical critique of the vocabulary of race by showing how "black" functions in American culture. His work inaugurates the project that Toni Morrison continues in *Playing in the Dark*, in which she proposes to examine "Africanism," "a term for the denotative and connotative blackness that African peoples have come to signify, as well as the entire range of lives, assumptions, readings, and misreadings that accompany Eurocentric learning about these people" (pp. 6–7). Ellison, too, examines how the ideology of racial inscription works in an unthematized way in American culture. In his view, what helps drive this inscription out of white self-understanding and into the political unconscious is the democratic ideal that is being denied. He plays the role of the analyst who employs a third-person critique to make this ideology explicit: "This unwillingness to resolve the conflict in keeping with his democratic ideals has compelled the white American, figuratively, to force the Negro down into the deeper level of his consciousness, into the inner world, where reason and madness mingle with hope and memory and endlessly give birth to nightmare and to dream; down into the province of the psychiatrist and the artist, from whence spring the lunatic's fancy and his work of art." (*Shadow and Act*, p. 99). One of the effects of such repression is the inextricable presence of race in every facet of what white culture understands as "white": "It is practically impossible for the white American to think of sex, of economics, his children or womenfolk, or of sweeping socio-political changes, without summoning into consciousness fear-flecked images of black men." (p. 100).[13]

One of the most vivid examples of Ellison's exposure of this racial ideology is the famous encounter in *Invisible Man* between Norton, the white trustee of the college, and Trueblood, a black farmer who has raped his daughter and who now spins his tale. In this scene, Ellison shows how Norton shifts his incestuous desire to Trueblood, how "black" becomes the social place to disguise his own desires and hate them as other. The other is not simply what white society excludes but a safe place for hiding self-referential statements. This scene follows a version of Freud's "splitting" off, in which the "good" feelings for the daughter are isolated and idealized, while the incestuous and destructive ones are contained and ennobled through the project of philanthropy for the black other. As Norton says, "I had a feeling that your people were somehow connected with my destiny" (p. 41).[14]

This racial ideology is not limited to white consciousness, however; the Invisible Man is complicitous with the system that defines the relations between him and Norton, and the text explores the cultural contradictions that appear in the Invisible Man's consciousness – from his desire to impress his torturers in the Battle Royal in chapter 1 to his desire to take up subject positions in Norton's fantasies: "I identified with the rich man reminiscing on the rear seat" (p. 39). This identification sets up the protagonist's struggle for autonomy, which for Ellison is the capacity to situate oneself in stories of one's oppression and traditions of achievement. What Ellison does that the poststructuralist genealogist does not is to narrate how he changed from the subject who internalized this system to the agent who could "slip the yoke" of this system and tell a genealogical story.

Ellison's portrait of the meta-theoretical work on traditions is

---

[13] Ellison says, "The anti-Negro images of the films were (and are) acceptable because of the existence through the United States of an audience obsessed with an inner psychological need to view Negroes as less than men" (*Shadow and Act*, pp. 276–77). In *Playing in the Dark*, Toni Morrison carries this point much further.

[14] See Selma Frailberg's interesting psychoanalytic reading of this scene. She says that Trueblood comes back after his exile and "thus reverses the classic fate of the incest hero. Instead of an Oedipus blinded we are given an Oedipus newly sighted. Norton is Oedipus blinded in the story, for when he is confronted with Trueblood's dream-sin, which is his own, he refuses to see and is carried from the scene unconscious" ("Two Modern Incest Heroes," pp. 658–59).

not a project one undertakes in graduate school but in childhood. Traditions are not laid out on a plate before the disembodied subject of critical theory. Critical perspectives are won through a personal struggle. Our lesson from Ellison is not just in the content but in the structure of his stories, and I will begin with the narrative dimensions of this structure as they are portrayed in *Invisible Man*. The Prologue announces the meta-critical work of the text, work that takes place within the world of the text and between text and reader. The theme of invisibility is as much about the text–reader relationship as it is about the relationships within the novelistic world. In the opening pages, the narrator tells the story of a fight with a white man on the street who does not see him; yet, the narrator is acutely aware that he is telling this story to someone who will undoubtedly inhabit many of the ideological positions of the white man in the story. The narrator is "signifying," to use Gates's term, on the reader in the telling, and he signifies in a way that is much like Jefferson's on Todd, in that he forces the reader to examine his/her self-understanding. This is a reciprocal interrogation that will involve authors (Dostoevsky, Kierkegaard, and Wright) and forms from European, canonical American, and African American traditions (slave narratives, the sermon, the blues). Unlike Frederick Douglass's slave narrative, in which the writing is the demonstration of equality, this text ties equality not to abstract rights and faceless individuality but to the recognition of differences. Ellison does not relegate to the margins what were for the white audience the unreadable dimensions of African American culture and experience, as Douglass is forced to do.[15] *Invisible Man* follows a plot of self-overcoming like "Flying Home" but with an important difference: It is a first-person retrospective narrative about how the protagonist comes to be able to tell the story. Instead of leaving the narrator off-stage, as in "Flying Home," Ellison foregrounds the narrator, or what I prefer to call the narrating self, as opposed to the experiencing self. Unlike James's third-person narrator (and the narrator of "Flying Home"), who foregrounds the movements of consciousness, Ellison's first-person retrospective narrative uses the distance between the narrating self of the present and experiencing selves of the past to

---

[15] See Gregory Jay's chapter "American Literature and the New Historicism: The Example of Frederick Douglass," in *America the Scrivener*, pp. 236–76, and William Andrews, *To Tell a Free Story*.

create a hermeneutic tension. Rather than beginning with the tale of his younger self, the narrator begins with a Prologue that is filled with literary and cultural allusions and told in a perplexing, taunting style. The reader's novelistic categories take a jolt, and we are made aware of the importance of both the act of writing itself and the site from which the hero's experience is remembered and recuperated, not simply transcribed.

Ellison dramatizes the work of critique and recuperation by having the protagonist's movement into the future push him backward into his personal and cultural histories. In *Shadow and Act*, he describes how the words of the Invisible Man's grandfather serve this hermeneutical function. The grandfather, whose "mask of meekness conceals the wisdom of one who has learned the secret of saying the 'yes' which accomplishes the expressive 'no' ... represents the ambiguity of the past for the hero, for whom the sphinxlike deathbed advice poses a riddle which points the plot in the dual direction which the hero will follow throughout the novel" (p. 56). For the protagonist, like Oedipus, the sphinx's riddle forces him to return from the issues of the present to his own past. The Invisible Man's backward movement is also psychological, as he regresses to recover lost emotional resources. The rebirth scene (chapter 11), for example, is not just a stripping away of the repressive socialized voice; it is a regression that helps to reconstitute the Invisible Man. His regression is both psychical and historical. In going back to his childhood, he rediscovers and reinvents the forgotten wisdom of the African American tradition at the same time that he gets back the feelings that social pain forced into a crippling shape. This is not an "excavation" of his historical or psychical past but a dialogue between past and present selves that places the process of discovery, not just the result, on the table. The Invisible Man's self-understanding is thus a personal and social achievement, so that the construction of social reality is inseparable from the self-constitution and historical reconstruction of what made this self possible. Ellison insists – like MacIntyre – on the narrative understanding of this identity that must accompany any genealogical account. As MacIntyre says, "The function of genealogy as emancipatory from deception and self-deception thus requires the identity and continuity of the self that was deceived and the self that is and is to be" (*Three Rival Versions of Moral Enquiry*, p. 214). For the narrating self, the experiencing self has internalized ideologies that have made him invisible to himself, not just to others. For Ellison, autonomy is not just about equal and respectful treatment; rather, it is about the formation of character and cultural critique. Thus, the hope expressed in the well-known last line of the novel – "who knows but that, on lower frequencies I speak *for* you" (*Invisible Man*, p. 568) – is that the text will transform the reader's self-understanding by speaking for, and not simply to or about, him/her.

Ellison's recuperative capacity is not just exercised on the African American tradition but on the "founding" texts of American democracy. His genealogy shows that racial vocabulary cuts all the way through the idea of democracy to become a constitutive aspect of American culture: "The fantasy of an America free of blacks is at least as old as the dream of creating a truly democratic society" (Ellison, *Going Into the Territory*, p. 104). The democratic impulse is imbricated with a racist, segregationist impulse. He notes that Jefferson drafted "a plan for the gradual emancipation and exportation of the slaves" (p. 105) and that Lincoln was involved "in a plan of purging the nation of blacks as a means of healing the shattered ideals of democratic federalism" (p. 107). Ellison looks at these wishes not just as a moral historian but as a therapist who wants to heal the psychic wounds of our histories: "When we consider how long blacks had been in the New World and had been transforming it and being Americanized by it, the scheme appears not only fantastic, but the product of a free-floating irrationality. Indeed, a national pathology" (p. 106). This exposure does not place the values of these texts beyond recuperation. What this requires is hermeneutics that can assess the potential of ambiguous texts, "All great democratic documents ... contain a strong charge of anti-democratic elements ... [I]t is by making use of the positive contributions of such documents and rejecting their negative elements that democracy can be kept dynamic" (*Shadow and Act*, p. 304). Moreover, he maintains a dialectical attitude toward the way cultural forms simultaneously enable and cripple, produce insight and blindness: "The English language and traditional cultural forms served both as guides and restraints, anchoring Americans in the wisdom and processes of the past, while making it difficult for them to perceive with any clarity the nuances of their new identity" (cited in Benston, *Speaking for You*, p. 174). For Ellison, his racial positioning facilitates, rather than inhibits, this interpretive process of critique and recuperation through which the democratic ideals of the American past become available to the present: "Negro Americans have developed an ability to abstract desirable qualities from those around them, even from their enemies, and my sense of reality could reject bias while appreciating the truth revealed by achieved art" (*Shadow and Act*, p. xx).

This interpretive capacity makes it possible for democratic principles to inform the site of narration, so that the point of his genealogical exposure is not just negative liberty and difference but a democratic future. In the Epilogue of *Invisible Man*, the protagonist reflects again on his grandfather's words that have haunted him throughout the novel: "Was it that we of all, we, most of all, had to affirm the principle [on which the country was built], the plan in whose name we had been brutalized and sacrificed . . . because we were older than they, in the sense of what it took to live in the world with others and because they had exhausted in us, some . . . of the human greed and smallness, yes, and the fear and superstition that had kept them running" (p. 561). This is not to say that I endorse all of Ellison's interpretations. For example, when he reads Twain and Melville to criticize twentieth-century fiction, since the former "took a much greater responsibility for the condition of democracy" (*Shadow and Act*, p. 104), Ellison idealizes them in a way that no one who has benefited from Toni Morrison's reading of *Huckleberry Finn* can do. My Ellisonian lesson is both ethical/political and methodological. The ethical/political point is made by my epigraph from Mouffe, in which democratic ideals are not dismissed but given new life.[16] These ethical/political points are gratuitous unless they are attached to new enabling theoretical narratives that supplement the ones provided by poststructuralism and recent Marxist theory. Ellison shows the need for such a story as a formal requirement independently of whether we agree with his reading of the history of democratic ideals. Sorting out the different levels of argument – meta-theory, theory, and first-order criticism, as we saw in chapter 3 – requires a

[16] Cornel West joins Mouffe in urging the Left to give up its rejection of liberal ideals as illusions: "Theorists tend to respond to liberalism's hegemony in the academy by disclosing the various exclusions of the liberal traditions, rather than reconstructing the creative ways in which oppressed and marginalized persons have forged traditions of resistance by appropriating aspects of liberalism for democratic and egalitarian ends" (*Keeping Faith*, p. 203).

thematization of these different levels and the creation of a dialogical relationship among the levels. Ellison's work suggests such a dialogue, and to see how he promotes it, we need to examine his idea of autonomy as narrative competence. This requires that we leave the genealogical frame and explore a cultural category that is dear to MacIntyre and communitarians but that is blocked by postmodern and poststructuralist discourse – character.

I introduce "character" into the critical space currently designated by "subjectivity" as the ethical/political correlate of bringing first-/second-person vocabularies into dialogue with third-person vocabularies. One of the virtues required by the contemporary democratic subject is the ability to see himself/herself and others simultaneously as subjects and as persons, as beings produced by social and discursive forces and as ethical/political beings capable of constituting themselves. That is, one needs the psychic mobility to be able to play the role of the genealogist as well as the role of the reviser of traditions. Ellison's work is attuned to the social and psychological conditions needed to nourish this virtue. For Ellison, like MacIntyre, the concepts of character and rationality depend on a notion of tradition, and tradition is the source of reason, not of mystification. As we recall from chapter 2, MacIntyre's attack on modern culture is that it attempts to set up a site for reason and identity outside all traditions and that this attempt leaves contemporary culture incoherent and impoverished. The desire to step out of one's past is all the more tempting and devastating for African Americans, because of racism, and we see this when the Invisible Man tries this route. However, Ellison brings to the concept of tradition what is missing from MacIntyre – the pulse of daily life, the conflictual possibilities of cultural pluralism, the complex reality of oppression, the need for the distancing vocabularies of genealogy, and the hope of democratic ideals.

I begin with "Harlem Is Nowhere," an essay in which Ellison gives an earlier version of the debate between the "vernacular tradition" and poststructuralism. In this piece, he discusses the pain and incoherence of cultural identity for those who come North to find not only a dizzying urban life but a new intellectual vocabulary: "Here the grandchildren of those who possessed no written literature examine their lives through the eyes of Freud and Marx, Kierkegaard and Kafka, Malraux and Sartre" (*Shadow and Act*, pp. 296–97). Ellison is sensitive to the loss of tradition that comes from moving North. "In the North he surrenders and does not replace certain important supports to his personality" (p. 298). This attention to needs helps keep the totalizing critical axe from falling on beliefs that cannot survive interrogation by contemporary philosophy. Ellison certainly believes that African Americans need the theoretical insights of Freud and Marx: "The Negro problem" is one "where Marx cries out for Freud and Freud for Marx" (p. 311); however, he does not let these third-person accounts evaporate either the wisdom of the tradition or the psychological needs for new forms of self-understanding and community. These needs will persist after aspects of tradition undergo ideology critique: "He [the Negro] leaves a still authoritative religion which gives his life a semblance of metaphysical wholeness; a family structure which is relatively stable; and a body of folklore – tested in life-and-death terms against his daily experience with nature and the Southern white man – that serves as a guide to action" (pp. 298–99). Ellison brings a therapeutic view to his ethical/political ideals, and his political therapy emphasizes the endless work of critical dialogue. Ellison is concerned with how we are going to live tomorrow and not just with what ought to be once the current mess is swept away. He investigates the conditions of positive freedom rather than just detailing the oppression from which we need to escape. To develop the way Ellison keeps the tension between genealogy and agency alive and productive, I will look at his famous debate with Irving Howe and at a later political critique by Donald Gibson.[17]

In "Black Boys and Native Sons," Howe criticizes Ellison for abandoning Richard Wright's socialist realism and retreating into a Modernist individualism. Ellison responds by attacking a Marxist, sociological reading of African American life because it ignores the language of self-constitution of that culture, reducing it to statistics and stories of domination. What Ellison does is show us how to combine the insights about subjection without giving up agency: "For even as his life toughens, even as it brutalizes him, sensitizes him . . . it conditions him to deal with life and himself. He must live it and consciously grasp its complexity until he can

---

[17] See Irving Howe, *A World More Attractive*, and Donald Gibson *The Politics of Literary Expression*. There has been a notable absence of political criticism in recent years on Ellison, as he has moved back into critical favor.

change it; must live it as he changes it. He is no mere product of his sociological predicament. He is a product of the interaction between his racial predicament, his individual will and the broader American cultural freedom in which he finds his ambiguous existence" (*Shadow and Act*, pp. 112–13). There are three key points in Ellison's response. The first concerns the self-understanding of African Americans of the past. As he says in another essay, "And isn't it closer to the truth that far from considering themselves only in terms of the abstraction, 'a slave,' the enslaved really thought of themselves as *men* who had been unjustly enslaved" (p. 254). His second point is a Jamesian one about the inseparability of language, ethics, and reference. Historical reality is disclosed and constituted through language, and this language establishes a relationship between the speaker and the object of inquiry as well as the audience. His third point, which follows from his second, is about the site of understanding in the present. This site requires future change to be connected to nourishing aspects of the past and present, a requirement that is often suppressed in Marxist criticism.[18] Ellison's message for us is that any third-person account that demands a total revolution ignores human needs for self and communal constitution, not just the mystified needs of humanism.

He makes the connection between the therapeutic and the political explicit when he says that the Lafargue Psychiatric Center in Harlem "represents an underground extension of democracy" (p. 295). Ethical/political goals must not lose sight of the community and tradition from which and to which they are addressed. Certainly, these goals require revision of the language of needs made by traditions; however, ethical/political agendas cannot ignore needs in their quest to bring about social change. Assuming the voice of the so-called "under-privileged child," Ellison says, "If you can show me how I can cling to that which is real to me, while teaching me a way into the larger society, then I will not only drop my defense and my hostility, but I will sing your praises and I will help you make the desert bear fruit" (*Going Into the Territory*, p. 75).

Donald Gibson develops Howe's criticism, attacking Ellison for his solipsism, his relativism, and his politics of isolated, disengaged

---

[18] In *Marxism and Morality*, Steven Lukes discusses how knowing what the "'self-transforming present' [the phrase is from Lukacs] is depends on knowledge of what the emancipatory future will look like" (p. 42).

individualism, a politics that he calls "the politics of retreat": "Ellison won the argument; Howe, if we discount the racism of his position, was right" (*The Politics of Literary Expression*, p. 93). Gibson says that Ellison believes that "race is an individual and not a group problem . . . If one denies the true and real existence of racial and class distinction, then one may say that such categories are inoperative and consequently irrelevant" (p. 64). Gibson claims that the novel points only toward the authenticity of escape: "One can only retreat into the cavern of the mind, for only there in the grotto of isolation exists unlimited freedom" (p. 92). Ellison does not deny the "collective identity" that Gibson wants; rather, he criticizes the crippling self-understanding of the collective identity of the time and insists that "collective identity" is not a pre-hermeneutic fact but an interpretation. The vocabularies of race and class are, first of all, part of the oppressor's language, and they must be reinscribed to become part of an enabling self-understanding. Ellison's insistence on individual interpretation is not a solipsism, because the text does not work in a pre-Wittgensteinian way with language and subjectivity. The individual as an ethical/political notion crucial to democracy needs to be separated from the individual as an epistemological category, as we noted in the Introduction and in chapter 2.[19] Ellison's relentless stripping away of the Invisible Man's sense of reality is a critique of the referential languages available at the time. His genealogies offer a language of reference just as his language of tradition does. Thus, I disagree with Howe and Gibson, not because they link art and politics but because they fail to see Ellison's critique of past referential languages and the creation of a new one.[20]

Thus, Ellison's genealogical sensibility cuts a deeper critique into the constitution of social identity than any socialist realism. In this sense, Ellison's third-person critique resembles a poststructuralist critique in its textual, rather than causal, exploration of the gaps in received categories of good and bad, the inside and outside

---

[19] The works of Hans Blumenberg, Rorty, and Mouffe all develop this distinction.

[20] The poststructuralist challenge to reference is often interpreted as the impossibility of reference. This interpretation has damaged Ellison criticism, damage that appears not just in Gates's deconstructive reading of Ellison but in Alan Nadel's otherwise excellent book. Nadel says, "Any attempt at 'reinterpretation' . . . suggests the validity of one interpretation over another. From a contemporary perspective, however, this is a very problematic assumption" (*Invisible Criticism*, p. 17). Ellison explicitly rejects this "view from nowhere" as an impossible and undesirable quest.

of the self, the optical metaphor of knowledge, etc. The Invisible Man says, "When one is invisible he finds such problems as good and evil, honesty and dishonesty, of such shifting shapes that he confuses one with the other ... I was never more hated than when I tried to be honest. On the other hand, I've never been more loved and appreciated than when I tried to 'justify' and affirm someone's mistaken beliefs" (*Invisible Man*, p. 559). Ellison's search leads him beyond good and evil. If he would reject poststructuralist determinism, he would appropriate poststructuralism's search for otherness, for ways to break through imprisoning social and linguistic forms.

Unlike poststructuralists, however, Ellison discusses the enabling figures and ideals of his own childhood with the same hermeneutic generosity he displays in his democratic therapy: "We fabricated our heroes and ideals catch-as-catch can, and with an outrageous and irreverent sense of freedom ... Gamblers and scholars, jazz musicians and scientists, Negro cowboys and soldiers from the Spanish American and First World Wars, movie stars and stunt men, figures from the Italian Renaissance" (*Shadow and Act*, pp. xv–xvi). Ellison now laughs at the naiveté of this play ("Looking back through the shadows upon this absurd activity" [p. xvi]) and confesses that he and his friends "did not fully understand the cost of that style but ... recognized within it an affirmation of life beyond all question of our difficulties as Negroes" (p. xvii). What Ellison affirms is the importance of play in breaking down patterns of socialization. These ideas were helpful, even though flawed, because they "encourage the individual to a ... state in which he makes – in all ignorance of the accepted limitations of the possible – rash efforts, quixotic gestures, hopeful testings of the complexity of the known and the given" (p. xv). Nonetheless, Ellison's experimentation was not a rootlessness, a view from nowhere: "And part of our boyish activity expressed a yearning to make any and everything of quality Negro American; to appropriate it, possess it, re-create it in our own group and individual images" (p. xvii).

Yet for all its insight, Ellison's hermeneutics of identity has features that perpetuate unfortunate patterns, and these patterns emerge in his understanding of development. What informs the unfolding of the plot of *Invisible Man* and his essays is the drama between father and son in the tradition of American literature as well as in Freudian analysis. There are several disappointing results. One is the stereotypical representation of women, which many have noted.[21] A second, related result is that the text is concerned with the authenticity of the self's personal vision and the judgment of the (grand)father rather than with the mutual recognition necessary to produce a less-damaged self. The idea of self-fathering plays a large role in *Invisible Man*, from the quest to decipher the grandfather's words to the Vet's advice to the hero, "Be your own father young man" (*Invisible Man*, p. 154), just as it does in canonical American literature of the nineteenth and twentieth century. My point is not that Ellison's narratives are gender specific but that the plots follow the pattern that cripples men and women, the pattern analyzed by Jessica Benjamin, which we discussed in chapters 3 and 4. Benjamin sums up the crucial point for us as follows: "The father–son relationship [in Freud], like the master–slave relationship, is a model in which the opposition between self and other can only reverse – one is always up and the other down ... This reversible complementarity is the basic pattern of domination, and it is set in motion by the denial of recognition to the original other, the mother who is reduced to object" (*The Bonds of Love*, p. 220). Nina Baym develops a parallel idea in her study of American literature, in which she finds plots that resemble Benjamin's, plots that she calls "melodramas of beset manhood": "The myth narrates a confrontation of the American individual, the pure American self divorced from specific social circumstances, with the promise offered by the idea of America ... In these stories, the encroaching, constricting, destroying society is represented with articulate urgency in the figure of one or more women" ("Melodramas of Beset Manhood," pp. 1152– 53).[22] To be sure, Ellison exposes the racial dimension of this myth, and he does not accept the "pure American self"; yet, he works within the Freudian plot of development, in which intersubjective relations necessarily break down. In *Shadow and Act*, he talks of how "father and mother substitutes also have a role to play in aiding a child to help create himself" (p. xv). His theme

---

[21] See Mary Rohrberger, "'Ball the Jack'" and Claudia Tate's "Notes on the Invisible Women in Ralph Ellison's *Invisible Man*.'

[22] Baym refers to many literary histories of America, including Eric Sundquist's *Home as Found*, which brings together Freud and previous readings, such as Richard Poirier's *A World Elsewhere*, and Annette Kolodny's *The Lay of the Land*.

of self-creation appears as moral damage if we see his parental "substitutes" as figures to play with rather than as persons who offer the challenge of recognition. Ellison's work offers tremendous insight into the problems of recognition, but it could not transcend the flawed models. Ellison's therapeutic sense leads him to talk about the need for parental recognition, but an inarticulate pain pushes him away from this process into the fantasy of self-creation. Since I do not have the space to develop this alternative here, I will note that Alice Walker gives an alternative narrative of empowerment in *The Color Purple*, in which Celie develops a voice *and* recognition through intersubjective relations that overcome power.[23]

If we have discussed Ellisonian meta-critical dialogue between tradition and genealogy, we have not yet brought liberalism into the conversation. If Ellison's subject recuperates the ideals of liberal democracy, he/she does not accept liberal instrumentalism and the disembodied subject. Richard G. Stern asks Ellison directly about the liberal tenet of neutrality toward a view of the good. Stern says, "The familiar liberal hope is that any specialized form of social life which makes for invidious distinctions should disappear. Your view seems to be that anything that counts is the result of such specialization" (*Shadow and Act*, p. 20). Ellison replies at first with a simple "Yes" (p. 20) and then develops his critique of liberalism later, when Stern asks about what equal access to all aspects of society would mean to African Americans: "Most Negroes would not be nourished by the life white Southerners live. It is too hag-ridden, it is too obsessed" (p. 22). Ellison goes beyond liberal and poststructuralist appeals to justice or to a politics of difference by making neo-Aristotelian claims about the good life. Ellison's politics of difference is not just defined in terms of exclusion but in terms of the ethical goods made possible through traditions. Because he defends goods and traditions, and not just difference *per se*, he never insulates these traditions from assessment. He thus avoids the relativism and undecidability left by the politics of difference that works only through genealogical critique but with no site of judgment (see chapter 3).

The good life question informs the relationship between equality and identity. The failure to recognize is a failure of equality, a

[23] See Cassie Premo, "Beyond Critique to Survival."

failure to grant respect and autonomy. For African Americans to be equal and autonomous requires – to recall Nancy Fraser's remark – "a degree of collective control over the means of interpretation and communication sufficient to enable one to participate on a par with members of other groups in moral and political deliberation" ("Toward a Discourse Ethic of Solidarity," p. 428). An "invisible man" has no chance for equality in the public sphere. Ellison's point in the opening anecdote in *Invisible Man* about the mugging by an "invisible man" and its subsequent report in the newspaper, has been rewritten in bold print with the trial of Rodney King. As Robert Gooding-Williams says, "If ever there were brute facts, we thought, then surely this fact – that Rodney King had been unjustly beaten and unforgivably abused – was one of them. Yet the attorneys who defined King's assailants knew better. They knew better because they know what Fanon knew and went to such great lengths to explain: namely, that in modern Eurocentric societies no black bodies can be kept safe from the assault of negrophobic images and representations" ("Look a Negro!," p. 165). Iris Young generalizes this lesson: "The culturally dominated are both marked out by stereotypes and at the same time rendered invisible" (*Justice and the Politics of Difference*, pp. 59–60). The public sphere cannot hear claims about the good life from those it writes out of public discourse. As Ellison says, "And though as passionate believers in democracy Negroes identify themselves with the broader American ideals, their sense of reality springs, in part, from an American experience which most white men not only have not had, but one with which they are reluctant to identify themselves even when presented in forms of imagination" (*Shadow and Act*, p. 25).

At the same time, Ellison does not think the ethical goods of ethnic traditions should transcend democratic principles but vice versa. In "The Little Man at Chehaw Station," he criticizes the rising appeal of ethnic identification:

We repress an underlying anxiety aroused by the awareness that we are representative not only of one but of several overlapping and constantly shifting social categories; and we stress our affiliation with the segment of the corporate culture which has emerged out of our parents' past – racial, cultural, religious – and which we assume, on the basis of such magical talismans as our mother's milk or father's beard, that we "know." Grounding our sense of identity in such primary and affect-charged symbols, we seek to avoid the mysteries and pathologies of the democratic process. But that process was designed to overcome the dominance of tradition by promoting an open society in which the individual could achieve his potential unhindered by his ties to the past.

(*Going Into the Territory*, pp. 19–20)

Ellison has several points. The first is simply empirical – most claims to ethnic purity are just false: "Elements of the many available tastes, traditions, ways of life, and values that make up the total culture have been ceaselessly appropriated and made their own – consciously, unconsciously, or imperialistically – by groups and individuals to whose own backgrounds and traditions they are historically alien" (p. 27). Secondly, the language of ethnicity is not only a language of self-constitution; it is a language contaminated by concepts of the dominant culture, which uses race, gender, and class to make invidious comparisons, as we have seen. Thirdly, what needs to be examined are the causes of the fear and pain that produce this quest for certainty in ethnicity – that is, we need third-person accounts.[24] Fourthly, in a liberal democratic society, democratic principles trump traditions in the public sphere. Traditions can make claims in the public sphere with democratic principles, not against them. Ellison's view of citizenship is not a liberal fight among competing interests nor a dogmatic communitarian view of the good life nor a radical revolution: "Democracy is not only a collection of individuals ... but a collectivity of politically astute citizens ... who would be prepared to govern" (*Invisible Man*, p. xvii).

Ellison can be read as anticipating Chantal Mouffe's understanding of citizenship, in which the opposition between the liberal citizen (who has a mere legal status) and the communitarian citizen (who identifies with the common good) is transcended. For Ellison, like Mouffe, citizenship is "a form of identification with the *respublica*" through "the common recognition of a set of ethico-political values ... It is an articulating principle that affects the different subject positions of the social agent ... while allowing for a plurality of specific allegiances and for the respect of

[24] Ellison is not always sensitive on this point. For example, in this same essay ("The Little Man at Chehaw Station"), he uses two anecdotes – one about a person's mixed ethnic codes and another about the discussion of opera in a black section of Manhattan – as if they formed arguments against any use of ethnic vocabularies. I read Ellison's anecdotes only as argument against the use of ethnic vocabularies as if they were pure.

individual liberty" (Mouffe, *Radical Democracy*, p. 235). The principles of liberty and equality produce a positive, but indeterminate, form of life. These principles are not simply rules that govern the struggle of competing interests, as the liberal view would have it: "For it is not a matter of establishing a mere alliance between given interests but of actually modifying the very identity of these forces" (p. 236). The urge is not for liberation beyond politics as we see in poststructuralism and Marxism, but for the preservation of a political culture.[25] (I will return to this point in the Conclusion of the book.) We can bring many of these Ellisonian insights to the present and conclude the chapter by comparing his views with those of Werner Sollers's recent work on ethnicity and the understanding of literary culture.

Werner Sollers distinguishes between descent and consent to talk about ethnicity in American culture: "Descent language emphasizes our positions as heirs . . .; consent language stresses our abilities as mature free agents" (*Beyond Ethnicity*, p. 6). Sollers takes this Ellisonian distinction to critique literary histories based on ethnic identities: "The emphasis of a writer's descent all but annihilates polyethnic art movements, moments of individual and cultural interaction, and the pervasiveness of cultural syncretism in America" ("A Critique of Pure Pluralism," p. 256). Sollers goes on to show how pluralism based on ethnicity has racist roots, another Ellisonian point.[26]

However, the dimension of the ethnic question that Sollers is not concerned with is the existential function of ethnic identification. The interpenetration of African American culture and mainstream culture does not mean that "black" dissolves as a category. The fact that one can talk about Elvis's connection to blues traditions, for instance, does not mean that race drops out either as a third- or a first-/second-person vocabulary for talking about his music. Thus, to take Public Enemy's denunciation of Elvis and their assertion of black nationalism as just an inaccurate ethnographic statement misses the role of "black" in self-understanding.[27] "Black culture" is an important part of the vocabularies of self-constitution, and it does not have to be a pure or essentialist

---

[25] See Sheldon Wolin, "What Does Revolutionary Action Mean Today?" and Mary Dietz, "Context Is All."
[26] Sollers pursues this point in "A Critique of Pure Pluralism."
[27] Public Enemy, "Fight the Power."

category in order to function this way. As Cornel West says, "What is distinctive about the Black church and Black music [is] *their cultural hybrid character in which the complex mixture of African, European, and Amerindian elements are constitutive of something that is new and Black in the modern world*" ("Malcolm X and Black Rage," p. 54, West's emphasis).

Racial positioning is not a matter of choice, and cultural mixtures that appear do not mean that racial subject positions are interchangeable any more than gender positions are. As Barbara Johnson says, "Jacques Derrida may sometimes see himself philosophically positioned as a woman, but he is not politically positioned as a woman. Being positioned as a woman is not something that is entirely voluntary" (*A World of Difference*, pp. 2–3). The critique of racial identities does not situate this new truth in a new first-person vocabulary that gives people a place to live in a racist society and does not account for the anger, resentment, and fear that fuel nationalism. As Houston Baker says in response to Anthony Appiah's discussion of the dissolution of race as a category in the discourse of science, "In short, Appiah's eloquent shift to the common ground of subtle academic discourse is instructive but, ultimately, unhelpful in a world where New York cab drivers scarcely ever think of mitochondria before refusing to pick me up" ("Caliban's Triple Play," p. 385). A racist society produces the existential need for a first-/second- person vocabulary of solidarity and pride; this need would not be as urgent in a culture that is not so intensely racist. Living in gendered, raced bodies means that one will be subject to certain discourses and have access to certain discourses in a way that those who are gendered and raced differently will not. Empirical ethnographic studies of "transethnic contacts" do not get at this existential dimension of race.

The histories both of African Americans and women generate a need for distinctive forms of self-understanding. These self-understandings are not essentialist but contingent and relational constructs that emerge from society's current configurations. Such constructions have referential value that works hand-in-hand with their self-constituting value. These values are not beyond critique nor do they require the compromise between politics and philosophy that is summed up in Gayatry Spivak's often cited phrase, "strategic essentialism."[28] This misreading keeps us in the false opposition between the shapeless play of differences (the poststructuralist truth) on one side and an essentialist identity on the other. Only the dream of a grand theoretical truth either about agency and tradition or about power and critique keeps us from seeing how we need to have both languages work in dialogue. The great lesson of Ellison's texts is that they testify to the ways our vocabularies of ethical and political self-constitution can draw on stories of determination and agency, as we seek to account for the histories of our pain, the legacies of our achievements, and the hopes for our futures.

[28] Spivak, *In Other Worlds*.

❖❖

Conclusion

❖❖

In order to summarize and extend the conclusions of my argument about agency, value, and interpretation, I will return to the debate on liberal education that opened the book and recharacterize the issues at stake. I look at the debate as a theoretical as well as an ethical/political conflict about the reproduction of the subjects of democracy, not the static question of the canon or the question of teaching negative liberty.

As we recall from the Introduction, conservatives such as Bloom and Bennett maintain that the curriculum needs to be centered around the canonical texts of the Western tradition if our society is to have social and philosophical coherence. Without such a commitment, they say, we will lose not only our common culture but the philosophical moorings that keep us from falling into relativism. Conservatives aim their attacks not just at radicals (poststructuralists or Marxists) but at liberals as well; for conservatives, liberalism's neutrality toward the good is too skeptical to resist the forces of relativism and nihilism. Radicals respond that conservative and liberal agendas propose exclusions and repressions that are manifestly undemocratic. It is not just that teaching canonical works does not represent the diversity of American historical experience but that teaching the canon in a hagiographic fashion leaves out the stories of power that are coextensive with the development of American culture. Radicals thus offer key insights at the same time that they fall silent about the site from which they understand these genealogies, and therefore about the kinds of democratic subjects they hope to produce. Education is about the empowering shapes of positive liberty and not just freedom from discursive networks. This positive liberty involves an account of texts that make the genealogies possible, of the democratic texts one seeks to recuperate, of the kind of agency that one affirms, or of the kind of ethical/political association that one envisions. Such agency is not formed through a denial of the genealogies of power but through a recognition of the forces that shaped and continue to shape our self-understandings. Instead, the radicals focus only on critique, while urging a revolution so profound that it is beyond discussion. This failure hands over to conservatives the power to define positive visions of how we should live.

Liberals try to resolve these disagreements by "teaching the conflicts," by maintaining institutions through which our differences can be discussed. Yet clearly teaching different texts in an *ad hoc*, pluralistic fashion leaves interpreters blindly following the whim of literary fashion. Teaching students to interpret behind a "veil of ignorance" or from an unspecified Foucauldian site is not the way to sustain democratic interpretation. In response to criticism that their neutrality is not neutral, liberals now say that their ideals are simply "our tradition," as we saw in Rorty and Rawls. However, while this move responds to the issue of foundationalism, such a revision does not satisfy either communitarian or radical understandings of the way ethical and political conflicts need to be presented. Liberals try to put out of play differences dear to these other theorists. Rawls does this by positing a common moral ground, while Rorty minimizes the articulation of difference by using a holistic problematic for language. Such a view of linguistic community deprives its members of the resources needed to formulate conflicting ethical goods or shapes of the self. Rorty and Rawls thus strive to preempt the conflicts that are important to their adversaries: poststructuralists, who are concerned with the otherness created by "our traditions"; communitarians, who are concerned with the complex ethical stories that precede and continue alongside liberalism; and identity politicians, who are concerned not only with their status as others but with the integrity and particularity of their traditions.

The rise of identity politics can be read as a response to liberalism's and poststructuralism's failures to dialogue with "others" excluded by dominant discourses in terms of their own self-understandings and languages. Poststructuralism blocks this empowerment since it gives no place to a constructing subject or to the possibility of an ethical/political substance not corrupted by power. The result is an indiscriminate valorization of otherness, a valorization that perpetuates the disenfranchisement poststructuralism seeks to overcome. Liberalism blocks the languages of traditions by stripping them of their particularity and by forcing the excluded to appear only through the categories of the dominant culture. But how do we define the interpretive process through which democratic subjects come to understand themselves?

The place to begin is not with the deracinated perspectives of liberals or radicals or with the homogenized and idealized canon of conservatives but with a tradition-based problematic that makes available the multiple self-understandings of the culture. Here we find rich axiologies of existence made available by problematics such as Taylor's, MacIntyre's, and Ellison's, and the complex interactions among traditions. Democratic interpretation begins "inside," not "outside," the historical embeddedness of citizens, with the narrative particulars that come from individual and collective visions of the good life. By focusing only on injustice and exclusion in the name of liberal neutrality or analyses of power, we deprive public debate of the stories and virtues of marginalized traditions. For an account of such traditions is necessary to the recognition of the citizens who inhabit them. By blocking out these stories, we hand over to the dominant discourses the power to control the first-/second-person vocabularies of ethical/political life. Of course, ideas of the good life will discriminate against other visions and foreclose certain possibilities. But a democratic education seizes on this opportunity to open possibilities for positive liberty, a positive liberty that is not just for marginal works but canonical ones. Reading canonical works, such as *The Ambassadors*, only in terms of power prevents them from being resources of the present. Once we start telling these recuperative stories that overcome the reductive opposition between humanist and poststructuralist readings of history, then we will want to look again at the relationship among language, value, and subjectivity in texts.

My goal has been to show how the traditions that inform democratic deliberation are not closed entities locked in deadly competition. An identity politics that totalizes one strand of the subject and a constructivist reduction of the subject to a discursive position both deprive democratic interpretation of a rich account of the hermeneutic circle, in which the stories of oppression and empowerment as well as the values that animate them are thematized. These are complex stories in which power and pain are imbricated with achievement. Thus, an exposure of Kant's racism and sexism without at the same time saying to what extent this critique depends on the Kantian ethical legacy fails to appreciate the complexity of our historical embedding. Feminist critics do the same thing when they idealize Glaspell through a gynocentric reading or dismiss her because of her complicity with the gender constructions of her time, constructions which are now seen as obvious, avoidable, and damaging. Such an ahistorical judgment leaves out the story that connects Glaspell to the interpreter.

My reading of "A Jury of Her Peers" was designed to exemplify a procedure for democratic interpretation that draws on the insights made available by the problematics of radicals, liberals, and communitarians. Reading in terms of an ethic of care that simply valorizes the women's self-understanding ignores not only their external and internal oppression but it also ignores the transformation of their identities in the story. The textual complexities foreclose the possibility of reading the work in terms of only one problematic – genealogies or female communities, or liberal injustices. Furthermore, Mrs. Hale's and Mrs. Peter's reading of Minnie's story offers a powerful lesson about the need to connect historically the text under consideration to the interpreter's self-understanding. The contemporary concern with unmasking oppression and exclusion risks abstracting itself from the recuperative story of the values that make such a critique possible and the future in which the problem is addressed. We cannot just vote up or down on the agency or oppression of our historical predecessors so that they are either Joan Scott's constructs or Linda Gordon's agents, to recall the discussion from chapter 3.

By urging radicals to put their stories of agency and the democratic ideals that inform them on the table along with their third-person stories, we can provide "zones of contact," to recall Mary Louise Pratt's useful notion from chapter 3, for all sides in the debate. These zones are embodied in institutions, such as schools. Refusing such points of contact in the name of a totalizing critique (radicals) or out of fear of relativism (conservatives) is a self-defeating and inconsistent self-righteousness. Arguments about the curriculum are going to be messy and contextual. What they require is a rich, nuanced deliberative space that is informed by the stories made available by these three theoretical perspectives but not determined by these theoretical commitments. Only then can dialogue connect democratic principles to the narrative particulars of citizens.

The constructed and constructing subjects come together in the inescapable interpretive agency through which individuals understand their pasts and their futures. When we talk about the value of the texts of Thomas Jefferson or Frederick Douglass, we are not weighing merits or counting demographic characteristics; rather, we are talking about how their texts participate in complex histories, whose shapes depend on the stories of our future hopes. The identities of these "we's" will, of course, always need to be contested; however, this contestation will have as its goal the broadening of the democratic project.

This project draws on liberal democratic ideals and institutions, which provide a context for such a debate. This space of deliberation is guided by the democratic ideals of autonomy, mutual recognition, liberty, justice, and equality – the liberal democratic values that are casually dismissed as part of neo-Enlightenment foundationalism – as well as the ethical/political goods of other specific cultural traditions. Entering the dialogue itself requires a commitment to the liberal virtue of self-consciousness and to institutions that support political culture. Our understanding of democratic liberalism can be elaborated if we think of it in terms of a tradition with particular goods and virtues, as the work of Salkever, Mouffe, Nussbaum, and Galston shows. The revised view of liberal virtues and traditions responds to charges by communitarians that liberalism encourages a skeptical detachment that corrodes belief and that fosters the fantasy of a view from nowhere. It responds to radical charges that the very terms of liberalism preclude deep critique by opening the space of dialogue to genealogies of power.

Unlike Rawlsian liberalism, which tries to achieve fairness through abstraction from cultural particularity, my idea here is to have democratic principles inflect the interpretation of different traditions within a political community in a reciprocal fashion. First, these principles modify the understandings of the particular traditions from the inside, as we see in Martin Luther King's democratic reading of Christianity or in Hannah Arendt's appropriation of Aristotle and Heidegger. However, the influence goes in the other direction as well. Feminist, racial, and neo-Aristotelian critiques of liberal theory have exposed the poverty of self-understandings of democratic institutions. Yet there is a tension between the public language of democratic life and the perfectionist views of individuals and groups. Hence, democracy must function as a kind of meta-tradition that is broader and thinner than an individual's ethical/political commitments at the same time that it functions as a first-order tradition. In such instances, democracy serves as a meta-language into which claims for a particular tradition must be translated in the public sphere. "Difference" gets its bite within the context of a democratic form of life.

My reading of Ellison's work sought to bring all these threads of the book together. Ellison narrates how he became a democratic subject by learning to tell liberal, genealogical (radical), and communitarian stories about himself and others. In doing so, he enacts the kind of dialogue between first-order discourse, theory, and meta-theory that we outlined in chapter 3. At the theoretical level, he draws on tradition-based problematics to articulate the resources of African American, American, and European traditions; on genealogical problematics to show how oppression is embedded in all the vocabularies of daily life and not just in laws; and on liberal democratic ideals in order to bring these stories together into a dialogue of enrichment and critique. At the meta-theoretical level, he sorts out the conflicts among the theories and makes the revisions necessary for them to work together. Lastly, and most importantly, he brings all these moves together in the story of a life, in which the capacity to tell stories of these three different kinds is won through daily struggle.

Ellison's democratic subjects acknowledge their need for nourishment from the cultures in which they are embedded, and they phrase the demands that these needs be met in terms of democratic ideals. The acknowledgment of embeddedness is not a philosophical concession but a new conception of citizenship that sees the resources of particular traditions as essential to the achievement of autonomy, to the rights of recognition, and to the demands for justice. His narrative is our guide for what a democratic education needs to provide.

Bibliography

Altieri, Charles. *Subjective Agency: A Theory of First-person Expressivity and its Social Implications*. Cambridge: Blackwell, 1994.

Andrews, William. *To Tell a Free Story: The First Century of Afro-American Autobiography, 1760–1865*. Urbana: University of Illinois Press, 1986.

Appiah, Kwame Anthony. *In My Father's House: Africa in the Philosophy of Culture*. New York: Oxford University Press, 1993.

Armstrong, Paul. *The Phenomenology of Henry James*. Chapel Hill: University of North Carolina Press, 1983.

Baker, Houston A., Jr. "Caliban's Triple Play." In *"Race," Writing and Difference*. Ed. Henry Louis Gates, Jr. Chicago: University of Chicago Press, 1986, pp. 381–95.

Baker, Houston A., Jr., ed. *Narrative of Frederick Douglas, An American Slave*. New York: Penguin, 1992.

"In Dubious Battle." *New Literary History* 18 (1987): 363–69.

Bakhtin, Mikhail. *The Dialogic Imagination*. Trans. Caryl Emerson and Michal Holquist. Austin: University of Texas Press, 1981.

Problems in Dostoevsky's Poetics. Ed. and tran. Caryl Emerson. Minneapolis: University of Minnesota Press, 1984.

Speech Genres and Other Late Essays. Trans. Vern W. McGee. Austin: University of Texas Press, 1986.

Bannet, Eve Tavor. *Structuralism and the Logic of Dissent: Barthes, Derrida, Foucault, and Lacan*. Urbana: University of Illinois Press, 1989.

Bardes, Barbara and Suzanne Gossett. *Declarations of Independence: Women and Political Power in Nineteenth-Century American Fiction*. New Brunswick: Rutgers University Press, 1990.

Baym, Nina. "Melodramas of Beset Manhood: How Theories of American Fiction Exclude Women Authors." In *The Critical Tradition: Classic Texts and Contemporary Trends*. Ed. David H. Richter. New York: St. Martin's Press, 1989, pp. 1146–57.

Benhabib, Seyla. *Critique, Norm, and Utopia*. New York: Columbia University Press, 1986.

"Introduction: Beyond the Politics of Gender." *Feminism as Critique: On the Politics of Gender*. Minneapolis: University of Minnesota Press, 1987, pp. 1–15.

Situating the Self: Gender, Community and Postmodernism in Contemporary Ethics. New York: Routledge, 1992.

Benhabib, Seyla, et al. *Feminist Contentions: A Philosophical Exchange*. New York: Routledge, 1995.

Benjamin, Jessica. *The Bonds of Love: Psychoanalysis, Feminism, and the Problem of Domination*. New York: Pantheon, 1998.

Benjamin, Walter. *Illuminations: Essays and Reflections*. Trans. Harry Zohn. Ed. with an Introduction by Hannah Arendt. New York: Schocken, 1968.

Bennington, Geoff. *Lyotard: Writing the Event*. Manchester: University of Manchester Press, 1988.

Benston, Kimberly, ed. *Speaking for You: The Vision of Ralph Ellison*. Washington: Howard University Press, 1987.

Bernstein, Michael André. "The Poetics of *Ressentiment*." In *Rethinking Bakhtin: Extensions and Challenges*. Eds. Gary Saul Morson and Caryl Emerson. Evanston: Northwestern University Press, 1989, pp. 197–224.

Bernstein, Richard. *Beyond Objectivism and Relativism*. Philadelphia: University of Pennsylvania Press, 1983.

The New Constellation: The Ethical–Political Horizons of Modernity and Postmodernity. Cambridge: MIT Press, 1992.

"Nietzsche or Aristotle? Reflections on Alasdair MacIntyre's *After Virtue*." *Philosophical Profiles*. Philadelphia: University of Pennsylvania Press, 1986, pp. 115–40.

Blumenberg, Hans. *The Legitimacy of the Modern Age*. Trans. Robert M. Wallace. Cambridge: MIT Press, 1983.

Brennan, Teresa. Introduction. *Between Psychoanalysis and Feminism*. New York: Routledge, 1989, pp. 1–24.

Butler, Judith. *Bodies that Matter: On the Discursive Limits of "Sex"*. New York: Routledge, 1993.

"Contingent Foundations." *Feminist Contentions*. New York: Routledge, 1995, pp. 35–57.

Callinocos, Alex. *Making History: Agency, Structure, and Change in Social Theory*. Ithaca: Cornell University Press, 1988.

Card, Claudia. "Women's Voices and Ethical Ideals: Must We Mean What We Say?" *Ethics* 99 (1988): 125–36.

Cascardi, Anthony. *The Subject of Modernity*. Cambridge: Cambridge University Press, 1992.

Chatman, Seymour. *The Later Style of Henry James*. Oxford: Blackwell, 1972.

Chopin, Kate. *The Awakening*. New York: Norton, 1976.

Christensen, Jerome. "Spike Lee, Corporate Populist." *Critical Inquiry* 17 (1991): 582–95.

Cixous, Hélène. "La Venue à l'écriture." *Entre l'écriture*. Paris: Edition des femmes, 1986, pp. 9–69.

Cohn, Dorrit. *Transparent Minds: Narrative Modes for Presenting Consciousness in Fiction*. Princeton: Princeton University Press, 1978.

Conley, Verene. *Hélène Cixous: Writing the Feminine*. Lincoln: University of Nebraska Press, 1984.

Connolly, William. *Politics and Ambiguity*. Madison: University of Wisconsin Press, 1987.

Identity and Difference: Democratic Negotiations of Political Paradox. Ithaca: Cornell University Press, 1991.

Culler, Jonathan. "Beyond Interpretation." *The Pursuit of Signs*. Ithaca: Cornell University Press, 1981, pp. 3–17.

"Communicative Competence and Normative Force." *New German Critique* 35 (1985): 133–44.

Davidson, Donald. "Paradoxes of Irrationality." *Philosophical Essays on Freud*. Cambridge: Cambridge University Press, 1982, pp. 289–305.

Inquiries into Truth and Interpretation. New York: Oxford University Press, 1984.

"A Coherence Theory of Truth and Knowledge." In *Truth and Interpretation*. Ed. Ernest LePore. Oxford: Blackwell, 1986, pp. 307–19.

Derrida, Jacques. "Limited Inc." *Glyph* 2 (1977): 162–254.

Positions. Trans. Alan Bass. Chicago: University of Chicago Press, 1981.

Dissemination. Trans. Barbara Johnson. Chicago: University of Chicago Press, 1981.

"Choreographies." *Diacritics* 12 (1982): 66–76.

Margins of Philosophy. Trans. Alan Bass. Chicago: University of Chicago Press, 1982.

"Deconstruction and the Other." Interview with Richard Kearney. In *Dialogues with Contemporary Continental Thinkers*. Ed. Richard Kearney. Manchester: Manchester University Press, 1984, pp. 105–26.

"But, beyond ... (Open letter to Anne McClintock and Rob Nixon)." Trans. Peggy Kamuf. In *Race, Writing, and Difference*. Ed. Henry Louis Gates, Jr. Chicago: University of Chicago Press, 1986, pp. 354–69.

"Some Questions and Responses." In *The Linguistics of Writing: Arguments between Language and Literature*. Eds. Nigel Fabb et al. New York: Methuen, 1987, pp. 252–64.

"Afterword: Toward an Ethic of Discussion." *Limited Inc*. Evanston: Northwestern University Press, 1988, pp. 111–60.

Dews, Peter. *Logics of Disintegration: Post-Structuralist Thought and the Claims of Critical Theory*. London: Verso, 1987.

Diamond, Cora. "Losing Your Concepts." *Ethics* 98 (1988): 255–77.

Dietz, Mary. "Context Is All: Feminism and Theories of Citizenship." In *Radical Democracy*. Ed. Chantal Mouffe. New York: Verso, 1992, p. 63–85.

Douglass, Bruce et al., eds. *Liberalism and the Good*. New York: Routledge, 1990.

Dreyfus, Hubert. "Beyond Hermeneutics: Interpretation in Late Heidegger and Recent Foucault." In *Hermeneutics: Questions and Prospects*. Eds. Gary Shapiro and Alan Sica. Amherst: University of Massachusetts Press, 1984, pp. 66–83.

Dubois, W.E.B. *The Souls of Black Folk*. New York: Signet, 1969.

Dworkin, Gerald. *The Theory and Practice of Autonomy*. Chicago: University of Chicago Press, 1988.

Dworkin, Ronald. "Liberalism." In *Liberalism and Its Critics*. Ed. Michael Sandel. New York: New York University Press, 1984, pp. 60–79.

Eagleton, Terry. *Literary Theory*. Minneapolis: University of Minnesota Press, 1983.

Ellison, Ralph. "Flying Home." In *Dark Symphony: Negro Literature in America*. Eds. James A. Emmanuel and Theodore L. Gross. Toronto: Free Press, 1968, pp. 254–74.

Shadow and Act. New York: Random House, 1972.

Invisible Man. New York: Vintage, 1981.

Going Into the Territory. New York: Vintage, 1986.

Farias, Victor. *Heidegger and Nazism*. Trans. Paul Burrell and Gabriel R. Ricci. Philadelphia: Temple University Press, 1989.

Fetterley, Judith. "Reading about Reading: 'A Jury of Her Peers,' 'The Murders in the Rue Morgue,' and 'The Yellow Wallpaper.'" In *Gender and Reading: Essays on Readers, Texts, and Contexts*. Eds. Elizabeth Flynn and Patracino P. Schweickart. Baltimore: Johns Hopkins University Press, 1986, pp. 147–64.

Fish, Stanley. "The Common Touch, or, One Size Fits All." *The Politics of Liberal Education*. Durham: Duke University Press, 1992, pp. 241–66.

Flanagan, Owen. "Identity and Strong and Weak Evaluations." In *Identity, Character, and Morality*. Eds. Owen Flanagan and Amelie Rorty. Cambridge: MIT Press, 1990, pp. 37–66.

Varieties of Moral Personality: Ethical and Psychological Realism. Cambridge: Harvard University Press, 1991.

Flax, Jane. "Is Enlightenment Emancipatory?" *Disputed Subjects: Essays on Psychoanalysis, Politics, and Philosophy*. New York: Routledge, 1993, pp. 75–91.

Foucault, Michel. *The Order of Things*. Trans. Alan Sheridan. New York: Random House, 1970.

Language, Counter-Memory, Practice: Selected Essays and Interviews. Trans. Donald F. Bouchard and Sherry Simon. Ithaca: Cornell University Press, 1977.

Power/Knowledge: Selected Interviews and Other Writings: 1972–77. Trans. Colin Collin et al. Ed. Colin Gordon. New York: Pantheon, 1981.

The Foucault Reader. Ed. Paul Rabinow. New York: Pantheon, 1984.

The Final Foucault. Eds. James Bernauer and David Rasmussen. Cambridge: MIT Press, 1988.

Frailberg, Selma. "Two Modern Incest Heroes." *Partisan Review* 28 (1961): 646–61.

Frank, Manfred. *What Is Neostructuralism?*. Trans. Sabine Wilke and Richard T. Gray. Minneapolis: University of Minnesota Press, 1989.

Frankfurt, Harry. *The Importance of What We Care About*. Cambridge: Cambridge University Press, 1988.

Fraser, Nancy. "Toward a Discourse Ethic of Solidarity." *Praxis International* 5 (1986): 425–29.

Unruly Practices. Minneapolis: University of Minnesota Press, 1989.

"False Antitheses: A Response to Seyla Benhabib and Judith Butler." *Praxis International* 11 (1991): 166–77.

Introduction. *Revaluing French Feminism: Critical Essays on Difference, Agency, and Culture*. Bloomington: Indiana University Press, 1992, pp. 1–24.

"Rethinking the Public Sphere." In *Habermas and the Public Sphere*. Ed. Craig Calhoun. Cambridge: MIT Press, 1992, pp. 109–42.

Fukuyama, Francis. *The End of History and the Last Man*. New York: Free Press, 1992.

Fuss, Diana. *Essentially Speaking: Feminism, Nature, and Difference*. New York: Routledge, 1989.

Gadamer, Hans-Georg. *Philosophical Hermeneutics*. Trans. David E. Linge. Berkeley: University of California Press, 1977.

"Destruktion and Deconstruction." In *Dialogue and Deconstruction*. Eds. Dianne P. Michelfelder and Richard Palmer. Albany: SUNY Press, 1989.

Truth and Method. 2nd. revised edn. Trans. Garrett Barden and John Cumming. Translation revised by Joel Weinsheimer and Donald G. Marshall. New York: Continuum Publishing Company, 1994.

Gallagher, Catherine. "Politics, the Profession, and the Critic." *Diacritics* 15 (1985): 37–43.

Galston, William. *Liberal Purposes: Goods, Virtues and Diversity in the Liberal State*. Cambridge: Cambridge University Press, 1991.

Gasché, Rodolphe. *The Tain of the Mirror: Derrida and the Philosophy of Reflection*. Cambridge: Harvard University Press, 1986.

Gates, Henry Louis, Jr. "Criticism in the Jungle." *Black Literature and Literary Theory*. New York: Methuen, 1984, pp. 1–24.

"'What's Love Got to Do with It?': Critical Theory, Integrity, and the Black Idiom." *New Literary History* 18 (1987): 345–62.

The Signifying Monkey. New York: Oxford University Press, 1988.

"Canon-Formation, Literary History, and the Afro-American Tradition: From the Seen to the Told." In *Afro-American Literary Study in the 1990s*. Eds. Houston A. Baker, Jr. and Patricia Redmond. Chicago: University of Chicago Press, 1990, pp. 14–39.

"The Master's Pieces: On Canon Formation and the African-American Tradition." *The Politics of Liberal Education*. Durham: Duke University Press, 1992, pp. 95–118.

Gibson, Donald. *The Politics of Literary Expression: A Study of Major Black Writers*. Westport: Greenwood Press, 1981.

Gilbert, Sandra. "The Second Coming of Aphrodite: Kate Chopin's *The Awakening*." *Kenyon Review* 5 (1983): 42–56.

Bibliography

Gilbert, Sandra and Susan Gubar. *No Man's Land: The Place of the Woman Writer in the Twentieth Century*. New Haven: Yale University Press, 1988.

Gilligan, Carol. *In a Different Voice*. Cambridge: Harvard University Press, 1982.

"Reply." *Signs* 11 (1986): 324–33.

"Moral Orientation and Moral Development." In *Women and Moral Theory*. Eds. Eva Kittay and Diana Meyers. Totowa. Rowan and Littlefield, 1987, pp. 19–33.

Glaspell, Susan. "A Jury of Her Peers." In *Best Short Stories of 1917*. Ed. Edward J. O'Brien. Boston: Small, Maynard, 1918, pp. 265–80.

Goldstein, Philip. "The Politics of Fredric Jameson's Literary Theory." In *Postmodernism/Jameson/Critique*. Ed. Douglass Kellner. Washington: Maisonneuve Press, 1989, pp. 249–67.

Gooding-Williams, Robert. "Evading Narrative Myth, Evading Prophetic Pragmatism: Cornel West's *The American Evasion of Philosophy*." *The Massachusetts Review* (Winter 1991–92): 517–42.

"Look, a Negro!" *Reading Rodney King/Reading Urban Uprising*. New York: Routledge, 1993, pp. 157–77.

Gordon, Linda. "Response to Scott." *Signs* 15 (1990): 852–53.

Graff, Gerald. *Beyond the Culture Wars: How Teaching the Conflicts Can Revitalize American Education*. New York: Norton, 1992.

"Teach the Conflicts." *The Politics of Liberal Education*. Durham: Duke University Press, 1992, pp. 57–74.

Gutmann, Amy. "Undemocratic Education." In *Liberalism and Moral Life*. Ed. Nancy Rosenblum. Cambridge: Harvard University Press, 1989, pp. 71–88.

"Democracy." In *A Companion to Political Philosophy*. Eds. Robert Goodin and Philip Petit. Cambridge: Blackwell, 1993, pp. 411–21.

Habermas, Jürgen. *Knowledge and Human Interests*. Trans. Jeremy Shapiro. Boston: Beacon Press, 1971.

"A Postscript to Knowledge and Human Interests." *Philosophy and the Social Sciences* 3 (1973): 157–85.

"Reply to My Critics." In *Habermas: Critical Debates*. Eds. David Held and John Thompson. Cambridge: MIT Press, 1982, pp. 219–83.

The Theory of Communicative Action. Trans. Thomas McCarthy. 2 vols. Boston: Beacon Press, 1983.

"Questions and Counter-Questions." In *Habermas and Modernity*. Ed. Richard Bernstein. Cambridge: MIT Press, 1985, pp. 192–216.

Autonomy and Solidarity: Interviews. Ed. Peter Dews. New York: Verso, 1986.

The Philosophical Discourse of Modernity. Trans. Frederick Lawrence. Cambridge: MIT Press, 1987.

Moral Consciousness and Communicative Action. Trans. Christian Lenhardt and Sherry Weber Nicholsen. Cambridge: MIT Press, 1990.

Justification and Application: Remarks on Discourse Ethics. Trans. Ciaran P. Cronin. Cambridge: MIT Press, 1993.

Hacking, Ian. "The Parody of Conversation." In *Truth and Interpretation.* Ed Ernest Lepore. Oxford: Blackwell, 1986, pp. 447–58.

"Styles of Scientific Reasoning." *Post-Analytic Philosophy.* Eds. John Rajchman and Cornell West. New York: Columbia University Press, 1985, pp. 145–65.

Hamon, Philippe. "Un discours contraint." *Poetique* 16 (1973): 411–45.

Hegel, G. W. F. *Philosophy of Right.* Trans. T.M. Knox. New York: Oxford University Press, 1952.

Philosophy of History. Trans. J. Sibree. New York: Dover Publications, 1956.

Phenomenology of the Spirit. Trans. A. V. Miller. New York: Oxford University Press, 1977.

Heidegger, Martin. *Being and Time.* Trans. John Macquarrie and Edward Robinson. New York: Harper Row, 1962.

"Letter on Humanism." *Basic Writings.* Trans. David Krell. New York: Harper Row, 1977, pp. 193–242.

Henderson, Mae Gwendolyn. "Speaking in Tongues: Dialogics, Dialectics, and Black Woman Writer's Literary Tradition." In *Reading Black, Reading Feminist.* Ed. Henry Louis Gates, Jr. New York: Meridian, 1990, pp. 116–42.

Hobsbawn, Eric and Terence Ranger, eds. *The Invention of Tradition.* Cambridge: Cambridge University Press, 1983.

Holmes, Stephen. *The Anatomy of Antiliberalism.* Cambridge: Harvard University Press, 1993.

Howe, Irving. "Black Boys and Native Sons." *A World More Attractive: A View of Modern Literature and Politics.* New York: Horizon Press, 1963, pp. 98–122.

James, Henry. *The Golden Bowl.* 2 vols. New York: Scribners, 1909.

The Art of the Novel. Ed. R. P. Blackmur. New York: Scribners, 1934.

The Ambassadors. New York: Norton, 1964.

Literary Criticism: French Writers, Other European Writers, The Prefaces to the New York Edition. New York: Literary Classics of the United States, 1984.

James, William. *Letters of William James.* Ed. Henry James. 2 vols. Boston: Atlantic Monthly Press, 1920.

Jameson, Fredric. *Marxism and Form: Twentieth-Century Dialectical Theories.* Princeton: Princeton University Press, 1971.

The Political Unconscious. Ithaca: Cornell University Press, 1981.

"Discussion of 'Cognitive Mapping.'" *Marxism and the Interpretation of Culture.* Urbana: University of Illinois Press, 1988, pp. 358–60.

"On Habits of the Heart." *Community in America: The Challenge of Habits of the Heart.* Berkeley: University of California Press, 1988, pp. 97–112.

Ideologies of Theory. Vol. I. Minneapolis: University of Minnesota Press, 1988.

Bibliography

Postmodernism, or, the Logic of Late Capitalism. Durham: Duke University Press, 1991.

Jay, Gregory S. *America the Scrivener: Deconstruction and the Subject of Literary History*. Ithaca: Cornell University Press, 1990.

Johnson, Barbara. *A World of Difference*. Baltimore: Johns Hopkins University Press, 1987.

"Response to Henry Louis Gates." In *Afro-American Literary Study in the 1990s*. Eds. Houston A. Baker, Jr. and Patricia Redwood. Chicago: University of Chicago Press, 1990, pp. 39–44.

Joyce, Joyce, A. "The Black Canon: Reconstructing Black American Literary Criticism." *New Literary History* 18 (1987): 335–44.

"'Who the Cap Fit': Unconsciousness and Unconscionableness in the Criticism of Houston A. Baker, Jr. and Henry Louis Gates, Jr." *New Literary History* 18 (1987): 371–84.

Kahane, Claire. "Object-relations Theory." In *Feminism and Psychoanalysis: A Critical Dictionary*. Ed. Elizabeth Wright. Cambridge: Blackwell, 1992, pp. 284–90.

Kant, Immanuel. *Critique of Judgment*. Trans. J.H. Bernard. New York: Haffner Press, 1951.

Groundwork of the Metaphysics of Morals. Trans. H.J. Paton. New York: Harper and Row, 1964.

Critique of Pure Reason. Trans. Norman Kemp Smith. New York: St. Martin's Press, 1965.

Kaston, Carren. *Imagination and Desire in the Novels of Henry James*. New Brunswick: Rutgers University Press, 1984.

Kerber, Linda. "Some Cautionary Words for Historians." *Signs* 11 (1986): 304–10.

Kolodny, Annette. "A Map for Misreading: Gender and the Interpretation of Literary Texts." In *The New Feminist Criticism*. Ed. Elaine Showalter. New York: Pantheon, 1985, pp. 46–62.

Kristeva, Julia. "Psychoanalysis and the Polis." In *The Politics of Interpretation*. Ed. W.J.T. Mitchell. Chicago: University of Chicago Press, 1983, pp. 83–98.

Tales of Love. New York: Columbia University Press, 1987.

Kuykendall, Eleanor H. "Questions for Julia Kristeva's Ethics of Linguistics." In *Thinking Muse*. Eds. Jeffner Allen and Iris Marion Young. Bloomington: Indiana University Press, 1989, pp. 180–94.

Laclau, Ernesto and Chantal Mouffe. *Hegemony and Socialist Strategy: Towards a Radical Democratic Politics*. Trans. Winston Moore and Paul Cammack. London: Verso, 1985.

Larmore, Charles. "Review of MacIntyre's *Whose Justice? Which Rationality?*" *Journal of Philosophy* (1989): 437–42.

Leland, Dorothy. "Lacanian Psychoanalysis and French Feminism: Toward an Adequate Political Psychology." In *Revaluing French Feminism*. Ed. Nancy Fraser. Bloomington: Indiana University Press, 1992, pp. 113–35.

Bibliography

Lukes, Steven. *Marxism and Morality*. New York: Oxford University Press, 1985.

Lyotard, Jean François. *Le Différend*. Paris: Minuit, 1983. (All quotations from this book are my own translation.)

"Histoire universelle et différences culturelles." *Critique* 456 (1985): 559–68.

The Postmodern Condition. Trans. Geoff Bennington and Brian Massumi. Minneapolis: University of Minnesota Press, 1984.

MacIntyre, Alasdair. "The Idea of Social Science." *Against the Self-Images of the Age*. London: Duckworth, 1971, pp. 211–29.

"Philosophy, 'Other' Disciplines and Their Histories: A Rejoinder to Richard Rorty." *Soundings* 45 (1982): 127–45.

After Virtue. Notre Dame: University of Notre Dame Press, 1984.

Whose Justice? Which Rationality? Notre Dame: University of Notre Dame Press, 1988.

Three Rival Versions of Moral Enquiry: Encyclopedia, Genealogy, and Tradition. Notre Dame: University of Notre Dame Press, 1990.

"A Partial Response to My Critics." In *After MacIntyre: Critical Perspectives on the Work of Alasdair MacIntyre*. Eds. John Horton and Susan Mendus. Notre Dame: University of Notre Dame Press, 1994, pp. 283–304.

Mansbridge, Jayne. *Beyond Adversarial Democracy*. Chicago: University of Chicago Press, 1983.

McCarthy, Thomas. *The Critical Theory of Jurgen Habermas*. Cambridge: MIT Press, 1978.

"Private Irony and Public Decency: Richard Rorty's New Pragmatism." *Critical Inquiry* 16 (1990): 355–70.

"Ironist Theory as a Vocation: A Response to Rorty's Reply." *Critical Inquiry* 16 (1990): 644–55.

Ideals and Illusions: On Reconstruction and Deconstruction in Contemporary Critical Theory. Cambridge: MIT Press, 1991.

McClure, Kirstie. "On the Subject of Rights: Pluralism, Plurality, and Political Identity." *Dimensions of Radical Democracy*. New York: Verso, 1992, pp. 108–27.

McGowan, John. *Postmodernism and Its Critics*. Ithaca: Cornell University Press, 1990.

McHale, Brian. *Postmodern Fiction*. New York: Routledge, 1987.

Meyers, Diana. "The Subversion of Women's Agency in Psychoanalytic Feminism: Chodorow, Flax, Kristeva." *Revaluing French Feminism: Critical Essays on Difference, Agency, and Culture*. Ed. Nancy Fraser. Bloomington: Indiana University Press, 1992, pp. 136–61.

Michelfelder, Dianne and Richard Palmer, eds. *Dialogue and Deconstruction*. Albany: SUNY, 1989.

Mitchell, W. J. T. "The Violence of Public Art: *Do the Right Thing*." *Critical Inquiry* 16 (1990): 880–99.

"Seeing *Do the Right Thing*." *Critical Inquiry* 17 (1991): 596–608.

Moi, Toril. *Sexual/Textual Politics: Feminist Literary Theory*. New York: Methuen, 1985.

Morrison, Toni. *Playing in the Dark*. New York: Vintage, 1993.

Morson, Gary Saul and Caryl Emerson. *Mikhail Bakhtin: Creation of a Prosaics*. Stanford: Stanford University Press, 1990.

Mouffe, Chantal. *Radical Democracy*. New York: Verso, 1992.

The Return of the Political. New York: Verso, 1993.

Mulhall, Stephen and Adam Swift. *Liberals and Communitarians*. Cambridge: Blackwell, 1992.

Munitz, Milton. *Contemporary Analytic Philosophy*. New York: MacMillan, 1981.

Murdoch, Iris. "On 'God' and 'Good.'" In *Revisions: Changing Perspectives in Moral Philosophy*. Eds. Alasdair MacIntyre and Stanley Hauerwas. Notre Dame: University of Notre Dame Press, 1983.

Nadel, Alan. *Invisible Criticism: Ralph Ellison and the American Canon*. Iowa City: University of Iowa Press, 1988.

Nietzsche, Friedrich. *Beyond Good and Evil*. Trans. Walter Kaufmann. New York: Vintage, 1966.

The Will to Power. Trans. Walter Kaufmann and R.J. Hollingdale. New York: Vintage, 1968.

Nussbaum, Martha. *Love's Knowledge*. New York: Oxford University Press, 1990.

Okin, Susan Moller. "Whose Traditions? Which Understandings?" *Justice, Gender, and the Family*. New York: Basic Books, 1989, pp. 41–73.

Ormiston, Gayle L. and Alan D. Schrift, eds. *The Hermeneutic Tradition: From Ast to Ricoeur*. Albany: SUNY Press, 1980.

Parekh, Bhikhu. "The Cultural Particularity of Liberal Democracy." In *Prospects for Democracy: North, South, East, West*. Ed. David Held. Stanford: Stanford University Press, 1992, pp. 156–75.

Parr, Susan Resnick and Pancho Savery, eds. *Approaches to Teaching Ellison's Invisible Man*. New York: Modern Language Association, 1989.

Parry, Benita. "Overlapping Territories and Intertwined Histories: Edward Said's Postcolonial Cosmopolitanism." In *Edward Said: A Critical Reader*. Ed. Michael Sprinker. Cambridge: Blackwell, 1992, pp. 19–47.

Pippin, Robert. "Hegel, Modernity, and Habermas." *The Monist* 74 (1991): 329–57.

Posnock, Ross. *The Trial of Curiosity: Henry James, William James, and the Challenge of Modernity*. New York: Oxford University Press, 1991.

Pratt, Mary Louise. "Ideology and Speech-Act Theory." *Poetics Today* 7 (1986): 59–72.

"Linguistic Utopias." In *The Linguistics of Writing: Arguments between Language and Literature*. Eds. Nigel Fabb et al. Manchester: University of Manchester Press, 1987, pp. 48–66.

"Arts of the Contact Zone." *Profession* (1991): 33–40.

Bibliography

Premo, Cassie. "Beyond Critique to Survival: Lessons for Life in *Meridian* and *The Color Purple*." *North Carolina Humanities* 1 (1993): 35–45.

Prince, Gerald. *Narrative as Theme: Studies in French Fiction*. Lincoln: University of Nebraska Press, 1992.

Public Enemy. "Fight the Power." *Fear of a Black Planet*. New York: CBS Records, 1990.

Rajchman, John. *Michel Foucault: The Freedom of Philosophy*. New York: Columbia University Press, 1985.

Rasmussen, David. *Reading Habermas*. Oxford: Blackwell, 1990.

Rawls, John. *A Theory of Justice*. Cambridge: Harvard University Press, 1971.

"Justice as Fairness: Political not Metaphysical." *Philosophy and Public Affairs* 14 (1985): 223–51.

Political Liberalism. New York: Columbia University Press, 1993.

Ricoeur, Paul. "Psychoanalysis and the Movement of Contemporary Culture." In *Interpretive Social Science*. Eds. Paul Rabinow and William Sullivan. Berkeley: University of California Press, 1979.

"The Question of Proof in Freud's Psychoanalytic Writings." *Hermeneutics and the Human Sciences*. New York: Cambridge University Press, 1981, pp. 247–73.

"What Is a Text? Explanation and Understanding." *Hermeneutics and the Human Sciences*. Cambridge: Cambridge University Press, 1981, pp. 145–64.

Temps et récit. Vol. I. Paris: Seuil, 1983. (All quotations from this work my own translation.)

Du texte à l'action. Paris: Seuil, 1986, pp. 379–92.

Time and Narrative. Trans. Kathleen Blarney and David Pellauer. Vol. III. Chicago: University of Chicago Press, 1988.

Rohrberger, Mary. "'Ball the Jack': Surreality, Sexuality and the Role of Women in *Invisible Man*." In *Approaches to Teaching Ellison's Invisible Man*. Eds. Susan Resneck Parr and Pancho Savery. New York: Modern Language Association, 1989, pp. 124–32.

Rorty, Richard. *The Linguistic Turn: Recent Essays in Philosophical Method*. Chicago: University of Chicago Press, 1967.

Philosophy and the Mirror of Nature. Princeton: Princeton University Press, 1979.

"A Reply to Dreyfus and Taylor." *Review of Metaphysics* 34 (1980): 39–46.

Consequences of Pragmatism. Minneapolis: University of Minnesota Press, 1982.

"The Historiography of Philosophy: Four Genres." In *Philosophy in History*. Ed. Richard Rorty et al. Cambridge: Cambridge University Press, 1984, pp. 49–76.

"The Higher Nominalism in a Nutshell: A Reply to Henry Staten." *Critical Inquiry* 12 (1986): 462–66.

Contingency, Irony, and Solidarity. Cambridge: Cambridge University Press, 1989.

Essays on Heidegger and Others. Cambridge: Cambridge University Press, 1991.

Objectivity, Relativism, and Truth. New York: Cambridge University Press, 1991.

"Two Cheers for the Cultural Left." *The Politics of Liberal Education*. Durham: Duke University Press, 1992, pp. 233–40.

Rosenblum, Nancy, ed. *Liberalism and the Moral Life*. Cambridge: Harvard University Press, 1989.

Said, Edward. *The World, the Text, and the Critic*. Cambridge: Harvard University Press, 1983.

Culture and Imperialism. New York: Alfred Knopf, 1993.

Salkever, Stephen. *Finding the Mean: Theory and Practice in Aristotelian Political Philosophy*. Princeton: Princeton University Press, 1990.

"Lopp'd and Bound: How Liberal Theory Obscures the Goods of Liberal Practices." In *Liberalism and the Good*. Eds. R. Bruce Douglass, Gerald M. Mara, and Henry S. Richardson. New York: Routledge, 1990, pp. 167–202.

Salusinszky, Imre. "Interview with Edward Said." In *Criticism in Society*. Ed. Imre Salusinszky. New York: Methuen, 1987, pp. 122–49.

Sandel, Michael. *Liberalism and the Limits of Justice*. New York: Cambridge University Press, 1982.

Introduction. *Liberalism and Its Critics*. New York: New York University Press, 1984, pp. 1–15.

Schott, Robin. "Whose Home Is It Anyway? A Feminist Response to Gadamer's Hermeneutics." In *Gadamer and Hermeneutics*. Ed. Hugh Silverman. New York: Routledge, 1991, pp. 202–09.

Scott, Joan. "Review of Linda Gordon, *Heroes of Their Own Lives*." *Signs* 15 (1990): 848–52.

Searle, John. *Expression and Meaning*. Cambridge: Cambridge University Press, 1979.

"What Is an Intentional State?" In *Husserl, Intentionality, and Cognitive Science*. Ed. Hubert Dreyfus. Cambridge: MIT Press, 1982, pp. 259–76.

Intentionality. Cambridge: Cambridge University Press, 1983.

Speech Acts. Cambridge: Cambridge University Press, 1969.

Seltzer, Mark. *Henry James and the Art of Power*. Ithaca: Cornell University Press, 1984.

Showalter, Elaine. "Tradition and the Female Talent: *The Awakening* as a Solitary Book." In *New Essays on The Awakening*. Ed. Wendy Martin. Cambridge: Cambridge University Press, 1988, pp. 33–58.

Silverman, Kaja. *Male Subjectivity at the Margins*. New York: Routledge, 1992.

Skinner, Quentin. "Modernity and Disenchantment: Some Historical Reflections." *Philosophy in the Age of Pluralism: The Philosophy of Charles Taylor*. Cambridge: Cambridge University Press, 1994, pp. 37–48.

Smith, Barbara Herrnstein. *Contingencies of Value: Alternative Perspectives for Critical Theory*. Cambridge: Harvard University Press, 1988.

Bibliography

Sollers, Werner. *Beyond Ethnicity: Consent and Descent in American Culture.* New York: Oxford University Press, 1986.

"A Critique of Pure Pluralism." In *Reconstructing American Literary History.* Ed. Sacvan Bercovitch. Cambridge: Harvard University Press, 1986, pp. 250–79.

Spivak, Gayatri. "Can the Subaltern Speak?" *Marxism and the Interpretation of Culture.* Urbana: University of Illinois Press, 1988, pp. 271–313.

In Other Worlds: Essays in Cultural Politics. New York: Routledge, 1988.

Staten, Henry. "Rorty's Circumvention of Derrida." *Critical Inquiry* 12 (1986): 453–61.

Steele, Meili. "The Drama of Reference in James's *The Golden Bowl.*" *Novel* 21 (1987): 73–88.

Realism and the Drama of Reference. University Park: Pennsylvania State University Press, 1988.

"Lyotard's Politics of the Sentence." *Cultural Critique* 16 (1990): 193–214.

"Narration and the Face of Anxiety in James's 'The Beast in the Jungle.'" *Analecta Husserliana* 28 (1990): 421–28.

'The Ontological Turn and Its Ethical Consequences: Habermas and the Poststructuralists." *Praxis International* 11 (1991): 113–33.

"Explanation, Understanding, and Incommensurability in Psychoanalysis." *Analecta Husserliana* 41 (1994): 367–76.

Contemporary Critical Theory: From Hermeneutics to Cultural Studies. Columbia: University of South Carolina Press, 1997.

"Ontologie linguistique et dialogue politique chez Bakhtine." In *Bakhtine et la pensée dialogique.* Eds. André Collinot and Clive Thomson. Forthcoming.

Tate, Claudia. "Notes on the Invisible Women in Ralph Ellison's *Invisible Man.*" In *Speaking for You: The Vision of Ralph Ellison.* Ed. Kimberley Benston. Washington: Howard University Press, 1987, pp. 163–72.

Taylor, Charles. "The Validity of Transcendental Arguments." *The Proceedings of the Aristotlean Society* 79 (1979): 151–65.

Human Agency and Language. Cambridge: Cambridge University Press, 1985.

"Justice after Virtue." In *Kritische Methode und Zukunft der Anthropologie.* Eds. M. Benedikt and R. Berger. Vienna: Braumü, 1985, pp. 23–48.

"What's Wrong with Negative Freedom?" *Philosophical Papers.* Vol. II Cambridge: Cambridge University Press, 1985, pp. 211–29.

"Cross-Purposes: The Liberal-Communitarian Debate." In *Liberalism and the Moral Life.* Ed. Nancy Rosenblum. Cambridge: Harvard University Press, 1989, pp. 159–82.

Sources of the Self. Cambridge: Harvard University Press, 1989.

"Rorty in the Epistemological Tradition." In *Reading Rorty.* Ed. Alan R. Malachowski. Cambridge: Blackwell, 1990, pp. 257–75.

Multiculturalism and the Politics of Recognition. Princeton: Princeton University Press, 1994.

Tronto, Joan. "Beyond Gender Difference to a Theory of Care." *Signs* 12 (1987): 644–63.

Veeder, William. "Strether and the Transcendence of Language." *Modern Philology* 69 (1971): 116–32.

Walton, Priscilla. *The Disruption of the Feminine in Henry James*. Toronto: University of Toronto Press, 1992.

Weinsheimer, Joel. *Gadamer's Hermeneutics: A Reading of Truth and Method*. New Haven: Yale University Press, 1985.

Wellmer, Albrecht. "Models of Freedom in the Modern World." *The Philosophical Forum* 21 (1989–90): 227–52.

West, Cornel. *Prophesy Deliverance! An Afro-American Revolutionary Christianity*. Philadelphia: The Westminster Press, 1982.

"Ethics and Action in Fredric Jameson's Marxist Hermeneutics." Ed. Jonathan Arac. Minneapolis: University of Minnesota Press, 1986, pp. 123–44.

The American Evasion of Philosophy: A Genealogy of Pragmatism. Madison: University of Wisconsin Press, 1989.

The Ethical Dimensions of Marxist Thought. New York: Monthly Review Press, 1991.

"Black Leadership and the Pitfalls of Racial Reasoning." In *Race-ing Justice, En-Gendering Power*. Ed. Toni Morrison. New York: Pantheon, 1992, pp. 390–401.

"Malcolm X and Black Rage." In *Malcolm X: In Our Own Image*. Ed. Joe Wood. New York: St. Martin's Press, 1992, pp. 48–58.

Williams, Bernard. *Ethics and the Limits of Philosophy*. Cambridge: Harvard University Press, 1985.

Williams, Sherley Anne. *Dessa Rose*. New York: William Morrow, 1986.

Wolff, Cynthia Griffin. "Thanatos and Eros: Kate Chopin's *The Awakening*." *American Quarterly* 25 (1973): 123–33.

Wolin, Richard. *The Politics of Being: The Political Thought of Martin Heidegger*. New York: Columbia University Press, 1990.

Wolin, Sheldon, "What Does Revolutionary Action Mean Today?" In *Radical Democracy*. Ed. Chantal Mouffe. New York: Verso, 1992, pp. 240–53.

Wood, Allen. "Habermas's Defense of Rationalism." *New German Critique* 35 (1985): 145–64.

Yaeger, Patricia. "'A Language Which Nobody Understood': Emancipatory Strategies in *The Awakening*." *Novel* 20 (1987): 197–219.

Young, Iris Marion. *Justice and the Politics of Difference*. Princeton: Princeton University Press, 1990.

Index

Index